CHILDREN
with FACIAL
DIFFERENCE

A Parents' Guide

Hope Charkins, M.S.W.

WOODBINE HOUSE • 1996

Published by Woodbine House, 6510 Bells Mill Rd., Bethesda, MD 20817.
800–843–7323.

Cover illustration ("Faces"): Shirley How, in cooperation with the National In-
stitute of Arts and Disabilities
Illustration of ear, page 169: Jason Chin
Photo credits: page 109, courtesy of Joseph G. McCarthy, M.D., Institute of
Reconstructive Plastic Surgery, New York University Medical Center; page
180, courtesy of Oticon, Inc., Somerset, NJ; page 181, 182, and 185, courtesy
of Phonak, Naperville, IL; page 186, courtesy of AVR Sonovation, Chanhassen,
MN

Library of Congress Cataloging-in-Publication Data

Charkins, Hope.
    Children with facial difference : a parents' guide / by Hope Charkins.
        p.   cm.
    Includes bibliographical references and index.
    ISBN 0–933149–61–1 (paper)
    1. Face—Abnormalities—Popular works. 2. Skull—Abnormalities—
Popular works. 3. Child rearing. I. Title.
RD763.C47   1996
618.92'09752—dc20   95–44576
                                                        CIP

Manufactured in the United States of America

10 9 8 7 6 5 4 3 2 1

To my husband, David, and my children,
Samuel Max and Molly Hannah,
and
to the memory of John J. Wasmuth, Ph.D.
He will be sadly missed.

About the author

Hope Charkins holds a master's degree in social work from San Diego State University. She works as a medical social worker for the Vermont Department of Health, Children with Special Health Needs. Along with her husband, she founded the Treacher Collins Foundation and now serves as its executive director. She has two children, one of whom has Treacher Collins syndrome.

About the cover illustrator

Shirley How is an artist with the National Institute of Art & Disability in Richmond, California, a visual arts center serving adults with developmental and physical disabilities. She was born with physical disabilities, including a facial difference.

Table of Contents

Acknowledgements

Many individuals, families, and organizations contributed to this book. I have had the opportunity to correspond, meet, and speak with people from around the world who have an interest—personal, professional, or both—in facial difference. Immediate and extended families of children with facial difference and adults with facial difference have welcomed me into their lives, and I am grateful. I owe a special thank you to the families who have opened their hearts to share their feelings, thoughts, concerns, triumphs, and disappointments with their contribution of photographs and Parent Statements.

While the personal experiences of my own and other families has guided subject selection for this book, a tremendous effort has been made to include accurate and up-to-date information, especially in the chapters devoted to science, education, health care, and health care financing. (If information was omitted or is erroneous, please contact Woodbine House at the address on the copyright page.) To this effort I would like to think the many people who have offered me *extensive* support: Dr. John Mulliken for medical editing; Dr. Tom Pruzinsky for psychosocial editing; Dr. Susan Hayflick for genetics editing; Dr. Sally Peterson-Falzone for speech and language editing; Dr. Linda Vallino for hearing editing; Pat Chibbaro, R.N., M.S., for advocacy editing and for information about family concerns during hospitalizations; Nancy Smythe for insurance editing; and Dr. David Drazin for writing the educational information.

I would also like to express my appreciation to: Dr. Joseph Murray for offering medical historical perspective on facial difference; Dr. Scott Bartlett, Dr. Joseph McCarthy, Dr. Jeffrey Fearon, Dr. Jeffrey Posnick, Dr. S. Anthony Wolfe for medical editing; Dr. Burt Brent for outer ear reconstruction editing; Elsa Reich, M.S., for genetic information editing; Dr. Robert Jahrsdoerfer for middle and inner ear information editing; Dr. Gary Lindner and Dr. Stephen Schusterman for dental editing; Dr. Sandra Meyer for educational information for hearing loss editing; Dottie McDonald, R.N., B.S.N., for feeding and eating information editing; Michael J. Dixon, Ph.D., for genetics information on Treacher Collins syndrome; Kit Bowry for helping tie up loose ends; and to the professionals and organizations who made an effort to connect me with a variety of families of children with facial difference, especially Patricia Severns, M.A.

Valuable input for the educational information incorporated into Chapters 6 and 7 was provided by: Dr. Susan Hollins, Dr. Ray Chin, Nancy Brogden, M.Ed., Jane Finlay, M.Ed., Ron Eberhardt, M.Ed., and Joanne Unruh, Ph.D.

For the availability of the photographs sprinkled throughout the book I would like to thank: Bill Lesiecki at Phonak, Inc., Preven Brunning at Oticon Corporation, Wendy Davis-Penn at AVR Sonovation, and Patricia Severns at the James Whitcomb Riley Children's Hospital in Indianapolis, along with the families of the children.

In writing this book, I am reminded of my son's tenuous early days and years of life, I am indebted to the people who nourished *his* body and *my* soul: Dr. Duc Ducnuigeen, Annie Lewis O'Conner, R.N., and Sherry Braun, R.D. with unconditional support, knowledge, and humor. They viewed Sam from a position of optimism and creative opportunities to develop his special strengths. Finally, special thank you's go to Nancy Divenere, who reviewed the manuscript of this book from the point of view of family friendliness and family centered care, and Nancy Smythe, who has patiently offered me support and guidance for a number of years.

I am especially indebted to the staff at Woodbine House: Irvin Shapell, Publisher; Susan Stokes, Editor; and Fran Marinaccio and Beth Binns. Their dedication, persistence and good humor have shaped this book immensely and they have been a joy to work with. Of far greater importance, however, is their vision for their "Special Needs Collection" and their interest in the inclusion of information for parents of children with facial difference.

Finally, I owe a special thanks to my family, for without their support this book would never have been written: to Dr. David Drazin, my husband, for providing me with childfree weekends to devote to the creation of this project, as well as his educational expertise; and to Sam and Molly for enjoying those weekends, pointing out to me what is important in life and what isn't, and for their willingness to share me with others during my travels and *lengthy* telephone conversations.

While it is not my intention to omit anyone from these Acknowledgements, I know that it can easily happen. If you assisted me with the writing of this book and do not see your name listed, I apologize.

Foreword

By Joseph E. Murray, M.D.*

Since the mid-1950s, craniofacial surgery has developed and advanced so dramatically that it is now possible to improve or correct almost all facial differences, whether congenital in origin or the result of trauma or disease.

These surgical breakthroughs are due almost solely to the imagination, skill, persistence, and teaching of one man, Dr. Paul Tessier of France. Born in Nantes, and a prisoner during World War II, he returned to work in Paris, where he established the first program for the management of craniofacial deformities, defects, clefts, or other differences in facial appearance.

By integrating his plastic surgery skills with neurosurgery, ophthalmology, maxillo-facial-oral surgery, and dentistry, he opened up the previously described anatomical "no-man's land" for corrective surgery. In addition, he conducted workshops on the complete management of these patients in Paris and around the world. I have been privileged to work with Paul Tessier in Paris and Boston for the past twenty-five years. Dr. Tessier was an active member of our Brigham/Children's/Harvard Craniofacial Centre.

---

* Dr. Joseph E. Murray is a graduate of Holy Cross College and Harvard Medical School. During World War II, he served on active duty in the U.S. Army Medical Corps, caring for hundreds of battle casualties, many with severe facial deformities and extensive burns. These experiences stimulated his lifelong study and treatment of facial differences and organ transplantation.

He performed the first successful human kidney transplant in 1954 between identical twins. As a result of his earlier pioneering work in human kidney transplantation, in 1990 he received the Nobel Prize in Medicine. Long interested in congenital facial anomalies in children, he performed the first mid-face advancement in the United States in 1975.

Currently he is Emeritus Professor of Surgery at Harvard Medical School, and Emeritus Chief of Plastic Surgery at The Brigham & Women's Hospital and The Children's Hospital (where he co-founded the multidisciplinary craniofacial clinic).

But surgical management is only part of the care and support that children with facial difference need. Specially trained nurses and social workers, as well as psychiatrists, psychologists, and other professionals, are integral parts of a well-balanced craniofacial program.

Most important of all is the need for strong parental relationships and understanding. These can strengthen the child's ability to cope with psychological and social issues. To fulfill these needs, regional and national parental support groups have been formed. These families, each affected unexpectedly at the birth of a child who is different, have come together for mutual support, to share information and experiences, and to help where family assistance is needed.

In today's rapidly changing health care delivery system, it is all the more important for parents to know what care and services their children need and where to find them.

The author of this book, Hope Charkins, has created a valuable resource of information for parents of children with facial differences. It covers the more commonly occurring conditions, as well as many of those less frequently seen. Every parent and teacher of a child with a facial difference can learn from her book.

Introduction

In 1987 when my son was born with Treacher Collins syndrome, the facial difference self-help movement had barely begun. During the early days of Sam's life, my husband and I longed for information about his condition and for resources to turn to. Living in a rural community in Washington state, we found neither.

Weeks after Sam's birth, we moved to the East Coast and I continued our quest to locate knowledgeable professionals, support and information organizations, and other families. I received letter after letter in response to my inquiries, informing me that craniofacial anomalies were not part of their database or expertise, but offering me good luck in finding information. I soon began to realize that the lack of information and support for my son's condition was not specific to any one part of the country, as I had hoped; *with few exceptions, it basically did not exist.*

During this time, my son was experiencing significant feeding difficulties, questions were raised about his need for a tracheostomy, I was beginning to encounter discrimination, and I struggled with state-run programs to obtain his needed speech and language therapy. While my plate was certainly overflowing, I hoped that someday I would be able to recount these experiences so that other families could easily access the information they might need about their child's facial difference, seek out appropriate services, and hopefully be spared the wealth of inaccurate information and discriminatory attitudes.

Since a child's and family's early days and years of life together are so critical, I have focused this book on the newborn period up through the preschool years. While later years are equally important, that would be another book! For similar reasons, I have also focused this book on congenital conditions of facial difference: that is, conditions children are born with rather than those that are acquired, such as through trauma, or developed, such as through disease. Perhaps another parent will pick up where I left off! You may also wonder why the term "facial difference" was adopted for this book rather than "facial disfigurement," "birth defect," "craniofacial anomaly," or other similar terminology. I first heard the term "facial difference" in 1989 at a meeting in New York City sponsored by the Institute of Reconstructive Plastic Surgery. This term, while perhaps less precise than other terms, offers a connotation that shows respect for a person's humanity rather than placing a label onto a condition that conjures up an image.

As you read from chapter to chapter, you will notice that the gender of pronouns alternates: "he" in one chapter, and "she" in the next. This language was purposefully used so that the material does not seem sexist or imply that only one sex has facial difference.

In looking back now over the events that have occurred since Sam's birth, I have come to believe the palm reader I consulted for fun in 1975. He identified a lucky crease in the palm of one of my hands. Perhaps it wasn't until the years between Sam's birth and the present that I have been able to see direct results of his prophecy. Since 1988 I have had the good fortune to be able to create countless opportunities to offer accurate information and support about Treacher Collins syndrome to families, professionals, and systems through my work with the Treacher Collins Foundation.

The resources available today for people with facial difference and rare conditions, their families, and professionals far exceed any dreams I had in 1987:

- From a medical perspective, the skill level and procedures of health care professionals have advanced beyond the early experimental years where little was known, and experienced professionals, interdisciplinary teams, and medical centers were few. The interdisciplinary professional community has supported an increased specialized interest in serving people with facial difference. They have organized to further the knowledge base by creating craniofacial-based professional organizations which support research, investigation, and training, and acknowledge the important role of the self-help movement. Thirty years ago, health care professionals not uncommonly advised parents of child born with facial difference to institutionalize their child. This is a travesty. I hope that this book, along with other educational materials and the availability of support groups, will prevent this from ever happening again.

- Support organizations for facial difference, both condition-specific and non-specific, have emerged internationally. While these types of groups can oftentimes have a difficult time being accepted by professionals, a great many craniofacial professionals recognize that support and networking with other people similarly affected with facial difference can be equally as important as the health care that is offered. When their child's condition of facial difference is viewed through the eyes of a connected and networking family, a variety of empowering events can occur: feelings of isolation can dissipate with connection with other families; education and educational materials can enable families to feel more in control of their child's health care and education, and an important part of their child's collaborative team; and, a feeling of unconditional acceptance and belonging with others who "have been there" can develop.

• From social and educational perspectives, the challenge of demystifying facial difference and focusing on the individual rather than the condition still continues. With the beginning of the Human Genome Project (a fifteen-year initiative to map every gene in the human body), people around the world are learning that we all have or carry differences of some type. As computers become more accessible and user-friendly, dissemination of information about facial difference is becoming easier and more widespread. With accurate information, families can educate their communities, and with education comes acceptance.

Access to information is not always what it appears to be. If you flip to the Reading List at the end of this book, you will find a wealth of publications. Unfortunately, some of these are written in language that is not easy to understand and few can be found at your local library or bookstore—the very places where families first turn for information when their child is diagnosed with facial difference. I am especially excited about this book because it is written *for families* and is available *where families go* when seeking information. Families don't need any special connections to professionals, organizations, medical centers, etc. to access this information. This is the way it should be.

ADVISORY BOARD

Editors

SCOTT P. BARTLETT, M.D.
Associate Professor
Division of Plastic Surgery
University of Pennsylvania

BURT BRENT, M.D.
Associate Clinical Professor of Plastic Surgery
Stanford University

JEFFREY A. FEARON, M.D., F.A.C.S.
Director, The Craniofacial Center
Medical City, Dallas

ROBERT A. JAHRSDOERFER, M.D., F.A.C.S.
Professor, Department of Otolaryngology
University of Virginia

GARY S. LINDNER, D.M.D., D.M.SC.
Orthodontist/Pediatric Dentist
The Children's Hospital, Boston

JOSEPH G. MCCARTHY, M.D.
Director, Institute of Reconstructive Plastic Surgery
New York University Medical Center

DOROTHY MACDONALD, R.N., B.S.N.
Clinical Coordinator, Craniofacial Centre
The Children's Hospital, Boston

SANDRA MEYER, ED.D.
Director, Correspondence Education
John Tracy Clinic

JEFFERY POSNICK, D.M.D., M.D., F.A.C.S.
Professor and Chief of Craniomaxillofacial Surgery
Georgetown Craniofacial Center
Georgetown University Medical Center

ELSA W. REICH, M.S.
Clinical Assistant Professor of Pediatrics
New York University School of Medicine

STEPHEN SCHUSTERMAN, D.M.D.
Dentist-in-Chief
The Children's Hospital, Boston

JOANNE UNRUH, PH.D.
Director, Special Education
Hartford, Vermont School District

S. ANTHONY WOLFE, M.D., F.A.C.S.
Clinical Professor of Plastic Surgery
University of Miami

Chapter 1

What Is Facial Difference?

Your child was born with a facial difference. This means that something about the physical, or outward, appearance of your child's face or head is different from most other children's. It also means that you probably have many questions and concerns about how your child's—and your family's—life may be different. Will your child have "average" intelligence? Will he always look like this? What about his health? Will the condition worsen? Will strangers stare at us wherever we go? Will he be able to attend the neighborhood school? Will future children have this problem?

Many of your questions are answered in this book; others can be answered only with time. But you should know at the outset that whatever the facial difference, your child is more *like* other children than *unlike* them. Like every child, your child has inherited family traits from his mother and father, including hair and eye color, stature, and creative, athletic, and other abilities. And like every child, your child has the potential to develop his own personality, interests, and skills and to pursue his own goals. As you watch him grow and develop, you will see which traits make him unique and which remind you of someone else in your family. You will recognize him as an individual with his own strengths and weaknesses—who just happens to have a facial difference.

This chapter discusses some basic information that parents often want to know about facial difference. Included are descriptions of characteristics and possible problems that occur with many types of facial differences. The chapter also explains what causes facial differences and discusses the chances of facial difference recurring in your family. A section on selecting and working with craniofacial experts will help you ensure that you and your child receive the support and treatment you need. Information about the years ahead will give you some idea of what to expect as your child grows older.

As you read through this chapter, keep several points in mind. First, because there are so many types of facial difference, all information included here will not be relevant to your child. Second, remember that research into the cause and treatment of facial differences is continually taking place. Although the scientific knowledge in this chapter is current as of the publication of this book, you should regularly consult your child's health care professionals and support organizations for the most up-to-date information. Third, this chapter attempts to explain complex medical and scientific terminology and concepts in language that is easily understood. Your health care professionals may use different terminology in discussing the same information with you. If you are in doubt, or have questions about what they are saying, do not hesitate to ask for clarification.

What Is Facial Difference?

"Facial difference" is a generic term for a variety of conditions that can affect the structures of a child's head and face—the bones and soft tissues such as nerves, muscles, and fat. Facial differences are either present at birth (*congenital*), or develop later as the result of disease or injury. This book focuses on congenital differences that result from underdevelopment or overdevelopment of the bones and soft tissues of the head and face. Technically, these types of facial differences are known as *craniofacial anomalies*.

Facial differences can affect a child's entire face, or they can occur only in the upper face, middle face, or the lower face. The upper face is from the eyebrows to the hairline; the lower face is below the nose; and the middle face is in between. Differences that occur in the middle and upper face are often called *craniofacial abnormalities*. Differences that occur in the middle to lower face are sometimes referred to as *maxillofacial abnormalities*.

Differences in physical appearance can range from minor (slight) to major (very noticeable). For example, a child born with a minor cleft lip might have only a small notch on one side of his lip, while a child with a severe cleft lip might have an opening that extends through the base of the nose. The number of physical differences a child has can also vary. A child who is mildly affected might have an incomplete cleft lip on one side and a slightly asymmetric nose, while a child who is more severely affected might have a syndrome that includes a cleft lip on both sides of the mouth, receded jaw, and depressed cheekbones. In addition to affecting a child's appearance, facial differences can also cause *functional problems* with breathing, eating, hearing, speech and language, and vision. *Most facial differences do not, however, affect intellectual abilities or potential.* How facial difference affects *your* child will depend on the specific type of facial condition he has, and whether these differences are mild, moderate, or severe.

Most facial differences are lifelong conditions. That is, they are not something that can be outgrown with time. Often, however, one or more operations can reduce or eliminate some of the physical differences, as well as improve functional problems with breathing, eating, hearing, speaking, and seeing. The surgical procedures for different types of facial differences are reviewed below and described in greater detail in Chapter 3.

Why Does Your Child Have a Facial Difference?

Perhaps the most nagging and painful question confronting parents of children with facial difference is WHY? Why does our child have a facial difference? Why did this happen to us? Perhaps you are afraid that you might have done something to cause your child's facial difference. Or perhaps you would like to know if you are likely to have another child with the same condition. For children with most of the conditions discussed in this book, the short answer to your "why" questions is that your child's facial difference resulted from a change in one or more of his genes. For some conditions, unfortunately, the cause is not yet known. This book explains what is currently known about the genetics of facial difference.

To give you the background you need to understand how your child's condition could have occurred, the next section offers a brief overview of genetics.

Some Basic Genetics

If you have been told that the cause of your child's facial difference is genetic, you may be perplexed. After all, if you, your spouse, and your relatives have "normal" faces, how could your child have inherited the condition from you? To understand how a facial difference can be called "inherited," it is necessary to understand a bit more about human genetics.

If your child has a genetic condition, it means that sometime during or before the prenatal period, something out of the ordinary happened to change his genes or chromosomes. Genes are the bits of chemical information in every body cell that serve as a blueprint for development of the embryo. Genes determine or influence all personal characteristics, such as eye color, height, and hair texture. Genes are strung together like beads, and the whole string of beads is a chromosome. Each cell ordinarily contains forty-six chromosomes—twenty-three given by the father, and twenty-three given by the mother. One of these twenty-three pairs (the *sex chromosomes*) determines a child's gender. The other twenty-two pairs of chromosomes are known as *autosomes* and contain the genes that determine all other characteristics.

Most of the genetic causes of facial difference that have been identified occur because of an abnormality in one or more genes on an autosome. These abnormalities arise from a genetic alteration (a change in the chemical blueprint) that can be acquired in one of two ways. First, one or both parents can have a gene alteration in their egg or sperm and pass it on to their child. For example, one parent might pass on a chromosome that is missing part of its genetic material, or one that is rearranged or contains too much genetic material. (This leads to a so-called "familial" or "inherited" facial difference.) Second, the gene alteration can arise anew (spontaneously) in the developing baby. Both conditions are genetic, but only the first is truly inherited.

Genetic conditions are classified according to the way they are passed on from generation to generation. The section below discusses the three most common inheritance patterns for conditions that cause facial differences.

Autosomal Dominant Inheritance. Most of the facial differences discussed in detail in this book, including Apert syndrome, Crouzon syndrome, Pfeiffer syndrome, and Treacher Collins syndrome, are "autosomal dominant" conditions. Autosomal dominant disorders affect a child if he receives altered genetic material from only one of his parents. For example, if a child receives an unaltered gene from his mother but an altered gene from his father, the altered gene will override the other gene, and the child will have a genetic condition.

Sometimes it can be determined that one parent passed on the gene for facial difference. The mother or father may have some or all of the features characteristic of a particular condition, even though he or she may never have been formally diagnosed. One parent may be so mildly affected that it is not until the birth of their more severely affected child that they are diagnosed. More often, however, neither parent shows (*expresses*) the features of the condition. There are two explanations for this:

1) The most likely answer is that the disorder occurred as the result of a new or spontaneous *mutation*. A mutation is a change that takes place in a gene. More specifically, a mutation is a deletion, addition, or rearrangement in one or more of the chemical units within a gene. The parent in whose egg or sperm cell the change occurred had no way of knowing that it happened, had no control over the change, and could not have prevented the change from happening.

2) Another possibility is that the condition occurred as the result of *germline mosaicism*. In germline mosaicism, one parent has some normal eggs (or sperm cells) *and* some egg cells that carry the gene change (mutation) for a genetic condition. He or she appears to be unaffected by the genetic condition but can unknowingly pass it on to a child. At present, there are no reliable tests that can determine in advance whether either parent has germline mosaicism.

If one parent carries a mutated gene for a particular autosomal dominant disorder, there is a 50 percent risk of passing on that gene to each child. That is, each time that parent has a child, there is a one in two chance that the gene will be transmitted to the child. If the gene is transmitted, the child *will* carry the gene and be able to pass it on to his own children and *might* exhibit the condition. In the unlikely circumstance that both parents carry the same altered gene, there is a 75 percent risk of passing on the gene. Each time the couple conceives a child, that child has a 75 percent chance of receiving either one or both altered genes. The risk of passing on an autosomal dominant condition remains the same for each and every pregnancy of the same parents. For example, if there is a one in two chance that each of your children will have the condition, that means that *each* child born has a fifty-fifty chance of inheriting the condition. It does *not* mean that if your first child has the condition then your second child probably will not have it.

If there is no evidence that either parent carries the gene for a particular facial difference, it is *not likely* that future pregnancies will result in a child with the same disorder. Geneticists usually set the chance of recurrence at 1 in 100. This is to account for the uncommon occurrence of germline mosaicism in one parent. Parents who do not have germline mosaicism actually have *no* increased risk for recurrence, whereas the very few who have germline mosaicism have a higher (up to 50 percent) chance. Unfortunately, it is currently impossible to determine whether or not a parent has germline mosaicism.

Autosomal Recessive Inheritance. An *autosomal recessive* disorder affects a child only if he receives an altered gene from both his mother and his father. If he receives an altered gene from one parent but not the other, he will not have the disorder. Instead, he will be a silent "carrier" of the disorder. Because he has one altered and one unaltered gene, he can pass the altered gene on to *his* children. If his spouse also happens to be a carrier for the same altered gene, there is a one in four (25 percent) chance that the child will get both altered genes and fully exhibit the condition. Only one rare type of facial difference—Carpenter syndrome—is known to be an autosomal recessive condition. Understanding the difference between dominant and recessive disorders may be helpful if you decide to do any further reading about genetic disorders.

Multifactorial Inheritance. The most common type of facial difference—cleft lip and/or palate—is usually passed on through what is known as "multifactorial inheritance." (Cleft lip/palate can also be part of a syndrome that is passed on through autosomal dominant or some other means of inheritance.)

What researchers mean by multifactorial inheritance is that the condition cannot be traced to any one cause. Instead, the difference probably results from the interaction of multiple genetic and environmental factors. In other words, some children are genetically more likely to develop cleft lip or palate. Then, exposure to certain substances or other external factors early in the pregnancy leads to clefting. Some environmental factors that have been linked to clefts include maternal nutrition before and during pregnancy, certain viral infections, or maternal use of drugs (both legal and illegal). It is unlikely, however, that a geneticist would be able to determine a specific environmental factor as contributing to your child's facial difference.

Geneticists do not entirely understand how multifactorial disorders are passed on, but research is continuing in this area. These conditions appear to be *polygenetic disorders*. That is, they are caused by a combination of changed genes, rather than a single changed gene. Whether children from families where cleft lip or palate has occurred have a cleft depends on the specific genes they inherit. For example, a child who inherited one altered gene would not express the disorder, but might have it if he inherited several altered genes. It is roughly estimated that a family with one child who has a multifactorial condition runs a risk of almost 5 percent (one in twenty) of having another child with the same condition. The risk for a third child is increased even more if a second child with the condition is born.

Unknown Causes of Facial Difference

It is unfortunately beyond the scope of this book to discuss the possible cause for every facial difference. Furthermore, the causes of many conditions of facial difference have not yet been identified. You should remember that the explanations of possible causes given above apply only to conditions of facial difference that are known to be *genetic*. If the cause of your child's facial difference has not yet been discovered, it may or may not be due to a genetic problem.

Not knowing the cause of your child's facial difference can be very frustrating, especially if you are contemplating having more children and would like to know whether your baby is likely to be born with a facial difference. To keep abreast of the latest research into the cause of your child's condition, consider joining a support group concerned with facial differences in general or your child's condition in particular. See the Resource Guide for some organizations that can help.

TYPES OF FACIAL DIFFERENCE

With the exception of cleft lip and palate, most of the conditions discussed in this book are relatively rare. So, even though you have a diagnosis for your child's facial difference, you may not have been able to find a great deal of information about the condition, or the physical, medical, and developmental characteristics that can accompany it. It is beyond the scope of this book to include *everything* that is known about each of these conditions. The sections below, however, provide the most important information for you to know in the beginning. Chapters 3 and 5 provide additional information about the medical and developmental issues you may encounter.

As mentioned earlier, this book focuses on conditions that are present at birth and result in abnormalities of the bones and soft tissues of the head and face. Many of these conditions are specific types of *syndromes*—recognized patterns of differences that occur in different areas of the body and that are considered to have a single and specific cause. A child is diagnosed with a particular syndrome when he has a cluster of characteristic features that are associated with that syndrome. These characteristic features can occur to different degrees in different children. Your child can have many, some, or only a few of the findings associated with a given syndrome. Although it is unlikely that your child will have all possible problems, being aware of potential difficulties can help you anticipate and deal with difficulties if they arise.

Cleft Lip and/or Palate

Cleft lip (split of the upper lip) and cleft palate (split of the roof of the mouth) are the most common congenital facial differences. Both types of clefts result from an incomplete fusion of skin, muscle, or bone during early fetal development (between the fifth and twelfth week of pregnancy). Cleft lip and cleft palate can occur separately or together as a child's only facial difference, or they can occur together with other characteristics of a syndrome or other congenital condition. For example, cleft palate can be one of several anomalies present in children with Treacher Collins syndrome, Pierre Robin Sequence, or Apert syndrome. (Most children with clefts do not have a syndrome.) A combination of both cleft lip and cleft palate is the most common, occurring 45 percent of the time (in about one in 750 live births a year). Both conditions interfere with the natural functioning of the mouth, and may cause problems with sucking, drinking, chewing, speaking, and hearing. In addition, the teeth may be out of position, misshapen, or rotated, or there may be more or fewer teeth than usual.

As mentioned in the section on genetics above, cleft lip with or without cleft palate and cleft palate can run in families. Usually, however, isolated cleft palate and cleft lip with or without cleft palate don't appear in the same family. Cleft lip with or without cleft palate and cleft palate are two distinct conditions. They have different timing during embryonic development and probably have different causes. Although the specific genetic abnormalities that cause common clefts is a subject of intense research, no one specific gene has been identified. There are likely many different genes associated with cleft lip/palate.

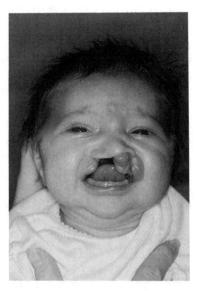

Cleft lip and palate cannot be prevented. The risk of giving birth to a child with a cleft, however, can be estimated under certain circumstances. For example, if one parent has a cleft lip, then has a child with a cleft lip, there is a 13 percent chance that future children will be affected. There is also one type of cleft lip/palate known as van der Woude syndrome that has a 50 percent chance of recurring. This type of clefting is associated with "pits" in the lower lip. It is an autosomal dominant condition known to be caused by a mutation on chromosome number 1.

There are no specific prenatal tests for cleft lip or palate. An experienced radiologist, however, can often use high-resolution ultrasonography to detect a split in the lip, often as early as the sixteenth week of pregnancy. A minor cleft lip usually cannot be detected, nor can an isolated cleft palate.

Cleft Lip

Normally, the lip forms in the fourth to sixth week of development within the uterus. Two tissue tabs grow in from the sides of the face to join with a central tab that grows down from the tip of the nose. If this union is not complete, the baby will be born with a cleft lip, or what was formerly called "hare lip." About 80 percent of the time, there will be a cleft (split) on only one side of the upper lip (unilateral), and 20 percent of the time there will be a cleft on both sides (bilateral). Most unilateral clefts (about 70 percent) occur on the left side.

Minor clefts involve a small notch in the upper lip or a slightly uneven nose (asymmetry). More severe clefts involve a complete separation of the upper lip, extending through the base of the nose. Usually the child's nostril is also displaced or malformed.

Clefts are more common in some ethnic groups than others. They appear to be most common in Native Americans, affecting over 3.6 of every 1,000 babies born. They occur in Japanese babies at a rate of about 2.1 in 1,000 births, and in Chinese babies in about 1.7 of 1,000 births. About 1 in 800 to 1,000 Caucasian babies have the condition, while only about 0.3 in 1,000 (1 in 3,333) African-American babies are born with cleft lip. In Caucasian babies, boys are more likely than girls to have severe cleft lip. Isolated cleft palate, however, is more common in girls.

Cleft Palate

The palate, or roof of the mouth, is composed of bones (hard palate) and a muscular, fleshy area at the back of the roof of the mouth (soft palate). Normally the palate is formed during the first eight to twelve weeks of fetal development. Bone and tissue grow in from the sides of the upper jaw to join in the middle. When the sides do not grow together properly, a cleft between the mouth and the nose results. Usually, the cleft appears as a hole in the roof of the mouth. Clefts vary greatly in width and length, depending on when and where the growth process was interrupted. The cleft can be only in the soft palate, or it can be in the soft *and* part or all of the hard palate. Sometimes a cleft occurs in the muscles of the soft palate, but does not affect the skin covering the muscles, so the cleft is not visible. This is known as a *submucous cleft palate.*

Children with cleft palates can have a variety of other problems, including frequent colds, sore throats, fluid in the ears, and tonsil and adenoid problems.

Operations to repair cleft lip and palate are discussed in Chapter 3.

Craniosynostosis: Single Suture and Multiple Suture

Craniosynostosis is the medical term for the premature closure of the seams (*sutures*) where the bones of the skull come together. This process causes distortion and underdevelopment of parts of the skull and often the face (usually midface). Craniosynostosis usually occurs before birth and is recognizable at birth. Rarely, however, it is not obvious until a child is one year of age or older.

To understand how craniosynostosis affects the head and face, it is important to understand normal development of the skull. The brain grows at a rapid rate before birth and during infancy, achieving about 70 percent of adult volume in the first year of life. The skull, which protects the brain, expands along with the brain. This expansion is possible because the skull is not made up of one solid piece of bone, but of several adjacent segments of bone. As the brain grows, it pushes the skull bones apart. New bone fills into the open seams (*sutures*) between the bones, so that the expanded brain continues to be protected by the skull. Normally, the skull is able to grow in several directions, including front to back and side to side.

Under normal circumstances, these seams (sutures) remain open to allow for further growth. The first seam to close is in the middle of the forehead—it closes by the age of two. Sometimes, however, one or more sutures of the skull fuses early—before birth, at birth, or shortly thereafter. When this happens, skull growth is altered. Once the bones join together at any point in a suture, head growth along the entire joint line is restricted. When one or more sutures fuse, the other, non-fused sutures are forced to compensate by extra growth. Distortion in the shape of the skull then occurs. The amount of distortion is directly related to the number of sutures that fuse prematurely.

If premature fusion (craniosynostosis) is not surgically treated, the proportions of your child's head and face (in some conditions) become increasingly altered. The head grows abnormally and becomes either too long, too wide, too tall, or a combination of these distortions. In some forms of craniosynostosis, the face becomes increasingly flat or concave, as the lower jaw grows normally and the upper jaw grows at about half the normal rate. The eyes can bulge because the bony areas around the eyes (*orbits*) are too small and shallow to fully contain them. This is known as *exophthalmos* or *exorbitism.*

Besides affecting how your child's face and head look, untreated craniosynostosis can cause other serious problems. First, the skull can become so constricted that there is increased pressure on the brain, causing brain damage and intellectual impairment. Rarely, pressure within the skull can also damage the optic nerve, causing impaired vision (blurry vision, decreased field of vision) or blindness. In addition, vision can be reduced because the corneas of the eyes become dry and vulnerable to injury when they are not completely covered by the eyelids. Strabismus, or eyes that do not coordinate with one another, is also common in certain types of craniosynostosis. Hearing loss due to nerve damage or fluid in the middle ear can occur, too.

If craniosynostosis is diagnosed and treated early, most of these complications can be minimized or prevented. See Chapter 3 for a description of surgical treatment options.

Other problems can occur even if your child receives prompt surgical treatment for craniosynostosis. A small nasal airway can cause minor to life-threatening breathing problems and contribute to speech problems. If the face is involved in craniosynostosis, teeth are usually very crowded. These and other problems with the teeth can also contribute to speech problems. See Chapter 3 for descriptions of the treatments that can improve the specific medical problems associated with craniosynostosis and Chapter 5 for information on helpful therapies.

The craniosynostotic conditions are separated into two major categories: 1) isolated or single suture craniosynostosis, involving just the head (conditions in which just one suture prematurely fuses); and 2) multiple suture craniosynostosis, involving just a child's head or his head and face, and sometimes also structures outside the head/neck area (conditions in which more than one suture prematurely fuses).

Single Suture Craniosynostoses

The single suture craniosynostoses occur spontaneously. In some families, they may be passed on from generation to generation as autosomal dominant disorders.

1. *Sagittal suture:* premature fusion of the suture between the two sides of the head, results in *scaphocephaly* (a "boat"-shaped skull). The head is long and thin.
2. *Metopic suture:* premature fusion of the suture between the two sides of the forehead bones, results in *trigonocephaly* (a triangular-shaped skull).
3. *Unilateral coronal suture (unilateral coronal synostosis):* premature fusion of the suture between one side of the forehead and side bones, resulting in *synostotic plagiocephaly* (an oblique or twisted skull).

Multiple Suture Craniosynostoses:

(Apert, Crouzon, Pfeiffer, and Saethre-Chotzen Syndromes)

The multiple suture craniosynostoses are called syndromes and are labelled with the names of the physicians who first described them. Most multiple suture craniosynostoses occur spontaneously. Once they occur, there is a 50 percent chance they will be passed on, as they are autosomal dominant disorders. There are more than 70 multiple suture craniosynostoses, but the best known are Apert, Crouzon, Pfeiffer, and Saethre-Chotzen syndromes. Researchers are actively trying to find the gene mutations that cause these conditions.

Apert Syndrome. Like other syndromes, Apert syndrome is so-called because it results in a combination of distinctive features. The major signs include:

- *Craniosynostosis,* resulting in distortions of the head and face. The large skull is typically short from front to back, wide on the sides, and overly tall. The eye sockets are slightly wide-spaced, the eyeballs bulge, and the eyelids are abnormally tilted downward at the sides.

- Misalignment and crowding of the teeth, due to underdevelopment of the upper jaw (*maxilla*). This makes it difficult or impossible for the teeth on the upper and lower jaws to make complete contact when clenched (*anterior open bite*).
- Cleft palate, which occurs in about 30 percent of children with Apert syndrome.
- Many children with Apert syndrome have either average or above average intelligence, but about half have mental retardation, or learning rates and abilities that are significantly below average. (Children who score below 70 on tests of intelligence are usually considered to have mental retardation.) Surgical procedures performed on the skull during the first year of life probably do not affect a child's cognitive abilities significantly one way or the other.
- Syndactyly, or webbed fingers, toes, or both. This webbing is always present, at least to some degree.

Syndactyly in Apert syndrome can be disabling and is difficult to correct surgically. This is because the webbing in the hands consists not just of skin, but also involves the finger (and toe) bones and joints. (In the feet, the webbing is sometimes just soft tissue.)

The fingers most seriously affected are usually the index, long, and ring fingers. There may be less webbing, or none at all, between the thumb and index finger, and between the ring and little fingers. Some children are born with all fingers fused. Often, the thumbs are short and curved away from the palm. The webbing makes it difficult or impossible for a child to move individual fingers independently. As a result, he may have trouble buttoning shirts, tying shoes, or using zippers. In addition, the child may not be able to completely straighten his elbows. The shoulder joints can also be affected.

Toes are frequently joined by soft tissue, with the tightest webbing between the second, third, and fourth toes. The first and second toes are often fused.

About 1 in 100,000 babies is born with Apert syndrome. The vast majority of time, the condition results from a spontaneous (new) mutation. Apert syndrome is an autosomal dominant genetic condition, so once it occurs, it can be passed on from generation to generation. It may not, however, be obvious that the condition runs in a particular family, perhaps because few adults with Apert syndrome have children. Indeed, familial transmission has only rarely been documented. The gene for Apert syndrome has been located on chromosome 10; it is called Fibroblast Growth Factor Receptor 2 (FGFR2).

Crouzon Syndrome. Crouzon syndrome is an autosomal dominant genetic disorder that results in an underdevelopment of the bones in the middle third of the face and skull. It occurs in about 1 in 10,000 to 1 in 25,000 births. The gene for Crouzon syndrome has been mapped to chromosome 10. It is called Fibroblast Growth Factor Receptor 2 (FGFR2) and is the same gene responsible for Apert and Pfeiffer syndromes.

Features include:

- Craniosynostosis, resulting in a high, flat, prominent forehead, and increased head width.
- Bulging of the eyes (exophthalmos) due to shallow, widely spaced eye sockets and downward slanting eyelids.
- Strabismus—a tendency for one eye to turn to the side or up rather than look straight ahead.
- A receded upper jaw, together with a relatively protruding lower jaw and prominent lower lip.
- Dental problems, including crowded, misaligned teeth.
- A high, arched, narrow palate.
- Hearing loss in about 50 percent of children.

The extent to which children with Crouzon syndrome have these features is quite variable. For example, eye bulging may be so minimal that it is not apparent to a casual observer. A child might also have some features to a severe degree and others to a mild degree or not at all.

Crouzon syndrome is usually present and recognizable at birth. Rarely, the early joining of the cranial bones (*synostosis*) can begin during the first year of life, and become complete by age two to three. Surgery on the front of the skull and upper eyes (*fronto-orbital advancement*), done in infancy, allows the skull and forehead to expand and increase in size. The surgery, however, may need to be repeated later. Surgical advancement of the midface is done in childhood.

Pfeiffer Syndrome. Pfeiffer syndrome is a type of craniosynostosis that is often confused with Crouzon syndrome. It is an autosomal dominant syndrome. Some people who carry the gene for the condition have a genetic mutation on chromosome 8 (FGFR1) and others have a mutation on chromosome 10 (FGFR2).

Features of the syndrome include:

- A tall head that is flat in the front and the back.
- Exophthalmos (bulging of the eyes), which can be severe or quite minor.
- A receded midface and relative prominence of the lower jaw.
- A high arched palate and crowded teeth.
- Thumbs and big toes can be unusually broad, but not always. This is often the key to the diagnosis of Pfeiffer syndrome. Sometimes there is partial syndactyly between the first and second toes and between fingers.
- Usually average intelligence (in the common form of Pfeiffer syndrome).

Saethre-Chotzen Syndrome. The features of this autosomal dominant condition are relatively minor. Often, the features are so minor that people who have the disorder are not diagnosed. As a result, the incidence is not known. Also because the features are not so obvious, Saethre-Chotzen syndrome is usually found in several generations of a family.

- Fusion of the cranial sutures sometimes produces an asymmetric head, flat on one side (*plagiocephaly*), and an asymmetric face.
- A low-set hairline with up-turned hair follicles (like a "cowlick") is typical.
- Ptosis, or droopy eyelids, is common.
- Ears are often low set and often have minor differences at the top of the ear and the folds.
- The nose is "beaked" and the septum (the partition between the nostrils) is deviated to one side (crooked).
- Fingers are short (*brachydactyly*) and often the second and third fingers (and/or toes) are partially fused.
- Rarely, the midface is receded.
- Intelligence is usually not impaired.

Saethre-Crouzon syndrome is commonly confused with either Crouzon or Pfeiffer syndrome or with unilateral coronal synostosis. It is definitely a different disorder, however, because the site of the altered gene lies on chromosome 7.

Carpenter Syndrome. Carpenter syndrome is a very rare form of craniosynostosis that results in an asymmetric tower-shaped skull, short neck, webbing between fingers and toes, and extra fingers. As mentioned above, it is the only condition of facial difference known to be passed on through an autosomal recessive inheritance pattern.

First and Second Branchial Arch Syndromes

The complex structure of a baby's face forms during the embryonic period (1–8 weeks of gestation) when six paired tissues from each side of the face and neck fuse. These tissues are known as the *branchial (or visceral) arches.* The first arches produce the nerves and muscles for chewing, the lower jaw, two of three bones in the middle ear, and a small part of the ears. The second arches produce the nerves and muscles of facial expression, one bone (stapes) in the middle ear, most of the external ears, and parts of the bone above the voice box (larynx). The third arches produce the nerves for swallowing and the remainder of the bone above the larynx. The fourth, fifth, and sixth arches produce the nerves for the vocal cords and the cartilages of the neck.

If anything alters either the production, growth, or migration of the cells that are in the branchial arches, parts of the face will not develop normally. Sometimes the facial differences that occur are symmetrical, suggesting that something altered both sides of one or more branchial arches. Other times, a problem occurs in only one side of the paired branchial arch(es), causing a one-sided facial difference.

This section discusses syndromes that result from problems in the development of the first and second branchial arches. The common feature of these first and second branchial arch syndromes is underdevelopment of the lower jaw (*mandibular hypoplasia*). Some syndromes are asymmetric, while others are symmetric. The asymmetric group includes microtia/atresia and hemifacial microsomia. The symmetric group includes Treacher Collins syndrome and Nager syndrome.

Microtia and Atresia

Microtia and atresia are technical terms for conditions that can affect how your child's ears look and function. Microtia refers to underdevelopment of the outer, visible portion of the ear (the *pinna*). This underdevelopment can result in an ear that looks otherwise typical but is small; in a miniature ear that is folded over and joined to the side of the head; in nothing but skin tags where the ears would normally be; or in a variety of different forms. Atresia refers to the closing or absence of an ear canal in the middle ear. Either microtia or atresia can occur alone or together. These ear anomalies may be the only facial difference a child has, or they can be just one feature of a syndrome, such as Treacher Collins syndrome or hemifacial microsomia.

In about five out of six children, microtia and atresia affect only one ear (unilateral). In one out of six children, both ears are affected (bilateral). When both ears are involved, the right ear is often more affected. In addition, the facial (seventh) nerve may not be located in the expected position, or, especially in children with hemifacial microsomia, the nerve is located closer to the skin. The facial nerve is responsible for movements of the face. If it is small or abnormally developed, some parts of the face do not have normal expression of emotions. The facial nerve can also be accidently damaged during surgery, resulting in paralysis or partial weakness. The more affected the external ear is, the more likely the facial nerve will not function properly and/or be in an atypical position.

Microtia and atresia are often associated with hearing loss. Most children have a moderate hearing loss and cannot distinguish sounds below a decibel level of about 40 to 60. (By comparison, people with normal hearing can hear sounds of 15 decibels or less.) With the help of a bone conduction hearing aid, though, these children can hear well enough to participate in conversations. This is because a bone conduction hearing aid sends sound right to the hearing bones, bypassing the ear canal and eardrum. Chapter 5 provides more information on measuring and treating hearing loss.

On average, 1 out of 10,000 babies is born with isolated microtia and atresia. Among Navajo Indians, however, the condition is much more common, occurring in about 1 in 1,200 births.

Hemifacial Microsomia

Hemifacial microsomia is the second most common congenital facial difference, next to cleft lip and palate. It is a complex condition, known by a variety of names: oculo-auricular-vertebral syndrome, lateral facial dysplasia, craniofacial microsomia, first and second branchial arch syndrome, and Goldenhar syndrome. What all these terms

mean is that there is usually an underdevelopment of soft tissue and bone on one side of the face. This underdevelopment results in facial bones that are smaller than usual. Sometimes both sides of the face are affected. Hemifacial microsomia can occur alone, or as part of a syndrome.

Common features of hemifacial microsomia include:

- One-sided (unilateral) or two-sided (bilateral) underdevelopment of the cheekbone, lower jaw, chewing muscles, temple, outer and middle ear, facial nerve, and facial muscles. Usually, one-sided smallness of the jaw is the most obvious facial difference.
- Hearing loss, related to underdevelopment (microtia /atresia) of the ear. The smaller the ear remnant, the more likely it is that hearing is diminished. Some physicians, but not all, believe that the greater a child's jaw deformity, the more likely it is that hearing (and the facial nerve) are affected.
- Dental problems, including delayed tooth development and sometimes missing teeth, on the affected lower jaw.
- The soft palate frequently moves to the unaffected side. This is because there is underdevelopment of the nerve supply and muscles on the affected side.
- The tongue can be small on the affected side, due to underdevelopment of the hypoglossal (twelfth) cranial nerve.
- Tags of skin and cartilage can occur in front of the ears.
- In about 50 percent or more of children, the facial nerve is weak on the affected side or both sides. Also, the facial

nerve may not be located in the usual place, or is closer to the skin than usual.

- *Macrostomia*—literally "large mouth," often due to a cleft or notch at the corner of the mouth—is present in one-third or more of children with the disorder.

Children with hemifacial microsomia can also have other differences of the head. Dermoid (skin) cysts are common. They can occur near the fusion lines of sutures (typically near the eyebrow) or in the midline of the face (in the nose region). About 5 to 10 percent of children have ocular (eye) dermoids located near the rim of the cornea, or less commonly, in the soft tissue around the eye. There can also be absence of sensation to the cornea of the eye (fifth cranial nerve) or a small eye (*microphthalmia*). Cleft lip/palate occurs in about 15 percent of children with hemifacial microsomia.

Besides the differences that occur in the head and neck, there may be differences in other parts of the body. This is called the "expanded spectrum" of hemifacial microsomia. Approximate percentages of children with each of these features are given. (The percentages add up to more than one hundred because many children have more than one feature.)

- Skeletal (40 percent): fusions of the cervical spine bones (neck); curvature of the spine; rib anomalies; or underdevelopment of the thumb or forearm.
- Cardiac (25 percent): these include structural differences or malformations of the heart and range from major problems, such as *tetralogy of Fallot* and *transposition of the great vessels,* to *minor aortic arch anomalies.* (See the Glossary for definitions.)
- Central nervous system (15 percent): intracranial cyst, underdevelopment of connections between the two halves of the brain, or hernia of the brain.
- Kidney (10 percent): usually an absence of one kidney, double ureter, fusion of the kidneys, and/or an abnormal blood supply to the kidneys.
- Pulmonary (10 percent): incomplete formation of the segments of the lung or an absence of a portion of the lung.
- Gastrointestinal (10 percent): imperforate anus (an anus with no exterior opening), either with or without an abnormal opening between the rectum and the vagina.

Hemifacial microsomia can cause problems ranging from only a slightly underdeveloped lower jaw to severe deformities of the skull and face. The disorder is apparent at birth, but sometimes the features become slightly more noticeable as the child grows. The degree of involvement, however, does not change with time. In other words, if your child starts out with mild differences, he will end up with mild differences. The condition can become more noticeable with growth, however, as one side grows normally while the other side does not.

Because there are so many different variations on how hemifacial microsomia can affect a child, a classification system is used to help medical professionals document the disorder and study the best treatment for each individual child. One such system— called the O.M.E.N.S.—helps physicians assess how hemifacial microsomia affects a child in five areas:

1. *O* for orbital (eye) asymmetry (how close in size, shape, and position the eyes are to one another).
2. *M* for mandibular hypoplasia. How severe is the underdevelopment of the jaw and the TMJ (temporomandibular joint)?
3. *E* for external ear deformity.
4. *N* for nerve involvement. Is the facial nerve impaired?
5. *S* for soft tissue deformity, underdevelopment of muscles and subcutaneous fat.

Each letter or anatomic feature is graded 0, 1, 2, or 3. The higher the number, the greater the severity of the difference.

During infancy and early childhood, your physician will probably pay the most attention to the "M" score, because jaw deformities can lead to special problems at this age. For example, newborns may have difficulty feeding, as well as breathing problems at night (*obstructive sleep apnea*), due to a narrowed airway. Chapter 3 explains how these difficulties can be medically treated.

Although hemifacial microsomia was first identified in the mid-1800s, its cause is still unknown. One theory is that the blood supply to the first and second branchial arches—where the primitive ears and neck of a fetus are located—is disturbed during the first four to six weeks of pregnancy. Often the condition seems to occur spontaneously and randomly. In some families, however, hemifacial microsomia appears to be passed on from generation to generation as a dominant condition. This means that some families who have one child with the condition have an increased risk of having another, while most families do not. It all depends on your family history. Hemifacial microsomia occurs in about 1 in 5,600 births, and is slightly more common in boys than girls.

Unfortunately, if you are concerned about having another child with the condition, there are no prenatal tests designed specifically to detect hemifacial microsomia. High resolution ultrasonography, however, can often pick up significant features of facial differences or asymmetries. Excess amniotic fluid (*polyhydramnios*) can also be a tipoff that this or another craniofacial anomaly is present.

Treacher Collins Syndrome

Treacher Collins syndrome is a very complex genetic condition that involves underdevelopment of many parts of the head and face. The hearing loss associated with the condition was first described in 1846 by Scottish physiologist Allen Thomson. The disorder is named after Edward Treacher Collins, however. He was an English ophthalmologist who wrote about several patients with the condition in 1900, gathering together major findings about the condition and identifying it as a syndrome. In Europe, Treacher Collins syndrome is also known as mandibulofacial dysostosis and Franceschetti-Zwahlen-Kleine syndrome.

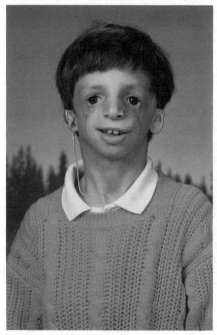

Except in very mild cases, Treacher Collins syndrome is recognizable at birth. It produces the same facial differences on both sides of the face, usually to the same degree. For example, if the right ear is mildly affected, the left ear will be, too. If the left side of the jaw is underdeveloped, the right side will be, too. In other words, the characteristic physical features are *bilateral* and *symmetric*. There is no facial nerve weakness; this fact and the symmetrical differences usually serve to differentiate Treacher Collins syndrome from bilateral hemifacial microsomia.

Common features of Treacher Collins syndrome include:

- Downward-slanting (*antimongoloid*) eyelids and eyes.
- Notching (*colobomas*) of the lower eyelids. There can be one or several notches. The notching can be slight or extreme. The notching can prevent the eye from closing normally, especially during sleep.
- Sparse or absent eyelashes in the inner one-third of the lower eyelids.
- "Sideburns," or licks of hair extending in front of the ears.
- Underdevelopment of the bones of the face, including the cheekbones (*zygomas*), lower jaw (*mandible*), and upper jaw (*maxilla*).
- An abnormal bite (*malocclusion*) related to underdevelopment, particularly of the lower jaw.
- A smaller than average face, which can make the mouth appear broad and the nose appear relatively prominent.
- Underdeveloped and/or malformed external ears.
- Hearing loss, usually conductive and severe, due to narrowing or absence of the ear canal or other middle ear abnormalities. See Chapter 5 for more information about hearing losses.

Less common features include:

- Cleft palate, with or without cleft palate, in about 20 to 35 percent of children.
- *Macrostomia*—a large mouth which may be due to a minor cleft at the corner of the mouth—in about 15 percent of children.
- *Choanal atresia*—a bony plate located above the soft palate, between the nose and the throat, which obstructs breathing.
- Strabismus—the tendency of one or both eyes to look inward, outward, or upward rather than straight ahead.

The underdeveloped facial features associated with Treacher Collins syndrome can cause a variety of complications. For example, because the infant's lower jaw is small, his tongue can take up so much room in his mouth that he has significant problems breathing. This problem may improve as he grows larger, but as a baby he may need a tube in his throat (*tracheostomy)* to make sure he receives enough oxygen. You might also have to use a special apnea monitor if your child has breathing problems at night. This device produces a loud noise to alert you if your child's breathing becomes too shallow or infrequent. Later on, an operation on the lower jaw (and sometimes upper jaw) is done to correct the airway problems.

Underdevelopment of your child's jaw can also cause eating and swallowing problems, especially if your child also has cleft lip or palate. The small lower jaw may not open fully. A feeding tube, a special nipple, and special formula might be necessary to ensure that your baby or young child receives adequate nutrition.

Finally, as mentioned above, your child will probably have a hearing loss, and could need a hearing aid and speech and language therapy to enhance his communication abilities. See Chapters 3 and 5 for more information on medical and therapeutic care for these problems.

One problem that Treacher Collins syndrome usually does *not* cause is mental retardation. Children with Treacher Collins syndrome have the same range of intelligence as any other children. Because of your child's physical appearance or use of hearing aids, however, people might sometimes jump to the conclusion that he has mental retardation. As Chapter 4 explains, this makes it especially important to nurture your child's self-esteem. And as discussed in Chapter 3, reconstructive plastic surgical procedures to improve your child's appearance can also help.

The precise cause of Treacher Collins syndrome is not yet known, but is an area of active research. Scientists initially identified a region on chromosome number 5 as the location of the gene responsible for the condition. Recently, they isolated the gene itself. This is likely to have some immediate benefits, but there is still much work to be done before it is understood how this gene causes the facial differences seen in Treacher Collins syndrome.

Treacher Collins syndrome is an autosomal dominant condition. Most cases are sporadic, the result of a new mutation of the gene. In other words, neither parent has an alteration of chromosome number 5. Instead, something happened to alter the fetal genetic material on one half of this chromosome pair. About 40 percent of the time, one parent has the Treacher Collins syndrome gene. The discovery of the Treacher Collins gene should lead to benefits where clinical diagnosis is difficult—for example, in determining whether a parent with extremely mild features of Treacher Collins syndrome actually has the condition, or in confirming that the parents of an apparently sporadic case are truly unaffected.

No matter how someone gets the gene for Treacher Collins syndrome, once he has it, he has a 50/50 chance of having a child with Treacher Collins syndrome with each and every pregnancy. Parents who are thinking about having additional children are often interested in prenatal testing for a variety of reasons—including arranging for improved medical care at delivery if another child with Treacher Collins syndrome is born. If you are concerned that future children might have the condition, prenatal testing may be available. The discovery of the Treacher Collins gene will make this test more accurate than ever before. It will not, however, be able to predict how mildly or severely affected your child will be. If you are thinking about prenatal testing, it would be advisable to consult a clinical geneticist before becoming pregnant. High resolution ultrasonography can also detect features of Treacher Collins syndrome prenatally, but usually not before twenty weeks of pregnancy. You should consult a radiologist who is experienced in visualizing the eyes, jaws, chin, ears, etc. Ultrasonography, however, is not a definitive diagnostic procedure and a fetus with mild features might not be detected. The best way to proceed might be to use genetic testing in conjuction with ultrasonography. Again, this is another area where it is advisable to seek advice.

Some physicians once believed that the condition becomes worse with each succeeding generation (called "genetic anticipation"). But they may have come to this conclusion because in the past, only people with mild symptoms of Treacher Collins syndrome were likely to marry and have children. Parents with mild features might not have been diagnosed until they had children with more severe, noticeable features. So it appeared that succeeding generations were more severely affected. In reality, though, the degree a child can be affected ranges from mild to severe, and there is no way to predict how affected a child might be based on his parent's features.

Currently, it is estimated that about 1 in 10,000 children is born with Treacher Collins syndrome. Geneticists at the major craniofacial centers believe that the frequency is higher, since many people with the disorder are so mildly affected that they have not been diagnosed. Even today, many parents are not diagnosed until after the birth of a more severely affected child.

Nager Syndrome

Nager syndrome (preaxial acrofacial dysostosis) shares many of the features of Treacher Collins syndrome. Children with Nager syndrome have flat cheeks and down-slanting eyes, almost total absence of the eyelashes, low-set, cup-shaped ears, and a very small lower jaw. In addition, they have asymmetric underdevelopment of the thumbs and forearms. Sometimes these children have genitourinary abnormalities or major heart anomalies, such as tetralogy of Fallot.

Pierre Robin Sequence and Associated Syndromes

The diagnosis of "Pierre Robin sequence" is given to infants born with severe underdevelopment of the lower jaw (*micrognathia*), a retruded (backward positioned) tongue (*glossoptosis*), and usually a cleft of the soft or hard and soft palate. The small mandible is thought to be the primary problem and responsible for the backward-positioned tongue and the occurrence of the cleft palate. Infants with Pierre Robin sequence can have life-threatening airway and feeding problems.

Sometimes additional problems can occur in a child with the "Pierre Robin sequence." If other problems *are* present, the child has a syndrome. The two most common disorders that cause the "Pierre Robin sequence" are Stickler syndrome and velocardiofacial syndrome (VCFS).

Stickler Syndrome

About 40 percent of infants with Pierre Robin sequence have Stickler syndrome. This is an autosomal dominant condition that has variable effects within a family. The syndrome involves skeletal abnormalities, arthritis, and eye problems. Eye problems include severe nearsightedness (usually before the age of ten), detachment of the retina, and cataracts.

Recent research has shown that most people with Stickler syndrome have a mutation within genes (two are known to date) that are responsible for various types of *collagen* (the structural protein in tissues).

Velocardiofacial (Shprintzen) Syndrome

About 15 percent of infants with Pierre Robin sequence are found to have velocardiofacial (Shprintzen) syndrome, called VCFS. In fact, this is the most common syndrome associated with an isolated cleft palate, accounting for about 8 percent of cases. Approximately 1 in 2,000–5,000 children are born with VCFS.

Children with VCFS have a typical facial difference. The face is long with a prominent upper jaw, flattening of the cheeks, and underdevelopment of the lower jaw. The opening of the eyelids is often narrow, and there may be a bluish coloring below the eyes. The ears are small with slightly thickened upper rims. The nose is prominent, and has narrow nasal passages and a square-shaped root (between the eyes). The upper lip is long and thin with downslanting mouth. Over one-half of children with VCFS have an obvious cleft palate or a hidden (submucous) cleft palate.

More than 50 percent of people with VCFS have multiple abnormalities of the heart. These include ventricular septal defect, right-sided aortic arch, tetralogy of Fallot, and aortic valve disease. These conditions are defined in the Glossary.

All children with VCFS have learning disabilities (LD). That is, they have more difficulty learning in one or a few specific areas than would be otherwise expected based on their intellectual abilities. For example, a child could have great difficulty with spelling or reading, but do well in other academic areas. Language development is often slow in children with VCFS, and psychological problems often occur. Children with VCFS are often described as having extremes of behavior.

VCFS is an autosomal dominant condition. Genetic studies of children with the condition show that a microscopic segment on the long arm of chromosome 22 is missing. Technically, this makes VCFS a "microdeletion syndrome." The genetic test for diagnosis of this condition, called "FISH analysis," can be performed in many university centers.

Other Facial Differences

Any condition that has been diagnosed in fewer than 200,000 Americans is considered an "orphan" or rare disorder by the National Organization for Rare Disorders. These conditions are considered orphan disorders because they are overlooked by most

A girl with Moebius syndrome.

researchers, drug companies, and medical professionals, who concentrate on more common conditions. Because these conditions are not studied as widely as other conditions, they tend to be misdiagnosed or under-reported.

Many of the facial differences described in this book are so uncommon as to be classified as orphan disorders. But there are also other, even rarer, conditions that cause facial differences. These include Juberg-Hayward syndrome, Miller syndrome, Moebius syndrome, oral-facial-digital syndrome, Freeman-Sheldon syndrome, cephalopolysyndactyly (Grieg syndrome), Baller-Gerold syndrome, craniofrontonasal dysplasia with orbital hypertelorism, and frontal encephalocele.

If your child has one of these diagnoses or another diagnosis not mentioned, this book can still be of value to you. A child with any facial difference needs to be evaluated and followed by an interdisciplinary craniofacial team, which is described below. Most of the information in the other chapters should also be helpful to you and your family. In addition, parent support groups have formed around many of these very rare craniofacial disorders. Some are listed in the Resource Guide. Your child's craniofacial team may also be able to help you locate these groups and the physicians who have focused their work on your child's particular condition.

Is Facial Difference a Disability?

Besides learning a specific name for your child's facial difference, you might hear a variety of terms associated with your child's diagnosis. These might include "special-needs child," "handicapped child," or "disabled child." But *is* he a child with special needs? Does he have a disability?

The answer lies, in part, on how you define these terms. Many people use them all interchangeably, so that if you agree that your child has some special needs, you also seem to be agreeing that your child has a disabling condition. Other people make distinctions among terms. Perhaps you will find the definitions developed by Dr. Thomas Strax helpful in clarifying how you look at your child's facial difference, as well as any accompanying speech, hearing, vision, or other problems.

According to Strax, an *impairment* is "something that someone lacks"—whether it be the ability to see, hear, or think as well as other people, or a specific body part. An impairment, according to Strax, can result in a *disability*—or difficulty performing a particular activity, whether it be reading a book, running, or dressing. So, if your child's hearing is impaired, he probably has some hearing disability.

In contrast to a disability, a *handicap* is more of a perceived than real problem—"It is socially imposed." A disability is only a handicap when society jumps to the conclusion that someone with a disability cannot perform a particular activity, when indeed he can, or expects him to participate in an activity when his disability impedes him from doing so. When your child's appearance causes others to treat him differently, it *could* be a handicap. For example, a facial difference could become a handicap if your child's teacher doesn't correct his mispronunciations because she mistakenly assumes that he can't do any better. Or it could become a handicap if neighborhood children don't include your child in games simply because he looks different.

If there *are* any disabling conditions—hearing, speech, vision, or intellectual impairments—associated with your child's condition, how they affect your child's life will depend on a variety of factors. As Chapters 3, 5, and 6 discuss, some of these factors include the medical, educational, psychological, and therapeutic care your child receives. Perhaps the most important factor is the attitude that your child and your family have toward his facial difference, and the support you provide him.

In the long run, whether you, your family, and your child choose to regard his facial difference as a disability is basically up to you. Some parents decide from the start not to perceive their child as having a disability, while others wait and see how their child will be affected. Many parents find that they must occasionally allow *others* to label their child as disabled in order to get needed services or benefits. This may happen, for example, if you seek special therapeutic or educational help for your child through the public schools. Under federal law, children cannot receive this special assistance unless they are diagnosed with a "disabling condition." Or your child may need to be diagnosed with a disability to qualify for certain types of financial assistance that will help pay for needed medical treatment and equipment. (See Chapters 6 and 7 for more information.)

No matter who might be labelling your child as disabled and why, you might do well to take the advice of Thomas Strax: "Do not assume that a disability is an inability. When we do, we severely limit the horizons of those with chronic illnesses and disabilities, and in doing so, we limit our own horizons as well."*

Working with an Interdisciplinary Team

The facial conditions described in this book are often quite complex, and can cause a variety of physical, emotional, and intellectual difficulties. Obviously, it would be impossible for one health care professional to have the knowledge and expertise to handle all of your child's needs. The solution is to work with a team of highly specialized health care professionals who each focus on a different problem that confronts your child or your family. When specialists from a variety of disciplines pool their knowledge and experience to help one child, they are known as a *multidisciplinary team or interdisciplinary team*. (The prefix "inter" implies that the various specialists are working together, while "multi" means only that there are several specialists.)

Some interdisciplinary teams meet together (as a group) with your child and your family. Others see your child individually, then come together as a group to discuss their findings and to plan treatment. In either case, all team members should work together to ensure that all your child's needs are met in a coordinated manner. When necessary, an interdisciplinary team will refer a patient to a specialist who is not a member of the team or is a consulting member.

---

* Thomas E. Strax, M.D., "What Price, Discrimination?" *Children's Health Issues*, Center for Children with Chronic Illness and Disability, Vol. 1, No. 1 (May 1992): 3.

If your child was not evaluated by an interdisciplinary team soon after birth, he should be seen by one as soon as possible. The genetics professional(s) on the team will confirm, whenever possible, your child's diagnosis. Sometimes during the initial evaluation, the geneticist will recognize features that could be a part of more than one condition or syndrome, and may not be sure of your child's precise diagnosis. It then becomes the job of the genetics professionals to "rule out" those conditions your child does not have. For example, children with bilateral hemifacial microsomia and Treacher Collins syndrome sometimes share many of the same features. So, too, can children with Nager syndrome and Treacher Collins syndrome. And cleft lip and/or palate often occur alone, but they can also be part of a syndrome. Early diagnosis of your child's specific condition is important so that all professionals working with your child know what to be alert to—especially potential breathing and feeding problems. The geneticist should provide you with a report outlining your child's diagnosis that you can share with other professionals.

Early evaluation is also important to assess cognitive, physical, speech, and language development and to plan treatment. The team should also notice other potential problems related to your child's condition, such as visual or hearing impairments, and recommend evaluation. In addition, the team usually wants to photograph your child and have x-rays taken. These visual images—together with measurements made with a tape measure or caliper—will provide the team with a baseline for monitoring your child's growth.

The interdisciplinary team can also help in many other ways. Members can answer your many questions, including concerns about why this condition occurred and whether it will occur again. They can offer emotional support and connect you with parent support groups and other resources. They can also provide service coordination or case management. A case manager or service coordinator is usually a nurse or social worker, but can also be the clinic administrator or coordinator. This professional can assist you in navigating through the systems that provide care for your child. He or she might, for instance, help you with paperwork or billing procedures at the hospital, ensure that members of the interdisciplinary team receive all reports relevant to your child, coordinate meetings between team members and other professionals your child might see, and serve as a resource to your child's pediatrician or other local health care professionals. Some parents like the assistance of a case manager or service coordinator; others prefer to do it all themselves. Either way, because so many conditions of facial difference are so complex and require on-going care by professionals from a variety of disciplines, it is important that someone coordinate your child's care.

The exact makeup of your child's team will depend on his needs and your concerns, as well as on the professionals available at your craniofacial center. Children with cleft lip and/or cleft palate who have no other facial differences are generally seen only by a "cleft palate team." Members of this team typically include an audiologist, nurse, orthodontist, otolaryngologist, prosthodontist, pediatrician, plastic surgeon, psychologist, and speech pathologist. Children with more complex cases or syndromes are seen by a "craniofacial team." Often the cleft palate and craniofacial teams are made up of many of the same specialists. Professionals who may be involved include: a craniofacial (plastic) surgeon, anesthesiologist, anthropologist, audiologist, dentist, epidemiologist, feeding specialist, geneticist, maxillofacial surgeon, neurosurgeon, nurse, nutritionist, occupational therapist, ophthalmologist, orthodontist, otolaryngologist, pediatrician, pedodontist, physical therapist, psychiatrist, prosthodontist, psychologist, social worker, and speech pathologist.

Below are brief descriptions of the professionals who may see your child at some time or be consulted about your child's needs, either as a member of his team or as an outside specialist. Chapters 3, 5, and 6 provide more information about how these professionals might work with your child.

Craniofacial Surgeon — A plastic surgeon who will probably direct and oversee your child's treatment. (See Plastic surgeon, below.) He is in this position because he has extensive experience and training in: treatment planning, operating on patients with facial difference, working in a team approach, studying ("following") patients with facial difference over many years, and holistically directing children's care and treatment. In addition to leading your child's team at the craniofacial center, he may also do your child's operations, or they may be performed by other surgical specialists on the team.

Anesthesiologist — A physician who specializes in administering drugs and gases to produce a loss of feeling and a state of sleep in the body so that a surgical procedure can take place.

Anthropologist — A scientist who specializes in monitoring and charting the size, weight, and proportion of parts of your child's body, especially the bones. (Many teams do not have an anthropologist. If there isn't an anthropologist on your child's team, another professional—perhaps a *medical anthropometrist*—will monitor bone growth.) This information could help to determine the best age for operations. The anthropologist may also gather information on growth for research purposes. For example, a team may feel it is important to gather growth information on all of their patients with Apert syndrome to see if they recognize any similarities, dissimilarities, or trends. They may also want to add this information to the scientific body of knowledge on that condition by presenting the information in a journal article, at a professional conference, etc. For information on participating in research, see the section on "The Future of Children with Facial Difference" later in this chapter.

Audiologist — A health professional who determines how well your child hears by administering tests and evaluating the presence of fluid in the ears. The audiologist prescribes hearing aids, if necessary, and provides on-going care to make sure the hearing aids work correctly. See Chapter 5 for more information.

Dentist — A doctor who diagnoses and treats problems with your child's teeth and the inside of his mouth by filling cavities and creating crowns and bridges. The dentist also prescribes preventive measures, such as fluoride treatments. If your child's dentist specializes in treating children, he will be called a pedodontist or pediatric dentist.

Epidemiologist — A scientist who specializes in studying the frequency, distribution, and causes of health problems, including facial difference. He may be required to report statistics to the state or to particular agencies, such as the Centers for Disease Control in Atlanta. It is not likely you will meet with this professional.

Feeding Specialist — A professional who is trained to help infants and young children who have problems either with the physical process of eating, or behavioral problems associated with eating. The feeding specialist often works with the nutritionist (see below).

Geneticist — A physician who specializes in inherited conditions and syndromes. Technically, geneticists are physicians with M.D. degrees, but you may also encounter "genetic counselors," who typically have a master's degree. One of these genetics professionals will diagnose your child's condition, and meet with you to explain: the features associated with the condition and why that is your child's diagnosis; why your child has this condition, if known (passed on from another family member, spontaneous mutation, etc.); whether you are likely to have other children with this or other genetic conditions; what to expect as your child grows; current research being done on your child's condition; and how to get in touch with researchers or support groups for the condition. At your request, he may put together a family pedigree—that is, gather information about your family history of genetic or non-genetic conditions, and then make a diagram or map of your family similar to a family tree.

Maxillofacial Surgeon — A surgeon who specializes in operations to treat skeletal problems of the lower half of the head and face (from the nose to the upper jaw). He or she often works with the plastic surgeon and/or neurosurgeon, dentist, and orthodontist.

Neurosurgeon — A surgeon who specializes in operations which require exposing parts of the nervous system (brain, spinal cord, nerves) and correction of the upper skull.

Nurse — A health care professional who assists in caring for your child under the direction of a physician. As a member of a craniofacial team, a nurse may coordinate your child's care or work closely with the nutritionist or developmental pediatrician to monitor your child's growth and development.

Nutritionist — A professional with expertise in how the human body takes in and uses nutrients for growth, energy, and maintenance. The nutritionist can advise you how to increase calories in formula or food if your child has a feeding or weight gain problem; work with the nurse to find the best bottle or nipple or to develop feeding strategies, such as a daily feeding schedule; provide suggestions about making the transition from a feeding tube to regular food.

Occupational Therapist — A professional who helps your child work on muscle strength and coordination so that he can improve his self-care skills (tooth brushing, handling utensils, grooming, etc.), as well as leisure and (school) work skills such as handwriting. An occupational therapist frequently concentrates on movements involving small muscles of the body (fine motor skills), in contrast to the physical therapist, who usually focuses on movements involving larger muscles (gross motor skills). Occupational therapy might be especially important if your child has a hand or other limb anomaly, such as with Apert syndrome or Nager syndrome. Before an operation, your child will need to be taught how to use his affected hands or limbs, and after the procedure he will need to be taught how to re-use his hands or limbs.

Ophthalmologist — A physician who specializes in diagnosing and treating eye problems, prescribes medications, and is skilled at delicate eye surgery. An ophthalmologist is different from an optometrist or optician. An *optometrist* is a specialist (not an M.D.) trained to examine the eye and prescribe corrective lenses, such as eyeglasses or contact lenses, to improve vision. Since he is not a physician, he is not qualified to diagnose or treat disease or injuries of the eye, or to perform surgery. An *optician* is a specialist trained to make prescription lenses used for correcting vision.

Orthodontist — A dentist who aligns and straightens teeth by using braces, retainers, etc., and who monitors and treats malocclusions (teeth that do not line up properly).

Otolaryngologist — A physician who specializes in treating conditions of the ears, nose, and throat, and infections in those areas. This physician, also known as an ear, nose, and throat specialist (ENT), provides important care for children who have cleft palate, on-going ear infections, or permanent or fluctuating hearing loss.

Pediatrician — A physician who specializes in the general medical care of children. Pediatricians who are part of craniofacial teams are usually developmental pediatricians—doctors with specialized training in monitoring development and in recommending treatment for delays in development.

Pediatric Dentist/Pedodontist — A dentist who specializes in the general dental care of children and has special training in managing unusual dental problems in children. Your child's team will generally include this type of dentist, rather than a regular dentist.

Physical Therapist — A professional who uses activities and exercises to help your child overcome problems with movement and posture, usually involving large muscles of the body. Evaluation and therapy can be especially relevant if your child had a "slow" beginning learning movement skills because he had feeding or breathing problems, spent time in the neonatal intensive care unit (NICU), or has hand or other limb anomalies.

Plastic Surgeon — A surgeon who builds, constructs, reconstructs, corrects, or improves the shape and appearance of body structures. He or she performs operations on the face, jaws, and head along with the maxillofacial surgeon and/or neurosurgeon. If the plastic surgeon is the director of the craniofacial team, he usually coordinates the treatment plan.

Prosthodontist — A dentist who specializes in making oral appliances such as dentures and bite plates—devices which improve the function of the structures in the mouth. He or she makes the appliances that the orthodontist uses, as well as crowns, bridges, caps, etc.

Psychiatrist — A physician who specializes in the study, treatment, and prevention of mental disorders such as depression, anxiety, and aggressive behavior. Psychiatrists can provide therapy to help with coping with a diagnosis, pre- or post-surgery concerns, and other family stress. They also help the other team members and parents to decide on when a particular surgical intervention should be done, based on the child's and parents' feelings. As a member of the craniofacial team, they could also be consulted if medication is needed for depression or another mental disorder.

Psychologist — A professional trained in understanding human behavior, emotions, and how the mind works. The psychologist can administer tests to determine intellectual abilities and to pinpoint emotional, social, or personality problems. As a member of the team, he or she also provides therapy to help parents, children, or other family members cope with concerns related to facial difference. The psychologist is most likely to be consulted at diagnosis, when planning the appropriate time for surgeries, and immediately before and after surgery. Also see the description of Social Worker, below.

Social Worker — A professional who monitors the social, emotional, and psychological growth and development of your child and family. He or she can help to identify and remedy problems associated with his facial difference. Sometimes there is overlap between what the psychologist and social worker do on a craniofacial team. Often, however, the social worker concentrates more on service-coordination and planning after surgery (discharge planning). The social worker may be more accessible to parents, especially in an on-going manner. On some teams, the psychologist provides the therapy and crisis management, while the social worker acts as a pipeline to the psychologist and provides on-going support. Both the social worker and the psychologist may also be involved with support groups, and refer families to them.

Speech and Language Pathologist — A professional who specializes in analyzing difficulties with speech and communication and ways to improve these skills. Chapter 5 explains how the speech and language pathologist may work with your child.

Not all craniofacial teams have the same philosophical approach—that is, they may differ in the types of operations they recommend; the timing of procedures; the number of operations; whether they put more emphasis on a child's abilities vs. disabilities; and their perceptions of the family's role in their child's treatment. For example, one team may recommend doing jaw or cheekbone surgery on a toddler that will need to be repeated at a later age, while another team may recommend doing the same surgery later with the hope that it won't need to be repeated. Teams can also have different psychological perspectives. Some teams may routinely coordinate operations with the child's psychological needs for an enhanced appearance, while other teams may be less concerned about this factor.

It is important for you to feel confident in the technical expertise and philosophy of your child's team. You may want to schedule evaluations with several teams in order to find the team you feel the most comfortable with. In selecting a team, consider the following points:

1. How much experience has the team had in caring for children with your child's diagnosis? Individually and collectively, team members should have had experience over a long enough period that they are familiar both with immediate and long-term complications and the changes that occur with growth. This enables them to anticipate and plan for problems.

2. Is the team willing to connect you with other patients and families with your child's diagnosis so that you can ask about their experiences with this team?

3. Are they willing to explain how their team works together and provide information about the institutions (hospitals, medical schools, colleges and universities, research centers, support groups) with which the team is connected?

4. Does the team recognize your need to get a second opinion when recommendations are made, especially for surgical opinions?

5. What are you looking for from the team and individual members? For some parents, the expertise of the profes-

sionals is a primary concern. For others, the personalities of the professionals ("bedside manner") is very important. Still others seek professionals who value their knowledge and experience as parents, or a combination of these and other factors.

To locate a craniofacial team, you can ask for a referral from a health care professional such as your pediatrician. You can also contact one of the craniofacial centers directly. Large national organizations such as the Cleft Palate Foundation and the National Foundation for Facial Reconstruction have listings of teams throughout the U.S. and Canada, and can offer referrals in your geographic location. Ask them to explain their criteria for including teams on their lists. Smaller, condition-specific organizations, such as the Freeman-Sheldon Parent Support Group and the Treacher Collins Foundation, may also provide referrals, usually to teams that treat many patients with that specific condition. Consult the Resource Guide for names and addresses of organizations that can help.

The History of Facial Difference

In a society that places great value on physical appearance, the history of facial difference reflects tremendous advances, as well as on-going challenges, for children with facial difference and their families. For much of recorded history, facial difference has commonly been associated with mental retardation and "badness." Throughout the world, there is documentation that children born with facial difference (and often their parents, too) were treated with hostility and accused of being evil.

In 1904, J.W. Ballantyne, a Scottish obstetrician, wrote a historical review of beliefs and attitudes about children with facial difference and their parents. According to Ballantyne, the ancient Greeks believed children with facial difference were created by the gods for their own amusement, or to warn, admonish, or threaten mankind. In Roman times and later in the Middle Ages in Europe, children with facial difference, and often the mother, were sacrificed to placate the gods.

In European folklore, children with physical deformities or mental retardation were thought of as the offspring of fairies, elves, or other sub-human beings, or as beings who had been substituted for nondisabled children. In most areas, the child was treated cruelly so that the elves would be coerced into returning the "stolen" child, but in some areas the child was thought to bring good luck and was treated well. A later myth was that the devil had performed the exchange as retribution for the sins of the parents.

A common belief throughout time has been that a pregnant woman can produce a child with a physical difference if, during the pregnancy, she sees someone with that difference, is frightened by animals, or witnesses disturbing events. This theory is represented in the writings of the Romans, Hebrews, and early Christians, as well as in India, China, Africa, Europe, and among the Eskimos. As late as 1708, King Frederick V of Denmark ruled that no one with a facial difference could show himself to a pregnant woman.

Theories about cleft lips in particular have abounded. A consistently common belief for the cause of cleft lip was that the mother saw a hare (rabbit) during pregnancy, or had stepped over a hare's lair. These beliefs were common in many European countries, as was the term "hare lip," which implied that a hare's upper lip and a child's cleft lip appeared similar. In the nineteenth century, tight corsets on pregnant women were suspected of causing congenital conditions such as clefts. It was also theorized that cleft lip was caused by the fetus lacerating its upper lip with its nails, and that cleft palate might be due to pressure of the fetus's tongue tip or to interuterine thumb sucking.

In the eighteenth century, society finally began making strides toward separating fact from fiction. William Hunter completed one of the first scientific studies refuting the belief that psychic trauma during pregnancy could lead to the birth of a child with facial difference. Gradually, more and more craniofacial conditions were identified and described in the professional literature. Still, there were no standardized treatments for these conditions for many years.

Over the past several hundred years, cleft lip repair has steadily improved. Advances in cleft palate closure have also occurred since the first repairs were attempted in the early nineteenth century.

It was not until after World War II, however, that surgical procedures began to focus on major congenital facial differences. During this period, Dr. Paul Tessier, a French plastic surgeon, began reconstructing the faces of soldiers who had facial injuries. By the 1960s, he had developed many of the craniofacial surgical techniques that are currently used. His techniques were based on two ideas: that a craniofacial skeletal difference must be either repositioned or reconstructed with bone grafts before the soft tissue can be repaired, and that the best approach to major craniofacial differences was to open the skull. Dr. Tessier is the acknowledged father of craniofacial surgery, a subspecialty of plastic surgeons.

Despite this progress, misperceptions about people with facial difference and their potential for a normal life lingered well into this century. As recently as thirty years ago, medical professionals often recommended that parents place newborn children with facial differences in institutions. And even when parents kept their children at home, they were often forced into fairly isolated existences because of the perceived stigma. At school, children with facial difference were often placed in classes for students with mental retardation, whether or not their intelligence was impaired.

Today, the outlook for children with facial difference is gradually brightening. Although many people are still uninformed about facial differences, society is slowly being educated by the media. Motion pictures, television talk shows, and magazine articles have chronicled a variety of children and their families, helping others to recognize and accept their humanity. More importantly, society is also being educated by people with facial difference themselves, as they attend school, socialize, and work in their communities. Better medical, therapeutic, and educational interventions, too, are helping to reduce physical and other differences that have historically made it difficult for children with facial difference to "fit in."

The Future of Children with Facial Difference

As the parent of a newborn or young child with a facial difference, it may be difficult to imagine what your child might be like as a third grader, teenager, or adult. Your focus right now is probably on his physical appearance and on any developmental or sensory problems associated with his condition. At some point, these concerns may seem less important and your focus will change. Although periodic operations may be part of your child's schedule in coming years, so too will scouting, band practice, sports, and other typical childhood activities.

One of the best ways for you to become educated about problems your child and your family might encounter is to contact a support group for parents of children with facial differences. Many adults with facial difference are willing to talk to parents about their experiences with operations, schools, social activities, therapies, etc. If you are concerned about an aspect of your child's development, such as speech and language development, you could also talk with an adult with your child's condition. Listen carefully to his speech and ask him about his speech and language development. You can find support groups through the organizations listed in the Resource Guide.

As your child becomes an adult, it will be important for him to talk with a geneticist about the chances of passing on his condition to his own children and about the choices available to him. With rapid advancements in medical research, it may only be a matter of time before a prenatal test is available or a procedure is developed to better correct your child's facial difference. You should periodically contact the research groups that have an interest in your child's condition to learn about medical advances and their investigative goals. One of these groups might even invite you or your family to participate as research subjects. Although your participation may not directly help your child, it may have benefits for future generations. Before agreeing to participate, you should fully understand the research project and the institution sponsoring it; give your informed consent; and make sure you feel comfortable communicating with the principal investigator. A support group for your child's condition can put you in touch with research groups and offer you educational materials to help you decide whether to be a research participant.

As important as the medical and scientific aspects of your child's condition are, try to keep them in perspective throughout the years. Although your child was born with a facial difference, he and your family can certainly be as much a part of the community as any other child and family. Adults with facial difference are fully capable of attaining high educational, professional, and social goals. Many adults with facial difference are prominent public figures such as celebrities or elected officials; well-respected professionals in law, medicine, music, and other fields; and happy, confident spouses and parents.

Conclusion

From a parent's perspective, the first few years are usually the most difficult. A diagnosis is made; your child is evaluated for feeding, breathing, and sensory problems; his intelligence is assessed;

and his development is closely monitored. Sometimes it seems like there is not much time for you to just enjoy your baby, play together, and have fun.

Fortunately, health care becomes easier for most children with facial difference as they become older and bigger. As your child's health becomes more stable, more enjoyable times will gradually begin, and you and your family will grow into a lifestyle that feels right and comfortable for you. True, your child and your family may face more psychological challenges than other families. Your child may have a harder time developing high self-esteem, you may need to cope with disappointment if operations don't work out as well as hoped, and everyone may grow weary of teasing and staring. Consequently, your child and your family will both need to work at accentuating the positive by offering support, nurturing self-esteem, and providing the opportunity for successful experiences. The challenge to you and your family is to remember that your child is a child first—a child who happens to have a facial difference. It's a big challenge, but one that you don't have to be a "super parent" to tackle. I should know. I've been there.

Parent Statements

Our son was diagnosed at birth with hemifacial microsomia/Goldenhar syndrome. He has left ear atresia, a misshapen skull, and a missing mandible.

�֍

Our daughter's microtia was diagnosed at birth, but we didn't find out she had hemifacial microsomia until she was thirteen months old.

✖

Our pediatrician missed Sarah's cleft of the soft palate when she was first born. After two days, a nurse in the nursery figured it out because Sarah was having such trouble nursing. The doctor gave me the news over the phone.

✖

Josh has Crouzon syndrome. He was seventeen months old when diagnosed.

✖

Pete was born at a rural hospital, but my OB recognized his features at birth. He had delivered a baby with Treacher Collins syndrome several years earlier. I was lucky. Without my OB's experience, the diagnosis could have been anyone's guess.

❌

In my pediatrician's twenty-five years of practice, he had never come across a case of craniosynostosis. He thought that Brittany's facial problems were a result of coming through the birth canal. He had me take pictures of her every two weeks to look for changes, but there weren't any. He sent us to have x-rays taken at a local hospital. The head of the x-ray department basically said to us that he didn't know why we were having x-rays taken because his son's head was a little disfigured at birth and he was just fine now. I'm certainly glad we didn't listen to him.

❌

Brittany was diagnosed with craniosynostosis, plagiocephaly at four months. We were very relieved to know there was something they could do for her. Then the doctor described the operation to us, stating that he would first cut her head from ear to ear, comparing the procedure to scalping someone. He next told us that they would remove her forehead, fix it, and put it back in. He stated that the whole procedure would take about eight hours. I felt ill and faint while looking at my beautiful baby and trying to imagine what she would have to go through. It's a maternal instinct to want to protect your child from any and all discomfort and pain.

❌

My daughter, Melissa, was born with a cleft palate and an underdeveloped jaw. She had difficulty breathing at birth and was transferred to a hospital, which, luckily for us, has an excellent craniofacial center. They were able to diagnose her as having Pierre Robin Malformation Sequence.

❌

Our daughter Lisa has Goldenhar syndrome. She was diagnosed within hours after her birth. The delivery room scene was traumatic. She let out one cry and then occluded her airway (because of the micrognathia), so she was surrounded by doctors and nurses. I could see how blue she was and that they were not able to intubate her, so I was very scared. I remember them wheeling me into the NICU after she was stabilized so I could see her, and her head seemed very distorted to me but not to the nurses. The next day she looked OK.

�֍

Henry, age ten, has Freeman-Sheldon syndrome. At birth, he was abandoned to a home for "Children of No Brain" in an Asian country because of his appearance. He was listed as "having multiple birth defects including cleft palate all the way up to between his eyes." (He *didn't* have a cleft palate!) He did have facial deformity, severe unrepaired club feet, contracted fingers, rotten teeth, and he drooled. He arrived at age six and was not officially diagnosed with Freeman-Sheldon syndrome until we took him to a specialist in Canada who specialized in conditions related to arthrogryposis. She says he's a "classic Freeman-Sheldon's child."

✖

Justine was born with Moebius syndrome. Her sixth, seventh, and partial twelfth nerve are paralyzed, which means she has no facial expression, her eyes do not move laterally, and her tongue does not lift to the roof of her mouth. She also has a small tongue and jaw, slight cleft palate, and deformed hands.

✖

After our daughter's birth, the OB who had done my pre-natal ultrasounds came hurriedly in to see me in the recovery room. This doctor had already been in to "view" our baby. He informed me that he hadn't seen any abnormalities in the ultrasounds and that the Treacher Collins syndrome "wasn't his fault." He then proceeded to tell me about another baby with Treacher Collins syndrome who had had to be air-lifted to another hospital two hours away and whose family had had to move there because of the medical complications of the child's care. I was shocked by the OB's behavior and his need to tell me this information.

✖

We were forwarded to a larger medical institution when our son was six weeks old. At that time we were given a description of what was wrong with him. When he was seven months old, we were given the name hemifacial microsomia, but not in writing, and we could only tell people he had something that meant under-development of bone and soft tissue. Now I think we were naive because we didn't ask for a written explanation of his condition. Finally, when David started early intervention, they received a written report of what David was diagnosed with. This was two and a half years after his birth. After an unexpected hospitalization when David was four, we were referred to Genetics. There we discovered his diagnosis to be more specifically called Facio-Auriculo-Vertebral syndrome because of some vertebral anomalies that were discovered.

✖

We knew something was wrong as soon as Laura was born. Our doctor could not identify the condition, so we were released the following day to go to a bigger hospital to see a neonatologist and a geneticist. They gave us the diagnosis of acrocephalosyndactyly (Apert syndrome).

✖

All the information we received was basically outdated and discouraging. Most of the information said that kids with Apert don't live through the first year. My reaction was to keep my heart guarded because I didn't want to become attached to Laura and then lose her. My prayer was that if Laura was going to die it would be early—not after a year of loving and growing. Praise God, she didn't! She's now six and a half and doing great.

✖

I did all that I could to have a healthy pregnancy. Still, Lyle was born with a bilateral cleft lip and palate. I was hurt deep inside. My emotional baggage that I usually don't even know is there came up and jumped all over my feelings. I hurt for the future of this little person. Then, while my husband was holding Lyle for me to see, I said, "Lyle, Mommy loves you," and that little person who was only minutes old turned his head to me at the sound of my voice. I was in love.

✖

I kept telling the doctors that I thought Kirsten's face was flat on one side and the fontanel was smaller than usual. But they kept telling me it was from the birthing process and then it was because I laid her on the right side to sleep all the time. Finally, when she was six weeks old, they diagnosed craniostenosis—her right suture was closed and she had a flattened right orbital arch.

✖

Theresa was born with choanal atresia (both sides of her nose were blocked with bony tissue), a cleft palate, and microcephaly. She had no ability to breathe or swallow at birth. I was given little hope that she would do well or survive. Her life expectancy was set at one year. Theresa is now twenty years old and can speak (although not always clearly), eat, and take care of all her physical needs. She is a great help to me, has a wonderful sense of humor, and is a joy to our family.

✖

Carla is our first and only child. It is a difficult decision to have another child, not knowing whether that child will also have a facial difference.

✖

In our extended families, there are several cases of cleft lip/palate, covering five generations (5 cases out of 200–300 people). We've had two more children since Drew was born with cleft lip and palate, and were naturally very concerned with each pregnancy.

✖

I was born with a cleft lip and palate myself. When I got pregnant, I was told there was a *slim* chance of having a child with a cleft— and it did happen. Our first child had a submucosal cleft palate, which was found at age seven, and our third child had a unilateral cleft lip and palate. My brother also has a son with a bilateral cleft lip and palate. So, there is a definite genetic event going on!

✖

What was very difficult for me early on was that the cause was unknown. I remember being told by the genetics people that some error in development occurs at about ten weeks gestation. I would go often to the calendar and search for some clue as to where I was or what I did that could have caused this to happen (even when my husband would point out that her twin brother was not affected). The intensity of that desire to know faded with time.

✖

After our daughter was born with Apert syndrome, we went to genetic counseling to see how or why this happened. For us, it was not genetic. Eighteen months later, we had another child who was OK.

�֎

The pediatrician I selected for my son told me that I had a 1 in 4 chance of having another child with Treacher Collins syndrome, so I might want to consider whether I wanted to have more children. I was never offered the services of a geneticist or genetic counselor. Many months later, I learned that the 1 in 4 chance was inaccurate. Our son's Treacher Collins syndrome was the result of a spontaneous mutation; there was no evidence of inheritance. And, if it had been inherited, there would have been a 1 in 2 chance of passing on the gene.

�֎

We went through genetic counseling and had a chromosome study completed. They felt the craniostenosis was an isolated occurrence and should not affect siblings.

✖

We were told that Lawrence's condition is genetic, so having another child was the hardest decision I ever made. Someone told us that you have to decide whether you are going to live in your child's world or have your child live in your world. Well, we've decided that we want Lawrence to live in our world, and since we always wanted three children, we're going to go ahead and have another.

✖

I simply want her to have a normal life, to go to school, make friends, and someday fall in love. My greatest concern is that she be happy in life.

✖

If there is any advice I can give to new parents, all I can say is look further into the person and you will find a loving, normal child who wants to be treated the same as anyone else in all ways.

✖

Remarkably, I always had a fear of having a child with a facial difference. After overcoming the initial shock, I am thrilled to say that I could not possibly love Cory more than I do.

❌

I take my daughter everywhere. She's beautiful. I don't try to hide her, and even if I wanted to, I couldn't. Her face is so visible.

❌

Chapter 2

✣

Adjusting to Your Child's Difference

From the moment I heard that my pregnancy test was positive, I started to dream about a little boy in a sailor suit with luxuriant dark curly hair like my husband's. I wondered who he would resemble. When my son was born and given to me to hold, I immediately noticed that he had dark hair, but it was not curly. I did not notice his facial difference until the doctor came into the recovery room to break the news. My husband nervously paced the floor while he listened to the details. I was still feeling euphoric after the birth, however, and naively asked if the problems could be fixed. The doctor's answer was not very positive or reassuring.

More than three months passed before my son was evaluated at a craniofacial center and I learned that the information given to me that day was not accurate. The correct answer to my question was "Yes, your son's problems can be fixed, but his hair still won't be curly."

Of course, this was not all I learned in the months following my son's birth. I also learned that having a child born with a facial difference is not something you learn to cope with overnight. You need time to think about what has happened and how you feel about it; you need information about your child's condition and what can be done to help her; and you need to find support wherever you can—from family, friends, professionals, other parents of kids with facial difference, and support groups. Perhaps most importantly, I learned that my son was more like other babies than unlike them.

I checked child development charts daily, but I would have done this with my first child even if he didn't have facial difference. Watching my son reach and exceed developmental milestones was a great relief for me and helped to confirm that he was a typical child. The more we became used to each other, the more I could focus on topics I had heard about from friends whose children weren't born with facial difference: my baby's developing sense of humor, personality, and attachment to me.

If you have a baby or young child with a facial difference, you have probably already learned many of the same lessons that I did. Whether you realize it or not, you have undoubtedly begun to cope with your emotions and the changes in your life. You may not realize, however, that the feelings you have are shared by many other parents of children with facial difference. You may be unsure whether your coping strategies are as effective as they could be. Obviously, no two people are alike, and what works for one person may not necessarily work for another. Even within the same family, emotions and strategies for coping with them may differ widely. There are, however, some ways of handling emotions that many family members and relatives find useful. This chapter will present some of these strategies for coming to terms with your emotions and explain where to turn for additional guidance.

A Baby Is Born

Growing up in our society, we typically learn that the anticipation and birth of a baby are joyous events. We watch it happen with others, and expect that our life will be no different. When your baby is born with a facial difference, the change in expectations can be overwhelming.

How and when you receive the news can affect your initial feelings about your child's condition. Parents who learn the news suddenly may react differently from those who find out after weeks or months of worry that there might be something "wrong" with their baby. Parents who learn about their child's condition from a knowledgeable, compassionate doctor may have a different response than those who are told by a brusque or harried doctor who is ill informed about facial differences.

Shock is often the first reaction when a facial difference is diagnosed prenatally or at birth. You were expecting a healthy baby. How could this be happening? You feel numb or detached or as if you have somehow stepped outside yourself and are merely observing what is going on, rather than participating. I remember getting up in the middle of the night to feed Sam and thinking I was in the middle of a dream. You may have trouble absorbing the information given to you about your baby's condition, especially if the language is technical. Shock is a normal reaction to a traumatic experience and protects you from being overwhelmed by emotions before you are ready to deal with them.

When diagnosis occurs long after birth, as sometimes occurs with Crouzon syndrome or very mild Treacher Collins syndrome, you may experience a range of emotions. Perhaps you have noticed a problem or delay that persists or is getting worse, such as hearing loss or atypical skull development. When you voice your concerns to doctors, you may be offered responses such as: "She'll outgrow it"; "Let's evaluate her again in six months"; or "Relax, you're trying too hard to be a good parent." It is easy to become frustrated if you sense that your observations are being ignored or minimized, and your child's condition is staying the same or getting worse. You may start to become distrustful of health care professionals, and shop around for second and third opinions. When you finally get a diagnosis, you may feel an immediate sense of relief that your observations were correct and validated by a professional. But this relief may also be accompanied by shock similar to that described above.

Stages of Adaptation

After the initial shock fades, the diagnosis of a facial difference often throws parents into a state of crisis. You may feel as if your world has been turned upside down, and may have no idea how to even begin making things right again. You might want to lie on your bed and stare at the ceiling all day, or you might want to cry on your spouse's shoulder, or you might want to get moving and search frantically for answers and assistance. No two parents (even spouses) experience exactly the same emotions and handle them in exactly the same way. Often, however, parents feel very isolated and think that nobody else could possibly understand what they are thinking and feeling.

In fact, there *are* others—both parents and professionals—who do understand what you are going through. Much has been written about the emotional reaction of parents when their baby is diagnosed with a medical condition soon after birth. Over the years, studies have found that parents move through a variety of stages when coping with the diagnosis of a chronic condition in their child. These stages are similar to the stages that people go through when a loved one is near death or has died. It is healthy and normal for you to experience these stages. You may go through all of these stages, or only experience a few. You may spend a great deal of time in some stages, but less time in others. No two people cope in exactly the same way. It is not an indication of mental illness or other disease to feel these emotions, or to feel different emotions than someone else in your family. These emotions are certainly nothing to be ashamed of.

The stages involved in coping generally include: shock; denial; sadness, anger, and anxiety; adaptation; and reorganization. Parents of children with facial difference may also experience a variety of emotions in reaction to their child's physical appearance. These can include: fear of how their lives will change because of medical, social, and other concerns; helplessness in the face of an unexpected situation that seems out of control; guilt about how and why this happened to their baby; and negative feelings connected with their child's appearance. Not all parents experience these emotions to the same degree. How deeply these emotions affect you may depend on factors such as the type of condition your baby has, how mildly or severely it affects her, your past experiences with people with facial difference, and other life events you may reflect upon. Also remember that you may experience these emotions in a different order than other parents do, and may remain in a particular stage for a longer or shorter amount of time.

There is no one right order or timetable for moving through the stages. As the section on "Marital Stresses" explains, you should bear this in mind if you and your spouse find yourselves at different stages at different times. What is important is that you eventually progress through each of the stages. There should be a general trend toward adapting to the changes in your family and your expectations, no matter how slow the adaptation process may be. If you find yourself "stuck" in one stage for too long, you may want to seek counseling from a psychologist, social worker, counselor, or other mental health professional.

As you move from stage to stage, feelings from previous stages may not totally go away. It is a gradual and flexible process. Everyone moves at their own time and with their own rhythm.

Denial

Once the shock has begun to settle, you may experience denial as a way to escape the facts or to cushion them. Some parents, for instance, perceive their child to be less severely affected than she really is. Others convince themselves that their child will outgrow her facial difference or may overlook signals that something is wrong with her feeding or breathing. Still others try to avoid their child and the reality of her facial difference by spending long hours away from home, perhaps at work. When your child has a highly visible condition, such as facial difference, however, you are reminded of the situation each time you see your child. Eventually, most parents are able to face the facts about their child's facial difference.

Sadness, Anger, and Anxiety

As you begin to confront the reality of your child's facial difference, you may experience a variety of emotions. Very likely, you will need to grieve or mourn for the perfect child you had expected, free from facial difference or other health problems. You may also feel sad when you think about some of the ways your life and your child's life will be different from others'. For instance, you may feel sad to think that your child may never be able to go anywhere without people staring at her. Or you may feel down because friends don't come to see the new baby and tell you how cute she is.

You may feel sad about many different things as your child grows and changes. When my son was young, for instance, much of my sadness focused on his hearing aid. I felt bad that all of Sam's clothes needed to have a pocket sewn in to hold his hearing aid. It also bothered me that no matter how I styled and cut his hair, strangers thought he was a girl because of the headband used to hold the hearing aid on his head. These days my sadness tends to reappear when Sam is participating in sports and can't localize sounds.

If you are like many parents, you may never completely get over your sadness. You may need to grieve periodically over the course of your son's or daughter's childhood—perhaps during periods of crisis or transition or around the time of surgical procedures. The sharpness of your grief will probably dull with time, however. And as you learn to cope, you may be able to put your moments of sadness behind you more quickly.

Besides making you feel sad, the anxiety of saying good-bye to your imagined child can leave you angry. This anger may be directed at anyone and anything. You may feel angry that fate, or God, or circumstances beyond your control "did" this to you or your child. You may be angry that doctors cannot make your child physically perfect. You may seethe when friends or family members say tactless things, or resent other parents for taking their "normal" children for granted. Sometimes parents feel so estranged or separate from their baby that they direct their anger at her. They may hesitate to bond with their child and even hope, consciously or subconsciously, that their baby will die so they won't have to cope with this new and unexpected situation.

For my part, I was angry at family members whose reactions to Sam's facial difference weren't terribly supportive. Some blamed the "other side" of the family; others kept Sam's facial difference a secret. I was also accused of making a big deal out of nothing, and was told, "Years from now, you'll laugh about it." Strangers, too, angered me with thoughtless comments about Sam's "deafness" or about how God must have chosen me because I was the ideal parent for a child with Treacher Collins syndrome. Especially maddening were the women who told me that they had pre-natal testing to make decisions about babies like "these."

Guilt

When a child is born with a facial difference, one of the first reactions that parents, family members, and others often have is that someone or something must be to blame. After all, things like this can't just *happen*, can they? Often, mothers think back over their pregnancy, searching for things they may have done to cause their child's facial difference. Was it because they stood in front of the microwave or lifted something that was too heavy? Was it because they drank an alcoholic beverage or had the nerve to wish for a beautiful baby?

Guilt may be especially difficult to deal with if one parent passed on the gene for facial difference, knowingly or unknowingly. The carrier parent may have thoughts like "You knew what could happen—you get what you deserve." He or she may imagine that others are angry at him or despise him for passing on the gene, even if no one says or does anything to indicate that this is the case.

Whether or not your child's condition was inherited, you may spend days or weeks playing the "if only" game. If only you had started a family earlier instead of waiting until your career was established, your child might not have been born with a facial difference. If only you had married your high school sweetheart, you would have had different children, free of facial difference. If only, if only. . . . It just seems impossible that this whole situation is out of your control; there must have been *something* somewhere along the line that you could have done differently.

Adaptation

As anxiety and other intense emotional reactions diminish, parents start to accept their newest family member and to respond to her needs. They also become able to absorb and evaluate information helpful to their child and their family and to look toward the future. Some parents find these steps harder to take than others.

This stage may mark the first time that you are able to put your child's condition in perspective and begin to attach and bond with your baby. (Bonding refers to the process by which an infant and a parent, most often the mother, psychologically attach to one another.) Bonding is very important for a child's long-term psychological development. If adequate bonding does not take place early in life, a child may develop emotional or behavioral problems, or her development may stop or be delayed.

For your baby to bond with you, she needs to experience your touch, feel loved and cared about by you, and have her needs adequately met in a timely manner. For you to bond with your baby, you need to feel as if she is "yours," develop loving, protective feelings for her, and enjoy spending time with her.

Unfortunately, when a baby is born with a facial difference, the bonding process can be interrupted. Sometimes babies with facial differences develop breathing problems and are placed in the Neonatal Intensive Care Unit (NICU). When this happens, the parents' first glimpse of their baby may be through the window of an isolette, an activity not conducive to bonding. In other instances, parents feel estranged from their baby or angry with her because of her facial difference. Bonding can also be delayed if physicians do not describe the baby's condition in a sensitive way, emphasizing the positive and encouraging parents to have physical contact with her.

By the time you reach the adaptation stage, you will usually have overcome these impediments to bonding. You will have begun to work through your emotions and to see that things might not be as unbearable as they first seemed. You will have taken care of your baby and learned that she needs and depends on you. You may have learned information that puts your child's condition in a more positive light. For example, you may have discovered that your child will likely not have mental retardation or deafness. You may be concentrating more on doing everything you can to help your baby instead of on your feelings about her facial difference. As bonding takes place, you will focus less on the negative aspects of your child and more on the positive.

Reorganization

During this last stage, you will be able to accept the birth of your baby with a facial difference and the impact it will have on your family. You will be able to view things in a more optimistic way. Consequently, you will be able to regroup and thoughtfully consider the needs of your baby and your family without overemphasis on your emotions. You will begin to experiment with coping strategies.

Also at this stage, you will begin to realize that you have needed to turn to your spouse or someone else close to you for support since your baby's birth. Some couples may draw closer during this period and others may drift apart. Couples who are best able to adapt to their baby usually do so by maintaining a strong relationship with one another. See the section on "Marital Stresses" for more information on coping as a couple.

Coping

When something out of the ordinary happens to us, we draw upon our personal experiences and try to make sense out of it. The same thing happens when a child is born with a facial difference. Some parents struggle with religious or philosophical questions or ideas in search of answers. Others turn to a more scientific approach. There is no one right way of coming to terms with what has happened. There are, however, certain coping strategies that often work better than others.

The most important thing you can do to get back on your feet emotionally is to take some of the pressure off yourself. This can be easier said than done when you are facing a challenge that never really goes away. Positive coping strategies that *may* help you stabilize your life include: 1) reaching out for support and communicating with parents of other children with facial difference; 2) seeking out information about your child's condition and the management of it; 3) emphasizing your child's strengths; and 4) keeping a sense of humor. These strategies are discussed in the sections below.

There are also some negative coping strategies that can help keep you and your family out of the mainstream of life. These include: 1) continuing to deny your child's condition; 2) emphasizing your child's differences and problems; 3) failing to provide your child with hearing aids or other devices or assistive technology to correct an impairment; and 4) becoming isolated from public places or family events for fear of the responses of strangers and extended family members. If you find yourself emphasizing any of these strategies, it might be helpful to consult a mental health professional, such as a psychologist, social worker, or a marriage, family, or child counselor. This professional can help you work through the stages described earlier so that you are able to function more adequately and accept your child's differences. Your child's cranio-facial team can refer you to an appropriate mental health profes-sional.

Reaching Out

Most families benefit from reaching out to others for support. By sharing stories and resources, asking questions, offering and hearing words of encouragement, you will learn that you are not alone with your fears, joys, struggles, and victories. You will learn that offering support yourself can be just as helpful as receiving it. Through my association with the Treacher Collins Foundation, I have found that parents are especially helped by receiving factual information about their child's condition, by having their concerns about issues such as feeding validated, by sharing reactions of fam-ily and friends, and by learning about surgical treatments and tim-ing.

The most profound experience I've ever had in offering sup-port began with a phone call from a new mom who was trying to de-cide whether to put her baby up for adoption. She wasn't sure that she could care for the child and called me to find out information that would help her make that decision. She started off the conver-sation by telling me that and how scared she was to call for fear that I wouldn't talk with her when I found out why she was calling. She ended up keeping her baby. We've kept in touch over the past three years, and she always says that she is glad she kept her baby—her child is precious and an endless source of joy to her and her hus-band. This is a clear example of how timely, accurate information delivered in a supportive way can make a difference in someone's life.

Support can come from professionals—a plastic surgeon, nurse, pediatrician, social worker, audiologist—or an organization or agency. It may also come simply from connecting with another fam-ily whose child has a diagnosis similar to your child's.

Many craniofacial centers offer support services such as parent-to-parent networking and support groups to families. Apart from these centers, there are also a variety of agencies and organizations which provide support for families of children born with facial dif-ference. Where you go for support depends upon the type of sup-port you are seeking.

If you want support dealing with your feelings about your child's facial difference, you may want to find a self-help or peer support group made up of other parents. Within the past several years, a self-help movement for facial difference has emerged and has been rapidly growing. There are organizations that focus on generic issues common to all facial difference. These include the Cleft Palate and Craniofacial Foundation, Let's Face It, About-Face, Children's Craniofacial Association, FACES, National Foundation for Facial Reconstruction, and Face of Sarasota. There are also organizations specific to particular conditions, such as the Treacher Collins Foundation, Prescription Parents (cleft lip and palate), Foundation for Nager and Miller Syndromes, Face to Face (Crouzon syndrome), The Goldenhar Research and Information Fund, Crouzon-Meniere's Support Network, and EAR - Ear Anomalies Reconstructed/The Microtia-Atresia Support Group. There are also center-based support groups that offer information and contacts to anyone, not just patients and their families: Craniofacial Foundation of America (Tennessee), Happy Faces Support Group (Arizona), Forward Face (New York), Foundation for Faces of Children (Massachusetts), Face to Face of Indianapolis. Each of these groups provides a variety of services to families, professionals, and anyone interested. Services usually include emotional support, networking with others, information and referral, educational opportunities and materials, and links with researchers.

If you want support for matters not directly related to your child's facial difference, there are other organizations that can help. For example, the Alliance of Genetic Support Groups, the Federation for Children with Special Needs, and the Beach Center on Families and Disability operate at a national level with goals that encompass general issues for any family of a child with a disability. Other organizations, such as the National Parent Network on Disabilities and Family Voices, are watchdogs and advocates for change in public policies. The Resource Guide at the back of the book offers contact information for these and other organizations that you may find helpful.

If you simply want to talk to another parent one-on-one, your child's craniofacial center may be able to give you the names of other parents. Your child's audiologist or therapists may also be good sources of names. There are also several organizations that offer parent-to-parent networking, including the National Organization for Rare Disorders (NORD) and Parent to Parent, which exists in most states.

Perhaps you feel as if you could not possibly share what you are thinking and feeling now with strangers. Don't feel as if you have to force yourself to do so, even if your spouse or someone else thinks you should. Not everyone feels comfortable asking for support. You might also feel the need for support later on. Parents who do participate in support groups or activities usually benefit from feeling they are not alone, learning about new resources and developing new skills, and receiving encouragement to pursue a satisfying lifestyle.

Seeking Information

The more you know about your child's condition, the better equipped you will be to actively participate in planning her treatment and education. You will learn what to expect and what questions to ask. You may find out about new procedures and devices that are popular in another area of the country but are still largely unfamiliar to your child's health care professionals.

When you begin to seek out information on your child's condition, you may feel overwhelmed. You may need to visit a medical library and ask a librarian to help you figure out how to use computer databases and indexes such as MEDLINE, MEDLARS, and the NORD database. Even then, the language may not be understandable to you. There are, however, services available that will do medical research for you (for a cost). See the Resource Guide for more information.

If you don't have a medical background, an easier place to start may be by contacting support groups to see if they have pamphlets, booklets, or videos that are easier to understand. Some organizations have bibliographies and lending libraries of information. And talking or corresponding with other parents of children with your child's facial difference are excellent ways of gathering information.

When consulting medical books and journals, try to stay away from information that is over ten years old. That information is often inaccurate and out-dated. Journal articles usually contain the most current information, but may be difficult to read because of the technical terms. On the other hand, basic medical reference books are more understandable, but may contain inaccurate information, especially about rare conditions. For information on rare conditions, *The Physician's Guide to Rare Disorders* can be helpful. You can also search for information on rare conditions on the NORD database or, for a small fee, you can ask NORD to send a printout of the information they have on a specific condition.

The members of your child's craniofacial team can be a great source of information on your child's condition and treatment. They may have a package of materials on your child's condition and can answer your questions and explain medical terminology. And if you're not sure of the accuracy of something you've read or heard, they can clarify it for you.

The more you learn, the more you'll understand. Before you know it, you'll be tossing around medical terminology, too!

Focusing on Your Child's Strengths

It can sometimes be hard to remember that your child has strengths and that you can enjoy her in the same ways that parents of children without facial difference enjoy their children. Especially when your child is young, medical professionals put much more focus on your child's weaknesses and deficiencies. Yet no matter what your child's condition of facial difference, you can probably find at least a handful of things about her that are endearing to you or that seem perfect to you.

If you find yourself focusing on a weakness or deficit your child was born with, it may help to find an offsetting strength. Perhaps she has your curly hair or your spouse's impish grin, an amazing talent for stacking blocks or a knack for painting and drawing. Maybe you love the sparkle in her eyes, her curiosity about the world, her loving nature, or her sense of humor. Even though it sometimes *is* necessary to focus on weaknesses, it is equally important to recognize strengths.

Keeping a Sense of Humor

In the beginning, it may seem as if everything that occurs in your life will center around the needs of your new baby and that you will need to shut out the outside world. Once your baby becomes medically stable, however, you can begin to relax, evaluate what has happened, educate yourself about what might happen next, and begin to refocus your life.

After a while, you and your family will begin to develop a unique lifestyle that is comfortable for you. When this happens, the way you and your family interact with the world outside your home will also change. As you begin to feel more comfortable accepting and responding to the needs of your child, you will begin to feel less isolated and more willing to rejoin the activities of the world. You will probably also become more willing or able to accept the challenges these interactions will bring. For example, you may not be so reluctant to take your child out in public and face the inevitable questions and invasion of privacy from strangers.

As you start to feel less vulnerable, you may notice that your sense of humor is being reactivated or starting to develop anew. This is a positive sign! Regaining your sense of humor means that you are able to look at your child's condition in a less intense light and find something positive and acceptable about your situation. These breaks from worrying are psychologically healthy and necessary to keep you from feeling continually overwhelmed or stressed.

I don't remember exactly when I stopped being so absorbed in Sam's facial difference. I had definitely started to lighten up by the time he was a toddler, though. One year at Halloween, I remember I was in a store looking at Halloween costumes. I found a pair of big rubber ears. I thought they would be perfect to buy for Sam as part of a costume. I saw this as a healthy sign!

The key in using humor to cope is not to use it to poke fun at, or degrade anyone. Being able to see the lighter side of things can be a turning point in your acceptance of your child's facial difference and her needs, and in your relationship to your child.

Marital Stresses

When your child was born with a facial difference, you and your spouse were immediately forced to adjust your lives to meet the needs of your baby. Whether you are a new parent or have other children, the stress placed upon you is tremendous and can be overwhelming. This stress may add to any problems your marriage had before the birth of your child. But it can also make your marriage grow stronger if you and your spouse can bind together as a family team, drawing strength and support from each other.

No marriage is quite the same as any other, of course. But there are some problems that often lead to conflicts among couples who have children with a facial difference. These include: different methods of coping; difficulty sharing emotions; uneven division of parenting responsibilities; and lack of time and energy to work on the marital relationship.

Minimizing Day-to-Day Conflicts

There is no one magic way to keep marital conflicts from developing. But again, there are some strategies that often help couples deal with these problems. First, it is vital that you and your spouse strive for open and honest communication. You can lay the groundwork for good communication by listening to one another without judging and by trying not to send the message that the other's thoughts or feelings are abnormal or extreme. Second, try to give your spouse the same kind of support you would like to receive from him or her. Respect his or her timetable for coping, and do not try to force him into the same stage of coping you have reached. Recognize that there are many valid ways of coping—by joining support groups, immersing yourself in reading, taking long walks to puzzle things out for yourself—and your spouse's way of coping doesn't have to be your way.

Third, try not to let one spouse take on sole responsibility for all decision making about your child and her future. It's quite possible that one of you will become more of an expert on your child's condition and her needs—perhaps because one of you has more time or inclination to do the research and networking. But ideally, all important information learned should be shared so that you can jointly make decisions.

Finally, do not let your relationship revolve solely around your child with facial difference. Your role as parent *is* important, but so is your role as a husband or wife. You and your spouse need to have other topics of conversation and socialize with other people besides families of children with facial differences. You need to have a life outside your family, just as other couples do. Every once in a while you and your spouse need to hire a babysitter and to do something as a couple, without your child. See Chapter 4 for information on finding a suitable babysitter.

Major Marital Conflicts

Sometimes couples face conflicts that cannot be easily resolved. One or both spouses may find that the stress is too much to bear, individually or together. These couples may find themselves being pulled in different directions, and separation or divorce may result. Conflicts that can lead to serious marital problems include: feeling stigmatized about having produced a child with a facial difference; blaming your spouse or his family for the condition or belief in mythology about the cause of the condition; being unwilling or feeling unable to be a good parent for a child with a facial difference; being unwilling to accept your child's differences; viewing your child as inferior or "subhuman"; and fearing that you might abuse or neglect your child.

If you or your spouse has any of the problems above, it is time for the two of you to evaluate your relationship. Some couples can do this on their own, and others prefer the guidance of a professional counselor. If your spouse refuses to engage in this dialog with you, you can still seek professional help on your own. The counselor can help you sort through your feelings and figure out where you and your marriage are headed.

In the end, some marriages fail, just as they do among couples who do not have a child with a facial difference. Sometimes this is actually in the best interest of the child, even though it can be very stressful for one parent to look after all of the financial, emotional, and physical needs of the family, as well as the needs of the child with facial differences. Keep in mind that for your child to feel good about herself, the quality of the support and love she receives is the key. Sometimes one devoted parent can support and love a child better than two parents who waste their energy arguing and fighting with one another.

Your Family and Friends

When a child is born with a facial difference, parents are not the only ones who need to adjust their expectations. Brothers and sisters, grandparents, other extended family members, and friends also need to come to terms with and accept your child's differences.

Different families react differently to the birth of a child with a facial difference. Often family stress increases, at least at first. Family members often need to learn how to cope with their emotions collectively, as well as individually. They may also need to become more flexible, rethink the roles of each family member, and figure out how to make the child with facial differences feel like a welcome and integral part of the family.

Experiment with different coping strategies. This is the only way to find out what works for your family and what does not. It is also important to remember that not everyone in your family needs to use the same coping strategies all the time. What works for your child's older brother may not work for her younger sister, just as what works for you may not work for your spouse. As a parent, you don't want to dictate to other family members how they should cope, but rather help them explore different ways of coping as the need arises. The sections below cover information to keep in mind when helping family members and friends adjust to your child's facial difference.

Siblings

Families of children with facial difference come in all sizes. Sometimes the child with facial difference is the only child. There may be a variety of reasons why: perhaps the parents had only planned to have one child, or they have financial concerns about having more children, or they are in emotional upheaval over the birth of the child with facial difference, or they may not have made up their minds yet about having more children. There are, in fact, a number of valid reasons for putting off

the decision: parents may want to wait for their child with facial difference to be more medically stable, or to work out problems in their relationship, or to find ways to improve their financial situation.

Whatever you and your spouse decide about having more children, it will be the best decision for you and your spouse at that time. You need not feel that you owe an explanation or apology to anyone, including yourself. Choices and decisions about childbearing and the timing of childbearing are highly personal. Remember, a family is not determined by the number of children you have. A single parent and one child are just as much a family as a husband and wife and four children. What is most important is how you and your child (or children) feel as a family.

If you have or are planning to have more than one child, your child's facial difference will definitely affect her siblings (brothers and sisters) in both obvious and subtle ways. These effects can vary from slight to very pronounced, depending on the ages of your children, your child's condition of facial difference, and other factors.

Especially if siblings are older, having a brother or sister with facial differences can be very confusing and overwhelming. If your children are old enough, they may realize that there is a crisis centered around the new baby. They will almost certainly notice that there is a great deal of excitement, talking in low voices, strong emotions, trip after trip to doctors and hospitals, and possibly the introduction of strange devices such as hearing aids, tracheostomies, and feeding tubes. Life as the siblings knew it has radically changed, and will continue to change. To make matters worse, they may not be given explanations for all the activity and changes, or the explanations may be too complex for them to understand.

Just as you do, brothers and sisters have many emotions to cope with and questions that need to be answered. In the beginning, however, it may seem impossible to handle their concerns on top of your own. You may feel as if you don't have the information you need to answer their questions, or as if you don't have a good enough grip on your own emotions to help them deal with theirs. Although these feelings are natural, it is essential to take steps to reassure your other children as soon as possible. Especially if they are quite young, a small amount of information may go a long way to reduce their concerns.

Depending on age, siblings usually have the following concerns about a new brother or sister with facial difference: How did the baby get the condition and are they in any way responsible? Does it hurt her to have a face or head that looks different? Can they "catch" the condition now or later? What should they tell their friends, their friends' parents, and strangers? How should they interact with the baby? How will the baby's needs affect their needs now and in the future (will she suck up all your love, time, and attention)? Is it OK to feel sad, angry, ashamed, etc. about the baby's facial condition?

Often children who have these concerns may not be able to articulate them. Consequently, you may need to do some mind reading to figure out what is bothering your children. Try to offer information in small doses at appropriate times. For instance, if you notice one of your children giving your child with facial difference a wide berth, you may want to let him or her know that your child's condition is not "catching." You may also want to *ask* your children if they are feeling a certain way or have a particular question. This way, you let them know that it is OK to have and express these concerns. Always give your children accurate information in language that is easily understood. And be persistent! If you aren't able to dispel a sibling's concerns with one explanation, try another.

When giving your other children information about their sibling's condition, be aware that you may need to correct erroneous information. Siblings may be confused by what they have heard from you, your spouse, or professionals, or by what they have figured out for themselves. Children often try to figure things out for themselves to stabilize their lives with explanations they understand and can be in control of. For example, they may conclude:

- that the baby was born with facial difference because they didn't want a new baby and they told you, or had a dream about it, or drew a picture about it;
- that the baby had to go back to the hospital (for a cleft lip repair) because they wished the baby would die or go away and live some other place;
- that everyone in the family should wear a hearing aid, have a trach or feeding tube, or have formula or food squirt out their nose. In my family, for instance, Molly was born more than three years after Sam, so she never knew any differently. She would ask me where her hearing aid was when she would see me put Sam's on him. (And when Molly was an infant, Sam asked me why *she* didn't wear a hearing aid.)

If your children's conclusions are incorrect, you need to gently correct them. Afterwards, watch and listen to your children to make sure they have gotten everything straight, and be prepared to repeat your explanation, if necessary.

To help your other children deal with their emotions about their sibling's differences, you may need to be a bit of a detective. Younger children may not be able to recognize what they are feeling or to put their feelings into words. They may misbehave to get attention because they are unable to express what they need. Older children may intentionally try to hide their emotions from you, thinking that their feelings are "bad." For example, a sibling might be angry and resentful at the amount of attention your child with facial difference is getting from you, but think that it is wrong for her to be mad at such a tiny, helpless baby. Sometimes children may keep their emotions to themselves because they think Mom and Dad have enough to worry about already.

You can encourage your other children to share their emotions by trying to look at the situation from their point of view. For example, you might ask, "How did you feel when I had to rush the baby to the hospital when she stopped breathing?" Or, "You looked uncomfortable when I fed the baby at the Scout picnic. Was it because of the special bottle that she uses?" As your children begin to open up to you, it is important to listen nonjudgmentally. Even if your children express sadness, anger, guilt, embarrassment, or other emotions that may not be pleasant for you to hear, be careful not to send the message that any of these feelings are wrong. Instead, you may want to let your children know that you, too, sometimes feel those emotions, but that there is an up side to things, too. For example, you might say to a younger child, "I feel sad that the baby doesn't have any ears, too. But when she gets older, the doctor can make her some ears."

Let your children know that their feelings are important to you. If you cannot discuss their feelings with them when you first become aware of them, set up a time to discuss them later. For example, say "I know you're very worried about the baby. I'll call you from the hospital and let you know how everything's going."

You are the best role model for teaching your other children how to deal with their sibling's facial difference. If you can openly, honestly, and respectfully discuss your child with a facial difference, your other children will learn that it is okay to talk about their brother or sister.

Coping emotionally will be an ongoing process for your children, just as it is for you. Your children will not only need to work through their initial feelings about the birth of a brother or sister with facial difference. They will also need to confront other emotions as they realize how having a sibling with a facial difference will change their lives. For example, as they begin to experience strangers' reactions to their sibling's appearance, they may need to come to terms with embarrassment or anger. It is therefore important to keep the lines of communication open throughout your children's childhood to help them deal with new concerns as they arise. Chapter 4 provides information about handling problems that can arise among siblings over the long term.

Grandparents

Grandparents anticipate the birth of a grandchild in a variety of ways. Often, they look forward to closing their own chapter on parenting responsibilities. The new chapter they expect to open may be filled with pleasurable expectations for the warm and indulgent relationships they will have with their grandchild. They may think about how they will boast about their grandchild with friends, and

view their grandchild as a window to the stability of the family's future. This link between grandparents and grandchildren can be very special, almost magical.

When a grandchild is born with facial difference, this link can become shaky or it can become strong. Research shows that grandparents *want* to be supportive and helpful, but feel at a loss for what to say or how to say it. Eventually, however, many grandparents become a source of boundless energy, support, and information to their children and grandchildren.

Before they can build a healthy relationship with your child, grandparents will need to cope with their feelings about her facial difference. They may experience the same stages of adjustment that you do. It has also been theorized that grandparents grieve not only for the loss of their expected healthy grandchild, but also for the pain that they expect you are experiencing.

How grandparents handle their own emotions can have a profound impact on you. Conflicts can arise if parents and grandparents are not in the same stages of adjustment at the same time, especially if the issues each person is dealing with are not resolved in the same way. For example, your parents might deny that your child was born with differences while you are struggling with feeding and other issues. You may overhear them telling their friends that everything is just fine, when the reality may be that your month-old baby hasn't yet regained her birth weight because of feeding problems, your three-year-old is making the demands on you that three-year-olds usually make, and your husband is working two jobs so that you can stay home with the kids. You're sad and grieving for your healthy baby, struggling to get through each day and night on small amounts of continually interrupted sleep, and have no prospect for any relief from this situation.

Some parents may feel weighed down by their parents' emotions, on top of their own. In addition, you might find that your parents are so wrapped up in their own feelings toward your child that they are unable to give you and your spouse support. Sometimes hostility between the generations breaks out if grandparents blame their child's spouse for causing their grandchild's condition and the problems they expect this to raise for the family.

It's hard to know what grandparents are thinking or feeling unless you ask. If you keep the lines of communication open, you can begin to understand their perception of the situation. You can then feel freer to point out differences between your thoughts and emotions and theirs and tell them what you need or want from them.

Of course, open communication can be risky business, since you're likely to find out the information you're seeking and it may not be what you want to hear. However, living with silence and always having to second guess can be painful and exhausting.

Even though you may need to be able to share your thoughts and feelings with grandparents, remember that it may not be an easy time for them, either. They may be doing the best they can for now, and they may not be sure what to say or do. They may be looking to you for a sign.

To help grandparents begin to cope with your child's facial difference, try offering them information about their grandchild's condition and how her needs may affect your family in the present and the future. You might start by giving them this book or an information packet from an organization for people with your child's facial difference. Supplying them with current, accurate information is essential, as many grandparents of today grew up at a time when they were taught to have a negative view of people with facial difference and disabilities.

Getting support from families and professionals might also help your parents. Support groups usually welcome grandparents to join them. And some craniofacial centers specifically encourage members of the extended family to attend clinics and programs.

How well grandparents eventually cope and rally around to support your family may depend upon your current and past relationship with them. The birth of your baby may not mend a rocky relationship, and might actually make the relationship worse. In the end, what will probably help grandparents the most is inviting them to get to know your child. Let them try their hand at feeding your child, or taking her out for a stroll, or babysitting, or doing any of the many activities any grandparent does with a grandchild. Chances are that the more the grandparents are able to look beyond your child's facial difference to discover the unique individual she is, the more their acceptance will grow. As the quality of support and love your child receives from her grandparents increases, she will feel better about herself and her place within your extended family.

Friends

Friendships usually begin on the basis of shared interests. They are maintained when each person's interests continue to grow in the same direction. Any major life event—marriage, divorce, the birth of a child, a new career—can change the flavor of a friendship. Changes that give you more in common with friends may draw you together, while those that give you less in common may cause you to drift apart. Having a child born with a facial difference is a change that often affects old friendships.

In the early stages of adjusting to your child's facial difference, you may have trouble interacting with many people in the outside world, including friends. Perhaps your friends react negatively or insensitively to your child or seem to ignore you. Or perhaps you are just afraid that they will react negatively, so you avoid them. You may think that they could not possibly understand what you are going through, or feel ashamed to tell them about the baby. For their part, friends may stay away for fear that they may say the wrong thing, or because they think that you want to be alone, or because they think you are too busy to see them, or because they are not comfortable with your child's differences—or for any number of reasons.

Some friendships are strong enough to withstand the emotional demands of your new circumstances; others are not. Factors that might determine which friendships endure include: your friends' abilities to empathize with you, their previous experience with children with facial difference or other health problems, how long you have been acquainted, and the basis of your friendship. In any case, don't be in a hurry to cross friends off your list. Give them time to adjust to your child's facial difference, to ask questions, to interact with your child—to understand how your new life might or might not mesh with their lives.

If friendships that seemed solid before your child's birth have started to dissolve, you might view this as a rejection of your child and of yourself for having produced this child. This may or may not be the case. You and your friends may simply be moving in different directions now, and what originally drew you to one another may not exert the same pull.

If you begin to fear future rejections, you might isolate yourself and your family, feel overly protective of your child and your family, or prefer to develop relationships only with parents and families of children with disabilities. To some degree, these activities can feel soothing and safe. And it is undoubtedly a good idea to get to know other families of children with facial difference. Not only can you gain a great deal of information and emotional support from other families, but you can also forge strong friendships with people who truly understand what you are going through. At some point, however, you and your family need to re-enter the world, which is predominantly composed of people who do not have facial differences. If this seems like an insurmountable task, a mental health professional may be able to help. Your child's craniofacial center can offer you a referral.

As you expand upon grounded friendships and develop new ones, you may find that these friendships are moving in a direction that is new and different for you. This is to be expected. Your life changed with the birth of your child with facial difference and it will continue to change. Your friendships will need to keep up with that change in order to stay intact.

Keeping Everything in Perspective

When your child was born with a facial difference, it may have seemed that what was supposed to be a joyous event had ended in tragedy. You may have felt alienated from family, friends, and the outside world, and felt your lives would never again be remotely "normal."

Once the initial shock subsided, you and your spouse began to view your life and your family's life in a different way than before the birth. You became more accustomed to your child's appearance, learned how her condition does and does not affect her capabilities, and developed an understanding of her needs and how to manage those needs. You may also have begun to look around and to discover that facial difference is more common than you thought. It is expressed in a variety of ways, has a variety of causes, and does not prevent people from living typical, fulfilling, and happy lives.

You have entered a new world where you will quickly become the expert on your child and her condition. As the world responds to you in a new way, you, in turn, will develop new strategies for responding to the world. Out of necessity, you will learn what works and what does not, and how to make the unworkable workable. When this begins to occur, it means that you are learning to keep your child's condition, and its effects on your family and the outside world, in perspective.

Over time, trips to the craniofacial center, visits with therapists, and encounters with curious strangers will become less stressful, more ordinary. Sometimes you might be caught off guard by a question or a stare; other days you may not even notice. Gradually, the overwhelming concern you felt over the number of ounces your baby drank in a twenty-four hour period or how to deal with questions at the supermarket will fade. Instead, you will find yourself complaining about waiting too long to see the surgeon, figuring out a tactful way to answer your mother-in-law's never-ending questions, and deciding between the big, brown stuffed bear or the little white dog that wags its tail for your child's birthday present.

This is a healthy sign! It means that you have reached a state of equilibrium, and no longer feel as if the world revolves around the needs of your child. The crisis has been resolved. For most parents, resolution means having your child followed at a craniofacial center where you feel comfortable; being able to adequately communicate with the professionals who work with your child; bonding with your child in spite of any obstacles her condition may present; accepting your child's differences along with her strengths; acquiring the support that allows you to regain a lifestyle which provides you with contact with the world; maintaining supportive relationships with family and friends; and loving and enjoying your baby as the parent of any newborn might do.

Conclusion

I have yet to talk with another parent who did not have vivid memories of the first few months of life of her child with facial difference. The highlights of these memories usually include taking part in the events surrounding the birth, understanding the diagnosis, telling family members and friends, reading information from medical books, meeting or talking with other families, and feeling like an outsider as you watch the world revolve from the isolation of your home or your baby's hospital room.

While many families' stories seem similar, everyone's experience is unique. Stories of overwhelmingly compassionate professionals who provided endless hours of support are contrasted with those of callous, harried, or anxious professionals who could not even make eye contact with parents. There are stories of extended families who have shown unconditional support, as well as stories of "friends" who have severed all ties with parents upon hearing the diagnosis of their newborn.

Whatever your particular blend of positive and negative experiences, this is the beginning of a new life for you, your family, and friends. You will learn how to adjust, how to evaluate, how to make choices, and how to develop insight. And perhaps most importantly, you will learn that you are not alone with your experiences, thoughts, and feelings. Somewhere else, whether it is around the corner or on the other side of the continent, someone has lived through the same events that you are facing and has built a life full of potential for their child and their family. You can, too.

Parent Statements

I am a pediatric nurse, so I knew what to worry about. I remember when she was just delivered, I noticed the skin tags on her face and knew something was wrong. I think the first 24–48 hours were frightening, not knowing exactly what she had, what it meant and the shock of it all. After that, I really saw her as my baby girl and fell in love with her.

❖

I think that initially our feelings were mostly shock. Then when doctors gave us a worst-case scenario, some of the shock wore off and we were left feeling disappointed and angry. When Michael was about five months old, we realized he could have been more severely affected and we started having some hope.

❖

I had learned to love the little boy in the adoption photos before he came to us. However, I was shocked when I actually met him. He was so tiny and looked like a sculpture abandoned half done. Within three days I had decided that even if nothing could be fixed he was mine forever.

The first seven weeks were very tough. We both felt responsible, but directed our anger at each other.

In the beginning, it was quite stressful because we felt so helpless—we had so many questions and very few answers about our daughter's condition. Gradually we realized that there is a lot more to her than the fact that she only has one ear—that in most ways she is just like any other child and that our capacity as parents to love is truly unconditional.

I have never had any negative feelings. It was love at first sight.

I blamed myself a lot in the beginning. I kept asking myself what I could have done to make him sick.

I wasn't really negative at first—just fearful that I might feed her wrong and injure her without realizing it because the cleft is not very visible.

Our initial feelings were more shock than negative. We had expected a typical baby, which wasn't the case. However, I had the baby I had always wanted, and loved her immediately despite her problems. I didn't have any other experience with babies to compare this one to.

I was born with a bilateral cleft lip and palate. My parents were very loving and life was very normal—except for many surgeries. Secretly, though, I dreaded the possibility that my children would inherit it. I put that part of my life away until Robert was born. Then I remembered all the pain I had gone through! My worst nightmare had become a reality! However, I quickly fell in love with his precious little face. His birth has actually turned out to be one of the greatest gifts of all.

✖

In the beginning we couldn't stop wondering why it had to happen and why to us. We felt better after learning that it was not because of anything we had done and that doctors had seen it before and could do surgery to correct it. We learned this when David was one and a half months old.

✖

It was easier for me to see past the facial difference when her personality was emerging and some hair was growing in. I think it was when she was around four months old.

✖

At age two, I brought him to a craniofacial center in New York City. Here, the doctors didn't seem "shocked." They had seen many cases of facial anomalies. My feelings became more positive as my guilt subsided. Other families had suffered this same "loss." We weren't alone.

✖

When Justine was very small, it was very hard to imagine how she could eat and talk without being able to move her face. I felt very alone, not being able to find anyone else with this rare syndrome. When Justine was eighteen months old, I met an eight-year-old boy with Moebius syndrome. I was very happy to see him eat me out of house and home in a few short hours. His mom assured me my daughter would eat—and eat she does now, all day long. She out-eats her two older brothers. Also, the boy we met talked and played with my boys, and they understood every word he said. It was interesting to see him talk clearly without moving his mouth, almost like a ventriloquist.

✖

Dad's very proud of him, but he much prefers Mom to Dad and can be a real brat to Dad.

✖

I went into therapy to help me deal with Cory's condition and to help both Cory and my son (who is older) deal with it. The therapist was extremely supportive and helped me to see how strong I was and to see that we were a "special" family.

�֍

It's taken me eleven years to get to this point of acceptance—to get over the pain and guilt I have felt overwhelmed by. Perhaps the most positive aspect has been meeting other children and their parents and seeing their courage and tenacity.

✖

Coping has not been easy. But at least we're still married. Our seventeenth anniversary is coming soon.

✖

Having Carla has bonded my husband and me together, giving us a common goal. It has also forced us to seek support and comfort from each other because we have no friends in a similar situation. This, too, has made our marriage stronger.

✖

When Katherine was a couple months old, I asked my husband something I had been wondering since her birth: Knowing what he did now, did he wish he had married someone else (and had a baby with no problems)? He quickly reassured me of his love and that he wouldn't change anything. He then asked me the same question, and from that point on, I feel our marriage was strengthened in a way that many people could not relate to if they didn't have a special child. We knew we loved each other when things were going well and when there were troubles as well.

✖

Since my husband and I delayed having a child until we were older (I was 36, he was 40), we wondered if we could have avoided this if we'd had a child earlier. I was wracked with guilt for not having a baby at an earlier age, since I could have, having been married over ten years.

✖

We didn't have a strong marriage to start with. It has taken a great toll on our marriage. I feel my husband isn't sensitive or involved enough. He feels I am too sensitive and overprotective and worry too much. He also blames me because I smoked during pregnancy.

I try not to dwell on why it happened, but on how I can help my son live a normal life.

※

The first year was the most stressful for us, and I think that support from family and friends helped us through. We have always been big communicators in our marriage and I am sure that helped. This was certainly the biggest challenge either of us had experienced. We handled things differently from each other at times. I benefitted from my husband's ability to prioritize and "chunk" things out. I tended to let my worries run ahead of things and he would help me focus my energy where it had to be. I think parts of us were revealed to each other that we didn't know before. I remember being amazed at how positive my husband stayed throughout all our ups and downs.

※

My other children have always accepted my daughter and don't act as if they feel she is any different.

※

Our children get along like most—some days they are best friends, and some days you can't believe they could ever be in the same room together. Her brothers only know her how she is, so they don't really come out and talk about it.

※

My other children are very supportive and caring toward their little brother. They both know the basics of Curtis's condition and can tell people about it just as well as I can.

※

Our daughter is only three months old, so she will grow up used to her brother's facial difference. It's not something we will try to hide or ignore.

※

We met a local family through a national support group and they were most valuable in sharing their experiences with surgeries.

※

Our support group has made all the difference in helping me and others deal with something we knew nothing about. We now feel we can educate others about what we have spent so much time and energy learning about. Also, my daughter has met more than twenty people with the same rare syndrome, and it has helped her talk about her facial difference, to know what it is, and to know that she's not the only person with the same problems.

✖

The Freeman-Sheldon Support Group has helped us immeasurably. We all learn from each other, and with FSS an extremely rare condition, Henry has met five other kids with it!

✖

Networking with other parents has been very educational and we actually learned more from other parents than we did from our doctors. Just sharing the same experiences with other parents and knowing someone who understands what the specific medical diagnosis is very uplifting.

✖

Kevin has caused me to grow into a better person. I can't be selfish anymore.

✖

We have learned that "what is inside is what counts" is really true. People put too much emphasis on looks.

✖

The person that helped me the most was the mother of a son who had the same thing our daughter does. She spent hours talking to me and my husband. She gave me the name of the best and most qualified person in my area to perform the operation Brittany needed.

✖

We've met so many wonderful people through trying to help Henry. During a long stay in Europe, he served as "ice breaker" everywhere we went and made friends with everyone.

✖

When my daughter was about eight months old, we joined the local chapter of a national support group. Until then, we were unaware that such a group existed in our area, and felt very isolated by our situation. Having other people in similar circumstances to talk to and share experiences with makes a tremendous difference and we have found it to be very therapeutic. We have also gained some much-needed perspective on our child's situation.

�

It's hard to have a facial difference when the world would have you believe that a pimple is a crisis.

✖

I have a happy, healthy baby. He is smart; he will make it. I just keep telling myself it will all be over with someday (speech disorders and surgeries) and my son and I will survive this. I won't let myself give up on my child.

✖

Since having Josh, I look at people differently. It's like I look at them more deeply, and I'm glad I was chosen to deal with this because I'm very good at taking care of him.

✖

She makes me stop and think about how lucky we are. We used to rush around without much silly time. Now the two babies and I spend our mornings in bed, just enjoying each other's company and making faces. The small, unimportant-seeming times end up being our most cherished moments.

✖

We feel privileged to be parents and to have learned from experience that any disfigurement does not define the person. The real beauty is what is on the inside. God gave David an extra special personality all his own so that others can see that.

✖

So many unknowns have come out better than predicted. We have met many wonderful people (I call them our guardian angels): other families, kids, teachers, therapists. This little person, who is only four, has taught us a tremendous amount about big things . . . like life . . . and what really matters.

✖

Chapter 3

✻

Medical Concerns, Treatments, and Professionals

When my son was a toddler, another parent told me about an eyelid operation that was "simple" and would greatly improve the appearance of the upper half of my son's face. Eager to learn more about the surgical procedure, I immediately called the coordinator of our craniofacial team and blurted out this easy answer. Gently, and with a great deal of diplomacy, she reminded me that my son's condition was very complex and there were no simple answers. And, anyone who was promising me simple answers did not fully understand his disorder.

While some of the conditions described in this book are more complex than others, all present a variety of health problems or potential health problems that parents should be aware of. This chapter reviews many of these problems and offers guidance on working with the health care professionals involved with your child.

Anesthesia

Most children with facial difference need an operation at some point in their lives—whether to repair a congenital deformity; improve functions such as speech, breathing, or hearing; or reconstruct the head or face following trauma. These operations are usually performed while the child is under general anesthesia. That is, the child is given drugs, gas, or both so that he can sleep comfortably during the operation.

Administering anesthesia to children with facial difference is often more complicated than it is for other children. In many children with underdeveloped lower jaws, the upper airway is smaller, narrower, or partially obstructed. This may make it difficult for the anesthesiologist to place a breathing tube in your child's nose or mouth. (This process is technically called *intubation.*) Intubation is particularly complicated in children with hemifacial microsomia and Apert, Crouzon, and Treacher Collins syndromes, due to narrowing of the nasal cavity and nasopharynx—the part of the pharynx (throat) above the soft palate. Another problem is that the mask used for administering anesthetic gases and oxygen might not fit well on children with an abnormally shaped face. Congenital heart disease or abnormalities of the cervical spine, present in many children with hemifacial microsomia, can cause additional difficulties. This is because children with heart disease need to be closely monitored for problems with oxygenation and blood pressure while under anesthesia. Cervical spine problems can make intubation more difficult.

Although it is possible to generalize about the difficulties that these conditions often cause, every child is unique. Unless there is an emergency, the anesthesiologist should meet with you and your child before the operation to find out how your child is different. The anesthesiologist should discuss your child's medical and surgical history, any previous anesthetic experiences, and the results of his most recent physical exam. (Physical exams are routinely done before an operation.) The anesthesiologist will also ask you questions about: your child's current medications, possible allergies, airway obstruction, disorders of the central nervous system such as seizures, congenital heart problems, clotting or bleeding problems, endocrine abnormalities such as thyroid disease or diabetes, respiratory tract infections, range of motion of your child's cervical spine (neck), hearing loss, and language delay.

If your child has any hearing loss or language problems, he and the anesthesiologist might have trouble communicating during the preparations before the operation. If your child is an infant or too young to reliably communicate, the anesthesiologist might talk to your child for comfort. If he is older, he might be asked to count, say his name, call out when the red light on his finger goes out, etc. These are techniques the anesthesiologist might use to test your child's consciousness, either going under or coming out of anesthesia. If your child can't hear or understand the directions, he can't respond. It will therefore be important for you to educate the anesthesiologist about ways of communicating with your child.

It is also a good idea to tell the anesthesiologist if your child has a tendency to have motion sickness (nausea). Motion sickness can be brought on by some types of anesthesia, and can be a problem if it causes your child to vomit and he subsequently breathes (aspirates) particles into his lungs. (Even without motion sickness, vomiting after surgery is common.) If the anesthesiologist knows about the motion sickness, he can take this into account and give specific drugs to prevent it.

The anesthesiologist will probably ask you about your concerns. But if he or she doesn't, speak up! Here are some questions you might want to ask: Does he specialize in giving anesthesia for children with cranial and facial differences? How many patients with your child's condition has he anesthetized? How long has he worked regularly with your child's surgeon? Does he specialize in children's anesthesia? If you aren't comfortable with the anesthesiologist, contact the surgeon immediately. For example, if the anesthesiologist says he has never worked with a child with your child's facial difference before, it is likely you will want to postpone the operation until a more qualified anesthesiologist is available. Parents can cancel an operation at *any* time. It is not advisable to go into the operating room with an anesthesiologist who has never before worked with children with facial differences.

Children often ask, "How will I be put to sleep?" There are two basic ways: 1) with an intravenous drug (IV), and 2) by breathing gas through a mask. If the IV route is chosen, your child may be afraid that it will hurt. If so, the anesthesiologist can use a new cream called Emla® to numb the skin before the IV is inserted. This cream must be applied 45 minutes to an hour ahead of time to be effective.

After your child is asleep, the anesthesiologist places the breathing tube through your child's nose or mouth. Nasal intubation is often used for patients with facial abnormalities. After intubation, anesthetic gas, mixed with oxygen, is used to keep your child asleep. Your child is carefully monitored by sophisticated machines throughout the operation. Blood pressure, pulse, respiratory rate, blood gases (oxygen and carbon dioxide), nerve sensitivity, and temperature are all watched.

Occasionally children with facial differences need a tracheostomy ("trach") to maintain an open airway during the operation. A tracheostomy is the creation of an opening into the trachea ("windpipe") through the neck; this is done after the child is anesthetized. A tube is inserted into the opening to facilitate the passage of air and/or to suction out secretions. A child with a facial difference should be considered for tracheostomy if he has a severely narrowed airway, a tongue that flops backward, a small lower jaw, or other atypical anatomy. Children with conditions with receded lower jaws (Treacher Collins syndrome, hemifacial microsomia, Pierre Robin sequence, Nager syndrome) need a tracheostomy more often than other children. If the anesthesiologist or surgeon feels it is likely that your child will need a tracheostomy, he will discuss this with you before the operation. In rare instances, an emergency tracheostomy is necessary if intubation cannot be accomplished. If your child already has a tracheostomy in place, his anesthetic procedure will be different from what is described here. The anesthesiologist should discuss this with you prior to the operation.

If the anesthesiologist anticipates that intubating your child will be difficult, ask to have a nurse come to the waiting room to let you know once your child is safely asleep and the operation has begun. When the operation is over, you should meet again with the anesthesiologist to discuss the intubation in depth. You should make sure that any problems that were encountered are noted in your child's medical records for use in future operations.

The breathing tube is usually removed (extubation) after the operation when your child is awakened in the operating room. If your child required a tracheostomy for the procedure, the timing of the removal of the tube is based on his future needs, such as breathing ability and possible further operations. Sometimes a tracheostomy is removed within a few days of the operation; usually it takes a while longer. You will be given detailed instructions on the care of your child's tracheostomy. Once the tracheostomy tube is removed, the hole generally heals rapidly. Sometimes it leaves a scar that can be "fixed" later.

Breathing

Breathing is one of the most basic functions of the body and must continuously take place for us to stay alive. Some children with facial differences, however, have trouble breathing through the mouth, nose, or both while they are awake and/or asleep.

These breathing difficulties are usually the result of partial upper airway obstruction. (Breathing problems that are the result of cleft lip and/or palate are discussed in the next section.) The age of onset and duration of the obstruction varies, depending on the type of facial difference. The most common causes of breathing difficulties are described below.

Choanal Atresia (or Stenosis). Choanal atresia occurs when soft tissue or bone blocks the back of the nasal opening, called the *choana* (the passage leading from the nasal cavity into the nasopharynx). Choanal stenosis (narrowing) is diagnosed when a catheter can't be passed through the nasal opening into the throat. In a newborn, this type of nasal blockage is an emergency, since newborns must be able to breathe through their noses to get enough oxygen. To provide an adequate airway, a tracheostomy might be necessary. Once the child grows bigger, he can breathe on his own, without the tracheostomy. Choanal atresia (or stenosis) is common in Treacher Collins syndrome, CHARGE syndrome, and several of the craniosynostosis syndromes, including Apert, Crouzon, and Pfeiffer.

Underdeveloped Midface. Sometimes an upper airway obstruction is due to underdevelopment of the maxilla (the upper jaw). The nasopharynx is constricted and the choanal openings can be narrowed or blocked. Normal growth of the adenoids (lymphatic tissue in the back of the throat), soft palate, and adjacent soft tissue can further reduce the available breathing space. These changes can cause breathing problems at birth or during the first year of life. These problems are most common in children with craniosynostosis disorders, such as Apert and Crouzon syndromes.

Hypoplasia of the Lower Jaw. Hypoplasia (underdevelopment) of the lower jaw can result in a hypopharyngeal obstruction (an obstruction of the opening into the larynx and esophagus). This is frequently a problem in babies with Pierre Robin sequence, who sometimes require a tracheostomy shortly after birth. As they grow older, children with this condition can have obstructive sleep apnea (see below). Enlarging tonsils and adenoids, from about ages two to five years, make the obstruction worse. Sometimes a small lower jaw makes it difficult, or virtually impossible, for an anesthesiologist to insert a breathing tube prior to an operation. Hypoplasia of the lower jaw is also very common in children with Treacher Collins syndrome and hemifacial microsomia.

Diagnosis and Treatment of Breathing Problems

Signs and symptoms that indicate that your child has an upper airway breathing problem include: *excessive* snoring (almost 100 percent of children with facial difference snore), irregular breathing, mouth breathing, daytime sleepiness, tiring easily, irritability, and frequent infections of the upper and lower respiratory tract (colds, strep throat). Airway blockage can also lead to failure of your child to thrive with poor growth rate. In older children, school performance can be lower than expected.

If you or your child's professionals suspect a breathing problem, you should have a formal "sleep study" done in a hospital center. During the study, your child will spend a night in the sleep laboratory. For the sleep study to be valid, your child must sleep through the night, just as he does at home (for at least six to eight hours and for approximately the same amounts of time in each sleep cycle). Before he goes to sleep, several electrodes will be attached with gel to his upper body and head. This does not hurt. He will then be asked to go to sleep.

While your child sleeps, information about the level of oxygen and carbon dioxide in his body, as well as heart and brain activity, will pass to a computer through the wires connected to the electrodes. The computer will process this information and chart it onto graphs (*polysomnography*). These graphs will be analyzed by a physician who specializes in sleep disorders. He or she will check to see whether your child has adequate oxygen levels during sleep.

Some centers also use videofluoroscopy to supplement the sleep study results. Videofluoroscopy is a special x-ray study that shows your child's internal organs on a fluorescent screen as he breathes. The results of these tests should be noted in your child's medical chart and consulted before any medications are prescribed prior to surgery. This is because children with partial airway obstruction can have breathing problems if given too much medication.

If testing shows that your child has an obstruction, he may be diagnosed as having *apnea, sleep apnea,* or *obstructive sleep apnea.* Apnea means that there are periods when the air flow stops for longer than ten seconds before the child starts breathing again. Sleep apnea generally causes at least thirty episodes of apnea in a seven-hour period of sleep. (The exact definition varies somewhat between sleep centers.) In obstructive sleep apnea, the child makes breathing movements, but for several seconds there is no air flow because of mechanical obstruction in the upper airway.

With early detection, these problems can usually be corrected, and possible complications such as cardiopulmonary (lung and heart) problems can be prevented. As mentioned above, one way of handling breathing problems is to do a tracheostomy if the child cannot breathe adequately. Such a tracheostomy usually is not permanent. Most children outgrow the need for a tracheostomy by the time they are five to seven years old. Some children need to open the tracheostomy tube while they are sleeping at night. During the day, the tube can be closed with a plug or valve (Passey-Muir) so that air passes around the tube and into the mouth and nose.

Other children might need to have their breathing checked with an apnea monitor. An apnea monitor is a device that is hooked up to electrodes on your child's body and "alarms" or makes a loud noise whenever your child's respirations (breathing in and out) do not occur in a normal pattern. Sometimes the alarm will be enough to awaken your child. Otherwise, you will need to wake him by shaking, so that he breathes more normally. Some children only need an apnea monitor during the night; others need to use it twenty-four hours a day. Although monitors are portable, they are cumbersome, so daytime usage limits mobility. Children usually do not need to use an apnea monitor long. They either outgrow the need for it or have a tracheostomy.

If your child has a breathing problem, you should learn CPR (cardiopulmonary resuscitation). Your child's doctor can direct you to an appropriate course offered by a hospital or the Red Cross.

How Clefts Affect Breathing

A cleft lip and/or palate also affect a child's ability to breathe, but in a slightly different way than described above. At birth, children with cleft lip and/or palate breathe through an open communication between their nose and mouth. That is, they don't really breathe through their nose or their mouth, but through the cleft. By the time the cleft is surgically repaired, usually by the age of one year, mouth breathing may have become an ingrained habit. In fact, research shows that 75 percent of adults born with bilateral cleft lip and palate breathe more through their mouth than through their nose.

There is another reason that children with clefts tend to be mouth breathers. Children with clefts, especially of both the lip and palate, often have a narrow nasal airway. (In adults with cleft lip and/or palate, the nasal airway is generally about 25 percent narrower than usual.) Thus, to take in enough air, people with clefts often need to breathe through their mouth.

Surgical correction of the nose and palate can further narrow the airway by leaving scar tissue in the airway or by causing cartilage to collapse into the airway. When considering an operation that is intended to improve appearance rather than function, it is therefore important to consider how breathing might be affected. It is especially important to consider how operating on a cleft might affect breathing when the cleft lip and palate are associated with a syndrome (other anomalies). That is, doctors should take into account how repairing the cleft might contribute to any airway obstruction already associated with the syndrome.

Dental Care

Most children with the facial differences described in this book need specialized dental care. Often they have missing, crowded, misshapen, or malpositioned teeth that do not fit together (*occlude*) properly. The enamel (the hard, protective covering) on their teeth can be poorly formed, missing, or unevenly deposited. This makes the teeth more susceptible to cavities. In addition, these children often need operations on the jaws and teeth. Consequently, they need the coordinated services of a pediatric dentist (pedodontist), an orthodontist, a maxillofacial surgeon, a prosthodontist, and/or a plastic surgeon. (The orthodontist specializes in treating teeth and the inside of the mouth with devices such as braces and retainers that gradually exert pressure to move the teeth into a better position.) Orthodontic wires and devices are usually placed on the permanent teeth in preparation for an operation on the middle or lower face, including the jaws. In some cases, treatment must begin before the permanent teeth erupt.

Here are some ways that conditions of facial difference commonly affect the teeth:

Apert and Crouzon Syndromes. The teeth are usually severely crowded. Sometimes teeth (both baby and permanent) are extracted to allow the remaining teeth to naturally space themselves. Occasionally, a child can be missing one or more teeth. Children with these syndromes usually require extensive orthodontic treatment at intervals during the eruption of teeth, and also later to support final operations on the jaw.

Cleft Lip and Palate. The baby (primary) and permanent (secondary) teeth closest to the cleft are most often affected—most often malformed, malpositioned, crowded, or missing. In addition, the upper jaw can be misshapen, making it difficult to get good mouth closure. As your child's baby teeth begin to erupt, the orthodontist will evaluate the position of the teeth and how they fit together (occlusion), and assess the overall growth of the jaws and the rest of the face. This monitoring usually continues until the permanent teeth erupt and the jaws are fully developed. Sometimes, a pediatric dentist who has experience in treating children with clefts might suggest earlier orthodontic treatment. An orthodontist then develops a treatment plan to align the permanent teeth. Sometimes a final phase of braces together with jaw surgery is necessary.

Primary repair of the cleft lip and palate is coordinated between the pediatric dentist and plastic surgeon. Sometimes orthodontic appliances are used to align the gums prior to surgical closure of the cleft lip. In later childhood (while there is a mixture of baby and permanent teeth), an appliance may be used to widen the upper dental arch. As your child approaches adolescence, the position of his jaws will again be evaluated. If necessary, he might have another operation to align them. If teeth are missing or gaps in the teeth remain, your child should see a prosthodontist—a dentist who specializes in improving the appearance and function of the mouth. The prosthodontist can replace missing teeth with bridges or implants. Proper care of the teeth holding the appliance is particularly important.

Hemifacial Microsomia. Although the lower jaw is small in hemifacial microsomia, there are few major dental problems. Sometimes teeth are missing or have short roots; often the teeth in the lower jaw are crowded. Because the lower jaw is both small and asymmetric, the teeth may tilt upward on the side predominately affected by the hemifacial microsomia. Occlusion for chewing is usually adequate, although the bite may be shifted toward the smaller side of the face.

Treacher Collins Syndrome. In children with Treacher Collins syndrome, the lower jaw is small and the teeth are usually crowded. Overbite and open bite is extremely common, since the lower jaw is always receded. The upper teeth often protrude markedly. Rarely, sudden growth of the jaw can occur or jaw growth can stop. Your child's dentist or orthodontist should notify the plastic surgeon or oral and maxillofacial surgeon if this occurs. Orthodontics will be used to align your child's teeth in preparation for the operation to elongate the lower jaw and move his receded chin forward. If, however, the bone distraction technique is used to bring the lower jaw forward, prior orthodontic treatment is generally not necessary. (Refer to the section on Bone Distraction, below.) In either case, more orthodontic treatment will be needed later to improve the bite.

Because dental problems are so common in children with facial differences, a pediatric dentist should examine your child's teeth on a regular basis as soon as his first tooth erupts. Early dental care should include a preventative approach of adequate daily cleaning, periodic fluoride treatments, and a nutritionally adequate diet.

Home Dental Care

Daily cleaning can obviously be difficult if your child's teeth are crowded or misshapen, or his mouth is small. As a parent, you must take extra care to make sure that brushing and flossing are daily rituals. When your child is young, you should do the brushing and flossing yourself. Use a toothbrush with a small head and soft bristles such as the Oral-B-20®. Regular fluoride toothpaste is fine, but use only pea-sized doses and caution your child not to eat it. Position yourself behind your child, supporting his head and tipping it back against your body to provide visibility and stability. Tablets that reveal plaque can be helpful in revealing spots where you need to take extra care in brushing. A floss holder such as the "E-Z Flosser"® or Floss-Aid® is especially useful in cleaning between crowded teeth.

Because of dental crowding and other problems, children with facial differences need more fluoride than usual. Be careful about using fluoride rinses with a young child, however. You must supervise rinsing because fluoride rinses have a high alcohol content and should not be swallowed. If you live in an area where there is no water fluoridation, your child should take a daily supplement.

As with any child, you can minimize problems such as cavities by limiting sugary foods in your child's diet. Be aware, too, that sticky sugary foods are especially bad. Foods like raisins or caramels can stick to the teeth and continue to bathe them in sugar for many hours. Avoid the temptation of giving your child extra sweets to "make up" for his special needs, as some parents do. Also, be careful not to substitute high fat, high cholesterol foods for sweet, sticky foods. An unhealthy cardiovascular system is not a good trade-off for dental cavities. The table below lists some good and bad snacks. If you are in doubt about foods to include in your child's diet, a dietician can give you guidance.

Good and Bad Snack Foods

Good Foods	*Bad Foods*
popcorn (low fat, low salt)	candy
cheese (low fat)	gum with sugar
natural fiber foods (granola, apple juice or other non-sweetened cereal)	refined fruit juices
	chips
breads	
fruits	

Choosing and Working with Dental Professionals

Your child's craniofacial team includes a pediatric dentist, orthodontist, and other dental professionals. Your child, however, also needs to have a local pediatric dentist and orthodontist. The dental professionals on your child's craniofacial team will likely provide comprehensive planning and treatments immediately before and after surgical procedures; your child's local dentists need to be able to continue the treatment plan. Between trips to the craniofacial center, the local dentist or orthodontist is also the ideal person to monitor jaw growth and dental growth and development, as well as to clean the teeth and check for cavities.

It is best to find local dental professionals who have experience working with children with facial differences. If they do not, you and your child may be comfortable with a professional who is willing to learn from and consult with your child's craniofacial team, and who is sensitive to your child's physical appearance. Ask the dentists on your child's team for referrals to pediatric dentists and orthodontists in your area. The American Academy of Pediatric Dentistry can also recommend appropriate dentists.

Any dentist you choose must be willing to work with your child's craniofacial team. Since your child will likely be seen more often by the local professionals, they need to contact your child's team whenever a problem or suspected problem arises.

Because your child will spend a considerable amount of time with the local dentist and orthodontist, it is essential that these professionals establish a caring, positive relationship with your child. Generally, pediatric dentists and orthodontists are tuned-in to communicating with children and are more sensitive to children's needs, especially regarding discomfort and self-image. A dentist with a sense of humor is *always* a plus! It's also important that dental professionals take care that you and your child feel relaxed and unhurried while in their offices. Finally, make sure that your local professionals are sensitive to your child's need to be included in decision-making processes as he grows older.

Nutrition

All babies need adequate nutrition in order to thrive. In addition, babies need a feeding experience that is loving, caring, and gratifying in order to bond with their parents. Babies with facial differences have the same needs for nutrition and love as other babies, but meeting those needs can be difficult. One reason is that structural problems of your baby's face and head can make feeding a frustrating, stressful experience. Another reason is that it may be psychologically difficult for you to look at your baby, feel close to him, and want to feed him.

To meet your baby's nutritional needs, be prepared to invest extra time in feeding him and to be flexible in trying a variety of feeding methods. Particularly if you are interested in breast-feeding, consult the feeding specialist, nutritionist, and nurse manager on your child's craniofacial team. They can give you a great deal of practical and emotional support.

Health care professionals agree that breast milk offers infants the best source of nutrition. But breast-feeding might not be possible for your child, or might be possible only with modifications. A lactation specialist can suggest ways to modify feeding positions and might be available for on-going support. The La Leche League also provides limited support to breast-feeding mothers of babies with cleft lip and palate.

If your baby is not able to breast-feed, you can pump or express the breast milk. Either parent can then feed your baby the milk in a bottle. Sometimes mothers are unable to produce enough

breast milk, or choose not to breast-feed or pump milk. If this is the case, you can use formula and your baby will still thrive. A pediatric nutritionist or pediatrician can determine the number of calories your baby needs, the best formula to use, and a schedule for feeding your baby.

Some babies are not able to get enough nutrition through a bottle and must be fed with a "feeding tube." The feeding tube is made of soft plastic, and can be inserted in several ways. A nasogastric (NG) tube is inserted through the nose, down the esophagus, and into the stomach. A gavage tube is inserted through the mouth and into the stomach. A gastrostomy (G-tube) is inserted through an incision in the abdomen directly into the stomach. Depending on his needs, the baby is then fed formula, liquids, or blenderized foods through the tube. Nasogastric (NG) and gavage feeding can only be done for a few months at most. The NG tube irritates the esophagus and can cause aspiration of food particles if not properly placed. If the child still needs tube feeding, he will probably need to be switched to a G-tube.

The goal is to move gradually from tube feeding to eating solid foods. Usually, as your child grows, his ability to feed orally improves because his ability to coordinate breathing and swallowing improves.

While your child is being fed by a tube, it is essential to provide some oral stimulation to prepare him for oral feeding. Stroke your child's cheeks, lips, and the area under his chin while you are feeding him. Or dip a pacifier in formula and place it in your child's mouth while you are tube feeding him. You can also give him small tastes of food from a finger, spoon, or dropper. In providing these types of stimulation, be careful not to stimulate the "gag reflex." Touch only the front third of his tongue. Also remember that your child should get some pleasure from these experiences. Learn to recognize his cues so you know when he has had enough oral stimulation.

With training, parents can feed their babies at home with a tube. Although this might not seem like a very nurturing way to feed your baby, you can still provide him with a loving and caring feeding environment while giving him adequate nutrition. If you have questions or problems, the nurse on the craniofacial team is typically the person best attuned to feeding issues. Some craniofacial centers have a "feeding team." Your child's pediatrician or a dietician may also be able to help.

To meet your baby's psychological needs, you need to provide opportunities for him to bond with you or your spouse during feeding. Typically, parents do this by holding their baby close, talking to him, and looking into his eyes while they feed him. If you have trouble doing this, talk with the psychologist on your child's craniofacial team. He or she can help you work through your emotional concerns about your baby's appearance so that you feel more comfortable feeding your baby.

The sections below explain some specific feeding problems that children with particular conditions may have.

Apert, Crouzon, and Pfeiffer Syndromes. Craniofacial abnormalities usually do not cause major feeding problems in these conditions. Your child should be able to latch on to the nipple and form a tight seal. But he may have trouble coordinating swallowing and breathing, especially as an infant, when he breathes primarily through his mouth. You may need to modify your feeding techniques, perhaps by holding your child in a more upright position while he drinks. Using a large cross-cut nipple or a Haberman Feeder can also help. In addition, be sure to give your child frequent pauses to allow for extra breathing. If he becomes overtired, use frequent, shorter feedings rather then fewer long feedings.

Sometimes, children with these facial differences need to be fed temporarily with an NG tube to supplement calories. Rarely, they may need a gastrostomy tube. Your child's feeding team can give you guidance about specific problems.

Cleft Lip. A baby with a cleft lip usually has difficulty creating suction. Feeding your child in an upright position and using a special syringe called a "cleft feeder" is usually helpful. With modifications, some infants are able to breast-feed. Extra and on-going support from a lactation specialist might be necessary, however. Following surgical repair, children are often fed with a cleft feeder until the incision heals (at least ten to fourteen days). To prevent infection and to ensure that the lip heals properly, you will need to take precautions to keep the stitches clean and to minimize straining and crying.

Cleft Palate. Babies with clefts of the soft palate usually have few problems feeding, whereas babies with clefts of the hard and soft palate can have extensive feeding problems. These babies usually have trouble creating enough pressure for sucking because of the leak in the roof of their mouth. Sometimes special nipples and bottles such as the Haberman Feeder can alleviate this problem. (See the Resource Guide for names and sources of special bottles.) A nipple with an enlarged, cross-cut opening that allows the milk to flow more freely is usually recommended. It also helps if the baby feeds in an upright position with the nipple placed directly on the tongue and lower lip. Placing a finger under the chin point helps to increase pressure on the nipple. Rarely, a dental appliance that fits into the roof of the mouth is needed to increase suction during feeding.

Hemifacial Microsomia. Babies with hemifacial microsomia may or may not have a feeding problem, depending on the severity of jaw underdevelopment and possible tongue weakness. Most do not have any special feeding problems, although they feed relatively slowly. Babies who have hemifacial microsomia and cleft lip/palate have the difficulties described above.

A baby with macrostomia (cleft of the mouth from the side) can have trouble forming a good seal around a nipple. This can make breastfeeding difficult or impossible. Mothers who have extended nipples, a good "let down" reflex, and the ability to "milk" their breasts are more likely to be successful. Usually it is best to hold the child upright or in a "football hold." It may be necessary to hold one side of the baby's mouth closed.

Bottle feeding a baby with a macrostomia is best done with a long nipple, Haberman nipple, or lamb's nipple. It is easiest if you hold the infant on a crossed leg so that he is looking toward you. It may help to swaddle him tightly so he cannot move his arms. Hold the macrostomia opening closed by using one finger to push the corner of the mouth from below the cleft toward the nose.

It is important not to overtire your baby when feeding. Feedings should not last more than twenty to thirty minutes. It is the amount of nourishment your child takes in over the course of twenty-four hours that is important. Your pediatrician, nurse, or nutritionist should be able to tell you how many calories your child needs per day.

Treacher Collins and Nager Syndromes. Babies with Treacher Collins syndrome often have a variety of feeding problems. The lower jaw can be so receded that the baby expends too much energy sucking, tires easily during feedings, and is unable to take in enough nourishment to gain weight. If the baby also has a cleft palate, he might be unable to produce enough pressure to adequately suck. In addition, some babies are unable to suck and breathe at the same time, or they have a tongue that flops back and closes the airway. An assessment of the ability to feed and breathe at the same time should be made within the first month of life. An oximeter (a device that measures oxygen concentration) is sometimes used while feeding to make sure the baby is getting sufficient oxygen.

Some babies with Treacher Collins or Nager syndromes need special bottles with long, extended nipples to feed adequately. The nurse on your craniofacial team or a pharmacist should be able to tell you where to buy these bottles, or you can contact the companies listed in the Resource Guide. Other babies may need a feeding tube or a feeding tube plus a tracheostomy so that they are able to breathe while feeding.

Feeding after Infancy

As children with facial difference grow and thrive, the ability to feed orally improves. Feeding is seldom a problem once a child with facial differences moves on to solid foods. This is especially the case if the child has had positive oral experiences throughout the first year of life. Introducing different foods and textures is made easier when a child has had the types of oral stimulation described earlier.

Occasionally, children with Treacher Collins or Nager syndrome develop *trismus*—spasms of the jaw muscles. They may also have a poorly working temporomandibular joint (TMJ)—the joint between the side of the skull and the lower jaw. Either problem limits how far the mouth can be opened or makes chewing difficult. If your child has one or both of these problems, you will need to work closely with the dental professionals on the craniofacial team.

Hearing and Communication

Many children with facial difference have diminished hearing. Hearing impairments can be present at birth, or can develop during childhood. Often, the hearing loss is a result of fluid in the middle ear and secondary infection (*otitis media*). It can also be caused by abnormalities in the structures of the middle ear.

Since hearing problems occur so frequently in children with facial difference, an audiologist should test your child's hearing as soon after birth as is medically possible. Later, if you notice that your child is not responding to sounds in a typical way or has an increasing number of ear infections, consult a pediatric otolaryngologist (ear, nose, and throat specialist). Hearing can often be improved by draining the built-up fluid from the ears and inserting tiny tubes through the eardrums. Sometimes a hearing aid is necessary, or, less often, an operation on the middle ear.

Because hearing is vital to the development of communication skills, potential hearing problems, their causes, and treatments are discussed in more detail in Chapter 5: Speech, Language, and Hearing Needs.

Vision

The craniofacial team will have a number of medical concerns after their first examination of your child. Usually the team will prioritize these concerns. That is, they will recommend taking care of the most important (functional) problems first and the less important ones later. If your child has breathing and feeding problems, visual problems are not quite so urgent. But once your child is tak-

ing in adequate amounts of air and food, his vision should be evaluated by a pediatric ophthalmologist—a medical doctor who specializes in diagnosing and treating children's eye disorders.

Visual problems are not a concern with every type of facial difference. The conditions that *are* associated with visual problems are usually those in which the orbits are affected. The orbits are the bony cavities which contain the eyeballs, as well as the associated muscles, blood vessels, and nerves. The orbits represent a bridge between the face and the cranium (skull bone).

Orbital problems are especially common in children with the craniosynostotic syndromes. Children with these syndromes have an underdeveloped midface (cheeks and upper jaw). As a result, they can have these problems:

- *exophthalmos,* or protruding eyes;
- *proptosis,* or bulging eyes;
- *orbital hypertelorism,* or widely spaced eyes;
- *exposure keratitis,* or inflammation of the cornea due to drying or irritation;
- *strabismus,* an imbalance of the muscles in which the eyes turn in different directions. If an eye just drifts temporarily, it is called a "phoria"; if the abnormal position is more constant, it is called a "tropia." More specifically, "exotropia" means the eye turns outward; "esotropia," turns inward; and "hypertropia," turns upward.

  Strabismus is also common in children with other facial differences. (Some researchers have reported that it affects as many as 79 percent of all children with craniofacial conditions.) Other visual problems often seen in children with facial differences include:
- *motility problems:* difficulty in coordinated movement of the eyes. Rarely, for instance in children with Moebius syndrome, there is a total paralysis of the muscles that move

the eyes to the side. In children with craniosynostotic syndromes there can be uncoordinated movement between the two eyes. This is caused by anatomic deformities of the orbits and resulting muscular imbalance between the eyes.

- *amblyopia:* diminished vision in one eye or both eyes. This loss of vision can be temporary or permanent. Amblyopia can occur if there is an underlying problem, such as strabismus, which results in blurred or double vision when both eyes are used. To see clearly, the brain suppresses the visual information from one eye. The unused eye then gradually loses the ability to process visual images. You may also hear this condition referred to as "lazy eye."

- *exposure keratitis:* damage to the cornea, the transparent "lens cap" covering the front part of the eye. Your child's corneas can be seriously damaged by dirt particles floating in the air, too much exposure to the air, or excessive dryness if they are not fully covered by his lids. This may occur either because of lid colobomas (notching), exophthalmos (protruding eyes), facial nerve weakness that prevents the eyes from closing, or absence of the normal nerves responsible for sensation in the cornea. If the cornea is permanently damaged, scar formation can make that area of the cornea so opaque that light cannot enter the eye.

- *epiphora:* excessive tearing. This can be caused by a congenital abnormality (blockage) of the tear duct system, or it can become a problem after surgical correction of the bones around the eye.

Treatment and Prevention of Vision Problems

Preserving and improving your child's vision requires periodic monitoring by an ophthalmologist. Strabismus can sometimes be improved by corrective lenses. More often, however, a surgical procedure on the eye muscles is required to straighten and align the eyes. To prevent amblyopia, the stronger eye is often patched for several hours a day, forcing the child to use the weaker eye. Sometimes an opaque contact lens is prescribed to be worn on the normal eye in order to strengthen the other. Corrective lenses, too, can help to correct amblyopia.

Fitting glasses can be a problem for children with certain facial differences involving the nose, cheeks, or ears. Usually, however, the oculist working with the craniofacial team can make the proper adjustments. For example, a child born without an external ear can use an elastic strap to hold his glasses in place until an ear is constructed by a surgical procedure or with a prosthesis.

As a parent, it is especially important for you to be aware of the possibility of corneal exposure and damage. You may need to use artificial tear solutions and lubricants, particularly at night, if your child's eyes remain open during sleep. Sometimes taping the eyelids closed is helpful. Excessive tearing does not usually cause major problems, but if it does, there are operations that can restore the function so that tears drain into the bottom part of the nasal cavity as they should.

Your child should have a baseline ophthalmologic evaluation before any craniofacial operation that involves the upper face. The evaluation should confirm how well he sees, the health of his eyes, and how his bones are different in shape from normal. This information will help the plastic surgeon, neurosurgeon, and ophthalmologist understand your child's orbital and facial anatomy. This examination is also important in selecting the timing and extent of specific procedures to repair the eyes and orbits. Generally, the orbits (and midface) are repaired by the plastic surgeon before the ophthalmologist does any procedures on the muscles to align the eyes. This is because craniofacial surgery can change the alignment of the eyes and vision, affect the tear duct system, or improve protruding eyes.

Syndactyly

As Chapter 1 discusses, children with Apert syndrome are born with syndactyly, or webbing between the fingers and toes. Children with Pfeiffer syndrome, too, can have partial syndactyly.

When syndactyly prevents a child from using his hands normally, operations are needed to straighten and separate the fused fingers. Most often, these procedures are done in stages, with the little finger and thumb being separated first. Skin grafts, usually taken from the lower abdomen, are used to provide the missing skin in the web spaces between the fingers. In Apert syndrome, the fingers are sometimes so tightly fused that one finger has to be amputated; sometimes two fingers are left fused. When the operation is performed by a surgeon who is experienced in these procedures, however, children with Apert syndrome almost always end up with five-fingered hands. Some surgeons also believe it is important to straighten the curved thumbs in order to help the child oppose the thumb to the other fingers. Most surgeons do not try to separate fused toes because this will not improve their function. Sometimes operations on the foot are needed to improve walking and make it easier to fit shoes.

Plastic Surgery

As defined by the American Society of Plastic and Reconstructive Surgeons, "reconstructive surgery is performed on abnormal structures of the body, caused by birth defects, developmental abnormalities, trauma or injury, infection, tumors or disease. It is generally performed to improve function, but may also be done to approximate a normal appearance." This is in contrast to cosmetic surgery (nose jobs, chin tucks, etc.), which is "performed to reshape normal structures of the body to improve the patient's appearance and self-esteem." Therefore, operations for children with facial differences should never be called "cosmetic surgery."

There is probably no one "right" surgical treatment plan for children with a particular facial difference. The number, type, and timing of surgical procedures for your child will depend on a variety of factors, including your child's age, the severity of his condition, bone and tissue growth, his developmental stage, and what kind of treatment plan your craniofacial team, your child, and your family agree on. (These issues are discussed later in the chapter in the section called "To Operate Now or Later?") There are, however, certain surgical procedures that are commonly performed on children with a specific facial difference. The information that follows

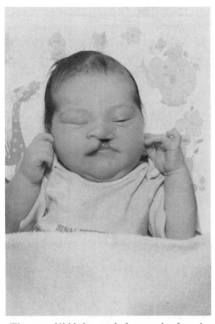

The same child before and after repair of a unilateral cleft lip and palate.

should provide you with a general idea of what could lie ahead for your child. Your child's craniofacial team can fill in the specific details about your child's treatment plan.

Cleft Lip/Palate. Surgical repair is the only treatment for cleft lip and cleft palate. Most often, the lip is closed first at one to three months of age, if the infant has gained enough weight and has no other major health problems. Cleft lip closure usually leaves a minor scar on the lip. Most surgeons correct the nose at the same time as the lip repair. A cleft palate is usually repaired later, between the ages of eight to twelve months, depending upon factors such as the size, shape, and extent of the split, as well as the surgeon's philosophy. The goals for both repairs are: a balanced and symmetrical lip and nose; normal speech; normal hearing; and functional and attractive teeth. More than one operation is often required to achieve these goals.

Before and after cleft lip closure, children are usually fed with a medicine dropper or cleft-lip feeder. Usually they wear arm restraints to keep them from touching the stitches or hitting the healing lip. Precautions must be taken to keep the stitches clean and to prevent the child from straining them in order to minimize scarring and to achieve the best cosmetic result.

When a cleft lip and/or palate is the only facial difference a child has, surgical repair is all that is needed. When a cleft occurs together with other anomalies (as part of a syndrome, for example), repair of the cleft is usually just a part of a larger treatment plan. For example, children who have other facial differences in addition to clefts can require medical procedures to improve breathing or feeding problems. The sections below discuss other facial abnormalities that require surgical correction.

Craniosynostosis. Surgical intervention can begin as early as two to three months of age. The first operation is designed to open the sutures in the skull that have prematurely closed and to move bone segments so as reshape the skull and forehead. Your child's cranial growth and brain development are then closely monitored to see whether further surgical correction is needed. This may be the case if the cranial bone(s) rejoin or if the condition is too severe to be corrected in a single operation. The child must also be monitored for possible development of increased pressure within the brain. As Chapter 1 explains, this increased pressure can lead to vision loss and brain damage. Later, between the ages of three and ten years, some children with craniosynostosis need operations to correct the shape and position of the forehead and/or the middle face. In addition, surgical procedures to adjust the occlusion of the teeth are sometimes needed after the teen-age growth spurt.

Hemifacial Microsomia. Children with hemifacial microsomia usually undergo a number of operations over the years. Corrective procedures may begin in infancy. If the corner of the mouth is enlarged (*macrostomia*), this cleft should be surgically closed in order to make the two sides of the mouth symmetric. Often the ear tags are removed or a notch in the eyelid is repaired while the infant is under the same general anesthetic. Also, if the infant has a misplaced ear lobule, some surgeons recommend moving this remnant during infancy.

In childhood, the goal of surgical treatment is to make the two sides of the face more symmetric and to improve the bite. This is usually accomplished by lengthening the lower jaw on the affected side to allow normal downward growth of the upper jaw. Often, usually in late adolescence, the upper jaw may have to be surgically corrected to allow it to mesh with the lower jaw.

The conventional procedure to build or lengthen the small side of the lower jaw involves inserting a bone graft from one of the child's ribs. A rib graft can also be used to build the arch bone of the cheek and the joint for movement of the jaw. Usually this procedure is done between six and eight years of age. Recently, a new technique known as "bone distraction" has been used to lengthen the jaw in children with hemifacial microsomia. This procedure is still in its early stages of development, but appears to have some advantages and some disadvantages compared to bone grafting for children with a small lower jaw bone. In addition, some surgeons are trying distraction for children as young as two years of age. See the section entitled "Bone Distraction," below. Orthodontic treatment before and after these operations may also be needed.

Another procedure frequently performed in childhood is construction of the outer ear(s) using rib cartilages (see the section on Microtia and Atresia below).

About 40 percent of children with hemifacial microsomia have some weakness (*paresis*) of the nerve that supplies movement of the facial muscles. The weakness usually occurs on the same side as the underdeveloped lower jaw. This causes a minor asymmetry of the lower lip, and the entire face can also be affected. Usually, children seem to have a small number of remaining nerve fibers rather than a complete absence (*paralysis*). For this reason, a form of physical therapy called "biofeedback" can be used, beginning when your child is about five to six years of age, to help him strengthen and activate his weakened facial muscles. Biofeedback is administered by a behavioral medicine team which includes a physician, psychologist, and physical therapist. Rarely, complicated surgical procedures involving nerve and muscle transfers are done to improve facial animation.

A child with a very small jaw and microtia can have less fatty tissue than normal in the cheek. More often than not, the face becomes more symmetric with growth as the "baby fat" on the opposite side of the face diminishes. Operations to lengthen the jaw also add to the facial contour. If the contour of cheeks continues to be a problem, however, fat tissue can be surgically added to the side of the face in adolescence.

Microtia and Atresia. Treatment of microtia and atresia has two goals. The first goal is to construct "normal"-looking ears that do not attract unwanted attention. This is done either by surgically building external ears from the child's own rib cartilage, or by attaching a prosthetic ear made from silicone rubber. Prosthetic ears can be made to adhere or clip on to the side of the face, or can be attached to implants placed in the bone, through a procedure called *osseointegration*. Usually, prosthetic ears are used only when surgical reconstruction is not possible or there is no experienced surgeon available to surgically construct ears. Some surgeons feel that prosthetic ears have little practical value for children and can actually make them feel *more* self-conscious. Each child is an individual, however, and your child's feelings should definitely be considered when deciding whether prosthetic ears would be helpful.

The second treatment goal is to improve hearing, if possible. This goal can sometimes be met by surgically opening the ear canal (*canalplasty*) and by middle ear construction. Neither procedure is usually performed if the child has normal hearing in the other ear.

Surgical construction of an external ear is best postponed until a child is at least six years of age and has enough rib cartilage to build an ear. And the operation on the middle ear generally does not begin until the outer ear constructive surgery is completed. Sometimes, especially if atresia is part of a syndrome, an operation to improve hearing is not advisable. In these cases, a hearing aid might be beneficial. For more information on treating hearing loss without surgery, see Chapter 5.

When choosing a surgeon to construct your child's ear, bear in mind that ear repair is highly specialized surgery. It is very important to ask the surgeons to show you photographic examples of ears that they have surgically created *themselves.*

Treacher Collins Syndrome. Most children with Treacher Collins syndrome require several surgical procedures over the growing years. These operations often continue into late adolescence or early adulthood, when facial skeletal growth is completed. The exact type of procedures your child will benefit from and when he receives them will depend on a variety of factors. Some of these factors include how severe his facial differences are, his attitude toward his differences, your philosophy about operations, and possible health problems, such as enlargement of tonsils and adenoids.

Beginning at birth, the growth of your child's facial bones should be evaluated at least once a year. The evaluation should determine how fast, how much, and in what direction the bones are growing. Based on this information, doctors will make recommendations about the extent and timing of surgical procedures for your child.

The surgical procedures for Treacher Collins syndrome can be divided into two major categories: 1) operations for the upper face (eyes, ears, and cheeks), and 2) operations for the lower face (the upper/lower jaws and chin). Often the first surgical procedure is to close clefts of the eyelids (colobomas) during infancy. Your child's small ears can be operated on as early as six years of age, provided he has enough rib cartilage to be used to build the external ear framework. Children with Treacher Collins syndrome often need a series of operations before bilateral outer ear construction is complete. Afterwards, they may be evaluated to determine whether surgery to open up the ear canal or construct the middle ear would likely improve hearing.

Elongation of the lower jaw can be done in childhood, usually between age six and eight. The final operations on the jaw, nose, and chin are done in early adolescence. Using *osteotomies* (bone cuts), with or without bone grafts, surgeons can make your child's jaw and chin larger or better proportioned, improve the airway, or correct an abnormal bite. Jaw distraction, a relatively new procedure to lengthen the jaw, has been used successfully in younger patients with Treacher Collins syndrome with severely receded lower jaws, feeding problems, and tracheostomies. Your child might also have an operation to build up his cheekbones. Currently, the preferred procedure is to transfer, or *graft*, skull (cranial) bone to the cheek area and along the floor of the eye socket. Some surgeons recommend performing the cranial grafts as early as four to five years of age to help the child appear more "normal" at a time when peer pressure is becoming increasingly important in his life. Other surgeons recommend delaying the operation until the teenage years. This is because children with Treacher Collins syndrome tend to resorb (dissolve) bone grafts, so cheek augmentation performed early often has to be repeated.

Bone Distraction

If your child has a receded lower jaw (mandible), it is possible that he might be considered for bone distraction, a surgical technique also known as the Ilizarov Technique or distraction osteogenesis. This method has been successfully used to lengthen the mandible on one or both sides of the face by as much as 35 millime-

ters. The technique is being studied and per-
formed in several cranio-
facial centers.

The operation is per-
formed in the hospital on
an in-patient basis. A surgical cut is made across
the child's mandible so
that there are two loose
ends of bone. Pins are inserted through the skin
and into the bone on
either side of the cut.
They are connected with
a bone-lengthening de-
vice called a distraction
rod on the outside of the
face. The next day, the
child is sent home; the
bone and wound are al-
lowed to heal for about
one week. Then, the dis-

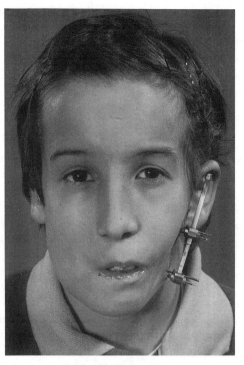

traction device is turned at the rate of one millimeter a day for up
to three or four weeks. This separates the two ends of bone it is attached to by the same distance. As the bone is gradually pulled
apart, the intervening gap is filled with new bone.

Supporters of this procedure point out several advantages over traditional approaches. The procedure is relatively simple, no blood trans-
fusions or bone grafts (harvesting bone from elsewhere in the body)
are required, and the newly formed bone is solid and seems to hold up
well.

There are also several disadvantages. First, long-term results
are not yet known. The technique has only been used in children
for a few years. Second, the pins leave scars on the outside of the
face. Third, although the procedure lengthens the jaw, it does not
move it out to the side or rotate the jaw forward. Fourth, not every
child with a receded mandible is a candidate for this procedure.
Currently, only certain children with underdevelopment of both
sides of the mandible (as occurs with Treacher Collins syndrome

and Nager syndrome) or moderate underdevelopment on only side (as in hemifacial microsomia) are selected for this procedure.

Some surgeons still believe that bone distraction is an unproven technique because long-term studies have not been done. If you wonder whether your child might be a candidate for bone distraction, you need to talk it over with the craniofacial team and find out their views on the procedure.

To Operate Now or Later?

Sometimes there is no question about the timing for your child's operations. For example, your child may require an immediate procedure if he has a functional problem—a problem that interferes with his breathing (tracheostomy) or nutritional intake (gastrostomy). Or an infant with craniosynostosis may require immediate surgical release of the fused sutures to relieve the pressure on the brain.

If, however, your child would benefit from an operation to enhance the appearance of his cheekbones or some other part of his face, there is often some leeway in choosing when to perform the procedure. Different craniofacial centers have different philosophies about timing of operations.

Surgeons also have different opinions about the need for operations. Some surgeons might recommend doing an operation as a means of solving a problem your child is experiencing, whether it is functional, reconstructive, or psychological. Other surgeons might recommend observing and evaluating your child's problem(s) over a period of time, and periodically consider surgical procedures. Some surgeons prefer to operate when a child is quite young, whereas others might prefer to operate when a child is older. For example, one surgeon might recommend waiting to begin outer ear reconstruction until the child is six years old and his rib cartilage is ready to be harvested. The surgeon might suggest fitting the child for prosthetic ears in the meantime. Another surgeon might be willing to begin the operations before age six if the child and his parents wanted the operation at an earlier age.

Whether your child's surgeon recommends operating early or later, he or she will usually allow time to evaluate your child's growth; wait for the craniofacial bones and tissues to become mature enough to be *harvested* (removed to be used in another part of his body, if needed); and project the best timing for the operations that will produce the most successful results. Over time, the surgeon will consider the following factors before making recommendations:

- your child's skeletal, dental, and soft tissue growth. The surgeon observes growth over time and makes comparisons to typical periods of bone and tissue growth in children without facial difference. He or she will then be able to estimate how much your child's bones and tissues may eventually grow.
- psychological issues such as developing self-esteem and body image.
- your child's developmental stage. This may affect your child's motivation to have operations. For example, physical appearance may be more important for an adolescent than a five-year-old.
- the most current advancements in the field and information about long-range effects of an operation.

Sometimes it seems as if there are no good or easy answers. So, a decision is often reached by weighing one factor against another and then making the best choice for you and your family. (You may hear this called the "risk/benefit ratio.") For example, would it be better to try bone distraction on a severely receded jaw even though long-term results are not known, or to build the jaw with well-studied conventional bone grafting? The decision to operate or not to operate is not made by one person alone, but by professionals and parents collaborating together.

It is important to remember that each of the congenital structural and functional problems described in this book poses complex treatment issues. In most instances, there are no simple or easy answers. That is one reason why the team approach is so valuable for patients with facial difference.

You and your child are an integral part of the decision-making process! You need to feel comfortable with the philosophical approach that your child's team takes, as well as with the professionals involved. You also need to feel free to change your mind about the approach you want the surgeon to take. If you and your child's surgeon strongly disagree about a philosophical approach, don't hesitate to change surgeons. Prior to scheduling an operation, you can always ask for a second opinion. Ask for a recommendation to another craniofacial center for this consultation.

Coping with Hospitalizations As a Family

Multiple operations and hospitalizations can become a part of life for children with facial differences. Still, whether it is your child's first hospital stay or his tenth, the stresses on your child and your family revolve around the same issues. Your child may be afraid of the unknown, of being hurt, or of being separated from loved ones. He may worry about missing school or about the lack of privacy and control he will have in the hospital. He may fear that the operation will change his appearance too much—so that he will not be recognized. You and your spouse may share your child's anxiety about being separated and may worry about his well-being. You may feel ambivalent about an operation scheduled for your child, at the same time you feel responsible for what happens to him. On top of everything, you may have financial concerns about the upcoming operations.

Although it is impossible to avoid all stresses related to hospitalization, there are some ways of handling both the pre-operative and post-operative periods that are more likely to reduce stress than others. The "pre-op" period is the day or so before the surgical procedure. During this time, your child will have a physical exam; x-ray studies; and blood and urine analysis, and other types of tests. Your child will accompany you to meetings with the surgeon, anesthesiologist, and other key medical staff members to discuss the upcoming procedure. On the day of the operation, your child will be "prepped" by changing into pajamas, taking a sedative, lying down on the stretcher, and saying good-bye to you. The "post-op" period occurs after the operation. This time involves meeting the surgeon and then your child after the operation; post-surgical care in the hospital and at home; and following through with care of the incisions.

Probably the most important thing you can do to prepare your child for an operation is to talk with him *before* the hospitalization, using words he can understand. Be *honest*. If something is going to hurt, don't say it won't. But if you can, follow up with a soothing statement such as, "It'll only hurt for a little while. I'll be there with you and you can squeeze my hand." If your child has had a previous bad experience, acknowledge that you know that, but reassure him that you hope it won't happen again.

In helping our son, Sam, deal with his feelings about previous unpleasant experiences in the hospital, I always try to find something funny to comment on and then we talk about it *a lot.* For example, once when a doctor was cleaning the post-surgical "crud" off Sam's ear, he talked non-stop to nobody in particular while Sam howled. (I don't think it really hurt him; I think he was responding to the doctor's insensitivity toward his needs.) Afterwards, we talked about it. We decided that sometimes your feelings get ignored, especially when the doctor (or nurse) is a "talker." Sam decided that if it happened again (and it has!), he wanted to squeeze my hand. So, if I anticipate anything will be scary or painful for him, I'm by his side ready for hand squeezing.

Another helpful strategy is to take a preoperative tour of the hospital facility. Most hospitals give children the chance to visit the pre-op area and the operating, recovery, and patient rooms; dress up in surgical clothes and masks; and press buttons on various machines to familiarize themselves with what will happen. Some hospitals have a "Child Life Department" staffed by specialists who can help psychologically prepare children—and siblings—for hospitalization. They often use play therapy to help children explore their feelings. This may involve the use of dolls or puppets to represent the child and other important people.

Staying with your child as much as possible, both pre-op and post-op, can help ease both of your minds. Most hospitals allow parents to spend the night ("room in") in the hospital. Some hospitals allow parents in the pre-op holding room, operating room, and/or recovery room, while others don't. Be sure to ask what the hospital policy is beforehand, so you and your child don't get a rude shock on the day of the operation.

During the post-op hospital stay, it is usually a good idea for the parent(s) to be actively involved in their child's care. You can keep an eye on what's happening to your child and question any procedures or medications that are of concern. You can also learn techniques, such as wrapping and rewrapping bandages or cleaning the sutures, that you will need to do at home. Most hospital nursing staffs welcome a parent's active involvement in their child's post-op care.

If your child has a lengthy post-op hospitalization, you will need to work out a schedule for being with your child. Some parents are able to stay at the hospital in shifts so that one parent is always available to their child. If only one parent is able to spend extended time at the hospital, nurses or volunteers are usually available to relieve you so you can eat, take a nap, take a shower, go outside for a walk, or just take a break. When your child is feeling well enough, you should encourage him to go to the play room, or visit with visitors or other hospitalized kids. When your child's interest in resuming typical kid activities reawakens, that's a good sign!

Perhaps the hardest post-op task for any parent is to help their child deal with his pain and his feelings about the results of the operation. The amount of pain your child experiences during the healing period will depend upon a variety of factors: his pain threshold; the type of procedure and its location; whether bone or skin was harvested; length of time in the operating room, under anesthesia (anesthesia can cause after-effects such as nausea, vomiting, and drowsiness); availability of pain medication and type used.

In many children's hospitals, the anesthesiology department has a "pain team" to consult and advise on the best ways to manage pain after an operation. For children older than five to six years, a technique known as PCA (patient-controlled analgesia) is often recommended. The child is able to push a button that allows a computer to inject a prescribed dose of pain medication into the intravenous line. The computer is set so that too frequent or excessive medication cannot be given. This set-up gives the child a sense of control over what's happening in the post-op period.

Whether or not your child has PCA, you will probably want to try to do interesting activities with him to take his mind off the pain. You might read to him, take a stroll in the hall, or go to the playroom. A new computer game, toy, book, or video may also take the edge off the pain.

In addition to being painful, your child's face may be swollen and discolored after the operation. So, it can take awhile before the results of the operation are clear. It is important to realize at the outset, though, that plastic surgery is not always as effective as you and your child might hope it will be. Unfortunately, some parents think their child will come out of the operating room looking like a fashion model. The reality is that an operation may not be able to bring a child's appearance within societal norms, especially when the child is severely affected. Usually, however, operations do improve the child's appearance enough so that he feels better about himself.

Try to hold off on judgments about the results of surgery and allow your child to decide for himself how satisfied he is with his new face. Your child may be happy and not want further refinements, even though you may see the situation differently. If your child is disappointed with the results, it is important not to make promises that you are not sure you can keep. For instance, don't say, "More surgery will make your cheeks look better," or "When we switch to another center, the new doctor will be able to fix everything."

Support your child if he is disappointed and suggest a wait-and-see approach. For some procedures, it takes awhile for the operative site to settle in after the swelling and discoloration are gone. You might also arrange meetings with the surgeon and possibly with the psychologist to discuss the operation. Remember, if your child is young, his level of satisfaction with the surgical procedure will likely reflect your attitude and comments. If he is older, however, he is more likely to formulate his own opinions.

Chapter 4 provides additional information about plastic surgery and its link to self-esteem.

Working with Medical Professionals

Chapter 1 introduced the concept of the craniofacial team and explained some of the reasons your child needs to be seen by such an interdisciplinary unit. On a day-to-day basis, however, your child will probably receive most of his routine care from your pediatrician and other local professionals who do not specialize in treating craniofacial conditions. Local professionals will provide therapy and primary care such as immunizations and well-baby checkups. The craniofacial team will see your child for periodic evaluations, usually annually. Local professionals can also provide follow-up care after an operation or other treatment provided by the craniofacial team.

In any case, local professionals and your child's team need to consult with, and coordinate services with, one another. They need to do so on an on-going basis, not just when a problem arises. They also need to have on-going communication with you, as you will be the one who manages your child's condition on a daily basis. In addition, you may need to help coordinate and maintain a loose relationship between local health care professionals and those at the craniofacial center. You might accomplish this by inviting local professionals to come to the craniofacial clinic with you or set up conference calls. The craniofacial reports should always be sent to the local professionals.

Sometimes local professionals and members of your child's craniofacial team might have different and conflicting recommendations. If this happens, educate yourself about the issue in question and encourage these professionals to communicate their differences with each other and with you. If the issue is still not resolved, it might be time to obtain a third opinion, preferably at another craniofacial center. You don't necessarily need to travel to the other center. Many centers will provide consultations over the telephone if you first send them facial photographs, reports, x-ray films, dental models, or your questions. Your child's pediatrician can be an effective "master of ceremonies"!

When choosing local professionals, try to find doctors, therapists, and dentists who have worked with children with your child's condition. If that is not possible, try to find pediatric professionals who have worked with children with facial differences. If that, too, is not possible, try to find professionals who are compassionate and express an interest in learning about your child's condition and are willing to be educated. Keep in mind that not all professionals are interested in working with children with facial differences. Trust your instincts to know whether the professional truly respects your child and enjoys working with him, and values you and your opinions.

If you feel that local professionals are not responding to your child's needs as you would like, contact the craniofacial center, explain your concerns, and ask for suggestions on ways to handle the predicament. Sometimes this might mean requesting a new referral and changing local professionals. Do not feel shy about requesting referrals. In doing so, you will provide your child with what you believe to be the best care. Professionals are aware that they must have comfortable working relationships with their patients and their families. They know that patients may choose to go elsewhere if they do not feel this is happening. You will not be hurting anyone's feelings by changing professionals. Other good sources of referrals might include other parents of children with facial difference and the local professionals who are liked and respected by these parents.

Making the Most of Visits to the Craniofacial Center

Once your child's condition stabilizes, he will usually be seen by the craniofacial team once a year, twice a year, or as crises arise. To feel good about these visits, most parents need to feel that they have control: they understand what is being discussed, their questions are answered, they are asked for their input, they are treated patiently and respectfully, and they are given the time and space to digest everything and make decisions.

Unfortunately, when you first start bringing your child to the craniofacial center, you can feel that your child's health is out of control and that you are at the mercy of the staff. You don't have to feel this way! Table 1 lists some questions you might want to ask to help you get a handle on the situation—*whenever* you are feeling overwhelmed or confused, not just at the first visit. Each time a new aspect of treatment is proposed or planned, you can use them as a framework upon which to gather information.

TABLE 1

QUESTIONS PARENT/PATIENTS MAY WANT TO ASK PROFESSIONALS

Diagnosis
1. How would you describe my child and his/her problems?
2. What is the major problem; what caused it?
3. What is your training and experience with this problem and its treatment?
4. Is my child unique or do others have the same condition?
5. Why have I not seen other children with this problem?
6. Where else are children with this problem treated?
7. What normal functions are threatened by the problem?
8. What kinds of tests should be done?
9. Is information from previous tests useful?
10. To whom can I go for a second opinion? a third opinion?

Treatment Planning
1. Have you treated this condition before?
2. How many patients have you treated for this problem?
3. I would like to talk to some of those families/patients. Will you introduce me to some of them?

4. What are the risks involved if nothing is done?
5. What are the risks involved in the treatment itself?
6. What is your treatment success rate? What do you consider successful treatment?
7. What other professionals will be involved with you in treatment of my child?
8. Will one treatment procedure correct the problem or will multiple treatments and long-term care be required?
9. If my child has surgery, will he/she need follow-up treatment? What kinds, where, and for how long?

Counseling

1. What aspects of my child's life can/will be affected by this condition? or the treatment?
2. Will this condition appear in other children I may have or in my grandchildren?
3. What can I tell my family and friends about the baby's problem, its cause, and hope for the child's future?
4. Is there a parent-patient group, or a support group?
5. How soon and how often do treatments start?
6. Where do we go for treatment? can we visit ahead of time to find our way around?
7. What instruction or training is given to the family/parent to meet the needs of at-home or carry-over care?
8. What is the cost of the treatment you propose?
9. Can you help me get funding for the treatments?
10. Why is there so little public information about this problem and its management?*

Other tips to help you feel in control and to make the experience a positive one include:

1. Write down questions in advance.
2. If you want to capture everything that is said, bring along a tape recorder.

---

* These questions were developed by Dr. Jane Scheuerle and first published in the *Parent-Patient Newsletter* of the Cleft Palate Foundation. Dr. Scheuerle is the Co-Director of the Tampa Bay Craniofacial Center and Professor of Communication Sciences and Disorders at the University of South Florida, Tampa.

3. Request that your name be added to the list of people who routinely receive all reports about your child (the "cc:" at the bottom of letters).
4. Especially if your child frequently sees the craniofacial team, keep a log, by date, of all phone calls and file all written materials in one place. It's easier to find the information you need if you keep everything together rather than scattered around your house.
5. If you have to travel a distance to the craniofacial center, consider combining the visit with a fun family experience, such as going to the zoo, eating out, staying in a hotel with a swimming pool, going to a museum, etc.
6. If your child sees a constant stream of professionals, you may want to instruct your child to call professionals by their title and first name ("Dr. Joe") to help de-mystify the person in the white coat. I've never yet met a professional who has complained!
7. Some craniofacial teams meet in an "arena." Parents and child sit at the front of the room and a number of professionals sit facing the family. This can feel somewhat like being "on stage." Parents can find the set-up overwhelming, and older children can be upset, feeling that there must really be something wrong with them if so many professionals need to come. From visit to visit, prepare your child for the team experience *before* you meet the team. If you don't like this "arena approach," you should tell the director of the team. A more individualized approach should be an option. Don't hesitate to request one.
8. If you have specific questions or specific reasons for the visit, gather as much information on the subject as you can before the visit—talk with other parents, contact support organizations, go to the library, etc. This will help you focus your thinking and ask good questions.
9. Ask the plastic surgeon's office for the names of other people with similar conditions or syndromes so you can compare notes about treatments, staff members, coping techniques, etc.
10. Be assertive!

One final note is in order about a common scenario that often confuses parents: namely, you go to the center and are offered a different treatment plan than was discussed on your previous visit. It isn't that the team is trying to confuse you or lie to you. After your last visit, the team may have become more knowledgeable about your child's condition and treatment. This knowledge may come either from experience or from new information gleaned from journals, conferences, or symposia. So, what seemed like the best treatment plan six months ago may not be the best one now. You should feel free, however, to speak up and mention any concerns you have about changes in treatment. "The last time we were here, I thought you said. . . . Now, it sounds like the opposite. Can you explain that to me?"

Taking Care of Yourself

In trying to keep up with your child's needs, it can sometimes seem like you are running a race that has no end. If too much is happening too quickly, or if you are feeling fatigued by the situation and cannot seem to catch up, it is time to slow down. Although you might use other parents as role models, comparing your abilities with theirs is not really helpful. In time, at your own pace, and on your own level, you will learn what you need to know about your child's condition so that you will feel you are making the best choices. You will learn: medical terminology; how to choose the best professionals for your child and your family; how to evaluate whether the professionals are providing the quality of care you are seeking; when to alert the professionals to changes in your child; how to collaborate with your child's professionals and work as an integral part of his treatment team; and, perhaps foremost, how to maintain a lifestyle that is comfortable for your family.

As you go about your day-to-day activities, you will become more and more accustomed to managing your child's health care issues. Some parents of children who wear hearing aids are so used to helping their child put on his hearing aid along with his clothes in the morning that they forget that not every child wears a hearing aid! While we all have our down days, if you find that daily reminders of your child's facial difference are quite painful, you might want to seek support from other parents or a mental health professional. Most parents experience these feelings from time to time, especially during a crisis or when something such as an operation or emotional confrontation has triggered these feelings.

Conclusion

Having a baby with a facial difference can be an overwhelming experience. During the nine pre-natal months, who expects that breathing problems, feeding difficulties, hearing loss, vision problems, orthodontia, and multiple operations will be primary concerns at birth and for many years to come? I know I did not.

In the beginning, my head whirled with information, names, and ideas amid an overwhelming feeling of disbelief and shock that this was even taking place. As the days of my young son's life turned into weeks and months and then years, however, I realized how much I knew and how easily I could explain this information to others.

I have learned how to make the best use of the professionals' expertise and our allotted time together during visits to the craniofacial center. My questions and comments are built on my experiences with my son from birth onward and my hopes and concerns about his future, as well as on all of the information—both factual and anecdotal—I have gathered over the years. This preparation allows me to have meaningful dialogs with his health care professionals, so that when we leave I feel satisfied with the responses.

Coping with my son's medical needs has not always been easy to do, and there have been many times when I have had to slow down and re-evaluate the pace and situation. But at least I feel as if I have some control of the situation, now that I have a better understanding of my son, his medical problems, and how to work with professionals to obtain the best possible care. With time, you too can gain this control.

Parent Statements

Very rarely my son will say that he wants to have the additional surgery, but then will voice his anxiety over the surgery itself. I let him know that his surgeon will let us know when it's time and we can make a final decision then. I reassure him that we love him and accept him for *who* he is always first.

✳

My child looks much better following his only surgery (frontal bone advancement).

✳

Justine was fed with a gavage tube for a year, and teaching her to eat involved much choking and a lot of time. She has had three ear tube surgeries and five major hand surgeries.

✖

Right now our biggest concern for Michael is that he receives all the medical help that will give him the best possible start in life.

✖

Our daughter says she feels more positive about herself since she has had the operations.

✖

I have a three-and-a-half-year-old son with a lymphatic malformation of the head and neck. He has had a trach since he was seven weeks old, and also had a G-tube until he was eleven months old.

✖

Our son takes a lot of Mom's time—trips to doctors two or three times a week as we repair and sort out one problem after another.

✖

My son likes the improvement surgery brings once the surgery is over. He doesn't like to plan or think about it ahead of time.

✖

My two-year-old daughter was born with a giant nevus on her face. She will undergo as many as ten surgeries in the next ten years to totally remove the nevus and all of the cells underlying the skin. All layers must be removed to prevent the formation of malignant melanoma.

✖

Gabriel's problem is that he has no suck or swallow and little facial movement in his mouth. He's on a suction machine and apnea monitor.

✖

Right now Josh is having problems with recurring upper respiratory infections and eye problems. He won't wear his glasses. I'm always afraid he's going to hit his head.

✖

One of the smartest things I've done is keep a book with copies of everything every doctor has written about our son. I also collect articles and pictures of his surgery so he can see them someday.

�֎

She takes a lot more time to feed, burp, and just sit to make sure she doesn't choke.

✖

I am having difficulty feeding Anna. She takes cereal in a bottle, and that's it. She chokes every time we try to give her fruits and veggies, even though they're very strained. I'm nervous, anxious, and pessimistic about feeding time.

✖

It was not until a month after Brittany's operation that I found myself crying non-stop. I went to a counselor and was told that I was depressed and the worst was over. The counselor explained that it was very common for people to suffer from post-traumatic stress syndrome after what we had gone through. The reason I had begun to cry after a month had passed was because I felt I had to be strong for my family and had therefore repressed all my feeling in the meantime. It took a few sessions before I finally worked through it.

✖

My number one concern for Brittany at the present time is her eyes. They float to one side. I was told by the ophthalmologist that there is nothing he can do for her until she is five years old.

✖

Feeding and breathing were difficult for Melissa, so at twelve days old, she underwent surgery to have her tongue attached to her lower lip. This is a rather severe measure, but it was necessary to keep her tongue from moving back and blocking the small airway. Melissa's tongue remained attached to her lip until her palate was closed at twenty-one months of age. Now, almost two years later, Melissa is thriving, and all-of-a-sudden tall for her age, compared with her first two years being just under the 10th percentile for weight, slightly better for height. Her jaw continues to grow and her somewhat flattened profile no longer looks unusual since her jaw is no longer receded.

✻

I fear she'll be somewhere and choke and they won't be able to establish an airway. I'll feel better when she has her jaw reconstructed.

✻

David's older sister doesn't understand why she always has to stay with grandparents when we take David for his appointments, and why when David comes back from trips to the doctors he has all kinds of stickers, gifts, and fun treats. She thinks we're having a fun time and that she is missing out on something. Our goal is to take her with us sometime so she can see what we actually have to go through each time we take David for his checkups.

✻

At nine and a half months our son had a bone graft surgery to his jaw that was done to help him with eating. When he was four, we discovered that the graft had come apart, but we felt it was a chance we had to take at the time for his benefit.

✻

Unfortunately, no health care professional ever made us feel hopeful. And we were involved in a major university-teaching medical center. They were more interested in treating my son's other medical problems: hydrocephalus and seizure disorder.

✻

A lot of doctors explained things using big medical terms that we didn't understand and we felt intimidated by them at times.

✻

Our pediatrician was very helpful. He kept telling us that he had a lot of hope for Michael and his future.

✻

The developmental pediatrician said, "You just never know—the more I learn, the more I learn I don't know much of anything." This was a lot more helpful to us than the neurologist who said, when our son was less than a year old, "Don't expect much."

✻

I think the health care professionals could have been more helpful in explaining what David would look like after his surgery—the swelling, bruising, and the mummy dressings, along with all the tubes connected to him. It is a shock to see your child look like that when you have no idea what to expect.

�֎

We've seen doctors who thought Henry was a wonderful kid. And then there was the craniofacial "expert" who said that all they could do was give him a better nose when he was grown, and that kids like him did better unrepaired because then people wouldn't expect so much of them . . . and that even repaired kids were still "funny looking."

✖

Doctors and nurses were generally very helpful and gave us direct information.

✖

We worry about having to make the right decisions for our child when there may be a difference of opinion from the medical field.

✖

On the day our daughter was born, we were told by a dermatologist that nothing could be done surgically until she was about ten years old. After several opinions from plastic surgeons, we began treatment at nine months of age. Physicians should not give opinions on something that they are not familiar with. This opinion caused us many months of unnecessary stress.

✖

The one thing I valued most in our pediatrician was his kindness. He is a very competent person, but was also loving and patient when we needed him most. Lisa was in the NICU for almost four months, so having someone we trusted and liked in charge made the rest of our life a little easier to bear.

✖

We appreciate hearing the good, bad, and in-between, but health professionals need to realize that so many senses and things are affected by a craniofacial syndrome that hearing all the information at once can be overwhelming.

✖

We have received a great deal of conflicting information regarding the benefits of outer ear reconstruction, making our decision that much more difficult.

※

Our pediatrician was very supportive. He researched and found a doctor who might be able to help Cory.

※

Since his diagnosis three years ago, Josh has been involved with seven different clinics, a craniofacial clinic, and a behaviorist. I have nothing but good things to say about the professionals who have worked with us.

※

The hospital staff was under-informed about clefts and was a little pushy about nursing when she *would not* and *could not* nurse.

※

When Katherine was only a few months old, I was worrying because every time I took her for a checkup, the doctor sent us for tests. It seemed she was always thinking there were other things wrong with Katherine (her hips, her intelligence), and I didn't feel she would scrutinize other babies the way she did Katherine. Although I could partially understand her reasons for doing so, I changed doctors before Katherine was two years old.

※

The cleft palate team we saw when she was five days old was outstanding with all the information and support. They were always there to reassure us that things would be OK.

※

Chapter 4

Self-Esteem, Family Life, and Strangers

When a baby is born, we think of her in terms of the dreamy future and of her as yet untapped potential: What will she become, how will she fit into the family, and what greatness will she achieve?

When a child with facial difference is born into the family, those dreams and questions may no longer seem relevant. If the child has a severely disfigured face or also has other obvious physical differences, such as a hearing impairment or webbed fingers, the issues become even more complex. Instead of wondering about the future, parents worry about much more immediate, concrete concerns: Does this mean the end of normal, happy family life? What do I tell the neighbors or the grocery clerk when they ask questions? How do I respond to the gossip, whispering, and thoughtless comments? And most importantly, what do I tell my child about his facial differences and why she was born this way?

There are certainly no easy answers to these questions. Attempting to give easy answers would only minimize the complexity of the issues involved in helping your child and your family develop healthy, well-balanced lives. You, your child, and the community you live in are constantly growing and changing. This means that what works one day may not work the next. ***As a parent, you simply can't expect to always know the right answers, especially at the right time!***

Although no one can tell you exactly how to deal with every problem related to family life and your child's self-esteem, there are some ways of dealing with these issues that generally work better than others. This chapter covers some of the problem issues families often confront, as well as methods that can be used to successfully integrate your child and your family into the community.

Self-Esteem

As a child grows, she develops a self-concept. That is, she comes to see herself as being a certain kind of person, with certain characteristics, who has a particular role in her family, her community, and the world. She also develops feelings about how she feels about herself—her self-esteem. If she has a good opinion of her self, then she is said to have high self-esteem; if she has an unfavorable opinion of her self, then she has low self-esteem.

To function in the world in a psychologically healthy way, people must like themselves, be realistically aware of their strengths as well as their limitations, and recognize their accomplishments and potential. This is all part of having a healthy (high) self-esteem. A child with good self-esteem isn't afraid to set high goals and take risks to meet them, as she doesn't feel threatened by failure. She can naturally feel positive about herself for being a talented musician. But she can also feel positive about participating in activities such as soccer where she is less talented, because she enjoys them and does not equate her level of competence with self-worth. In addition, her high self-esteem enables her to feel like an equal when interacting with other people.

Without good self-esteem, children may feel worthless, inadequate, helpless, and inferior. These feelings can contribute to mental health problems and problems socializing.

Self-Esteem in Children with Facial Differences

". . . disfigurement does not define the person. . . ."
(Thomas Pruzinsky, 12/18/92)

In any child, self-concept reflects not only how she feels about herself, but also how her family and community respond to her. If Mom, Dad, teachers, and friends all treat her as if she is a competent and lovable person, she will naturally come to see herself as competent and lovable. But if people continually act as if there is something "wrong" with her, she may come to believe that this is true, and her self-esteem will suffer.

Unfortunately, society often reacts negatively to children with facial differences. This is because our society places a great deal of importance on attractive facial appearance. As sociologist Frances Cooke Macgregor has observed, "In all human relationships, it is the face that is the symbol of or synonymous with the person . . . focus of attention whenever people meet. . . ." (1990, p. 250).

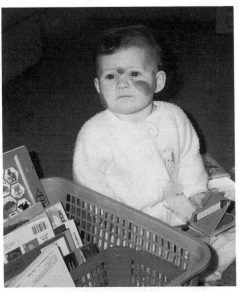

In our society, the first thing that happens when people meet is that they look at each other, see the other person's face, and often make an on-the-spot decision about whether to continue the interaction. There are certain expectations about how the interaction will take place, including length of time of eye contact, and the distance between the people involved in the meeting. While we generally do not consciously think about these factors, they do take place and have been documented by researchers.

When someone with facial difference participates in a conversation, the social interaction is often changed and different. Macgregor has identified three ways in which social interactions may be affected:

- **Privacy is violated.** In public, most people enjoy a sense of privacy and anonymity. For people with facial differences, the privacy boundaries seem to be non-existent. The customary social graces of politeness seem not to matter, as though the person with facial differences was an object instead of a person. People with facial differences are routinely asked personal questions about their faces.
- **Social interactions are "strained."** Others may be uneasy about being around a person with facial difference or avoid her altogether. They may show their discomfort by keeping a greater than average distance from the person, making less eye contact, or prematurely ending the contact. When social interactions are consistently strained, the

person with facial differences can anticipate what might happen. However, when these reactions occur inconsistently, social interactions might produce alternating feelings of anxiety and relief.

- **The message that people with facial differences get from these "strained" social interactions is that their appearance is causing these events to take place.** In anticipation of these events, they can become inhibited and socially withdrawn, and focus on their appearance in a negative way. They may feel ashamed of their appearance, and feelings of impotence, anger, and humiliation may develop.

On top of these uncomfortable social interactions, a child with facial difference may constantly feel as if she is being stigmatized. As Chapter 1 discusses, people with facial differences have historically been thought of as deviant, have been targets of prejudice, and have been victimized by discrimination.

Not surprisingly, your child with facial difference may develop her self-esteem based on her appearance. That is, she may base it on how she perceives the appearance of her face or on how she thinks others perceive the appearance of her face, rather than on seeing herself as "more than a face." The importance of facial appearance may be reinforced each time she goes to see a health care professional for a problem related to her facial difference. When reconstructive surgeries take place, she may get the message that her face needs to be "fixed" to make her more socially acceptable. Or she may believe that your parental love depends upon her having reconstructive surgeries that make her appearance more pleasing to you.

According to Ms. Macgregor, research shows that adults with facial differences always feel vulnerable about their appearance. As they grow older, their impotence and anger may become evident. Perhaps surgeons and medical technology have not been able to offer them the face they had hoped for. Or perhaps parents, family, and mental health professionals have not understood them as well as they wanted them to. As a result, they may feel as though they live a life of compromises, making do with less: both in work and in personal choices, such as a marriage partner. They may feel as if they spend too much time and energy just trying to live in society—time and energy that could be channeled in other directions.

Being aware of the many ways your child's self-esteem *could* be harmed, you can take steps aimed at preventing harm. As a parent, you can help her learn not to think of herself as just a face. You can teach her that her life does not need to be a life of compromises. You can encourage and inspire her to have goals and ideals and to reach for them. The next sections provide a starting point.

Building Your Child's Self-Esteem

"We overestimate their weaknesses, and underestimate their strengths. . . ." (Macgregor, 1979, p. 108)

At a very early age, your child will sense your attitude toward her appearance and the special issues involved in raising her. Her attitude toward her facial differences and herself will therefore reflect your abilities to cope with her appearance, any other physical differences she has, and the reconstructive surgical concerns. The first step, then, in building your child's self-esteem is to ensure that you don't inadvertently convey any negative attitudes about her condition. Chapter 2 should help guide you to the beginnings of acceptance of your child's facial differences. If you are finding the road to acceptance especially rocky, you may also want to follow the suggestions in the section "When to Seek Professional Help," below.

Just as there are many methods you can use to cope with feelings about your child's condition, there are also many methods she can use. If your child is old enough, she may have figured out some of these methods herself. Many children with facial differences do. Since some of these methods are more effective than others, however, it is important for you to determine which methods, if any, your child is using. If necessary, you can then guide her to a more effective coping manner. The following sections review the most common methods used by children with facial differences.

EFFECTIVE AND INEFFECTIVE COPING STRATEGIES

Denial

Denial is the most common coping method used by children with facial differences. They may rate their appearance as less severe and more pleasing than a professional would. Although this is a form of denial, it is not an unhealthy denial. It allows a child to acknowledge that she does have a difference, but keep it in perspective so that all of her energy is not concentrated on that one aspect of her life.

A good way to learn whether your child uses healthy or unhealthy forms of denial is to observe how she perceives her facial differences. Does she focus on her appearance as a reason for why she can't do things (unhealthy), or focus only on what she wants to do or participate in (healthy)?

Generally, children start noticing differences at around age five or six. They may notice that some part of their face looks different from that of others. Their awareness may be that the *other* person's face looks different! Or, they may realize that their face looks different.

As your child gets older and starts understanding more, she will undoubtedly wonder why she needs to see so many medical professionals. There must truly be something wrong! At this point, it would not be helpful for you to deny your child's condition. Instead, either you, medical professionals, or both need to put the condition in perspective for your child. In this type of discussion, you need to emphasize your child's strengths and abilities, while realistically explaining her physical differences. Your child should be told the truth, but in a way that will still allow her to feel good about herself. If your child thinks of herself as a "freak," she may not want to participate socially; if she takes it in stride, social interactions should be easier.

You can expect the subject of your child's differences to come up many times over the course of her childhood. You and your child may need to re-visit certain topics many times. As your child matures and experiences life, she will probably want and request increasingly sophisticated information and support from you. Over the months and years, you will need to use trial and error to find out what approach to answering questions and dealing with concerns works best for your child. Your long-range goals should be to help your child understand that facial difference does not define the person.

Anger

Some children openly express their anger at having been born with a facial difference, and others hold their anger inside in the form of depression or withdrawal. If your child is angry because of her facial differences, her anger needs to be dealt with, regardless of how she expresses it.

If your child is often angry, don't immediately assume it is because of her facial difference. Start by asking "why": "I notice you seem to be mad a lot. I saw you hit your brother yesterday for no reason. Why do you think you're mad so much? It doesn't seem like you can have much fun if you're mad all the time."

If your child indicates that her anger is related to her facial difference, or you deduce that it is, it is time to talk with your child. The psychologist or another professional on the craniofacial team who provides emotional support can prepare you for this discussion, or sit in on the discussion. You can start by asking your child how things are for her at school, with sports, etc. When the focus of the discussion comes to her facial differences and her anger, it is important to try to understand why she feels as she does. Unless you as a parent have a facial difference, you are not going to truly *know* what your child is feeling. However, you can validate her feelings and clear up any misunderstandings she may have.

The issue of fairness will often enter into the discussion. Your child may say something like "It's not fair that I was born with little ears and I have to have all these operations." You can validate the unfairness of the situation while trying to help your child see things in a more positive light: "Yes, you're right—it's not fair. I'm sorry that you were born with little ears. But you were born with strong legs, you can read, and you can make beautiful art projects. And, Dr. Jones is going to make ears that are just right for you." Of course, this may not be the end of the discussion, as you child may come back with something like, "But now I have to go to the hospital and have operations. It'll hurt." Your discussion could continue on like this, jumping from one topic to another that is making your child anxious (depending on her age and willingness to communicate). This discussion may need to occur many times over before your child is ready to focus on something besides the unfairness of it all. At the end, however, you will have a better insight into the roots of your child's anger.

If your child won't talk with you, is a threat to herself or others, or is out of control, professional counseling may be the safest option. If so, you should be willing to take part in it as well. You may have something to do with your child's anger—perhaps by being overprotective and holding her back because of your fears. If so, you need to know, so you can work on being more helpful to your child.

It may take a while, but at some point your child will feel more accepting of herself as a person with a facial difference. Ideally, she will learn to think of herself as a child like any other child who just so happens to have a facial differences. Remember, however, that it is not easy for *any* child to develop good self-esteem, and there are plenty of challenges along the way.

Discovering Talents and Abilities

Another way of coping is for a child to excel in an activity, such as a sport, drama, music, computer games, or academics. She is then recognized—at least in part—for her abilities, rather than her facial appearance.

If your child doesn't find activities she enjoys on her own, provide her with opportunities to discover and develop her skills. Obtain a listing of activities and classes that are available in your community. Then let your child choose several that she might enjoy and which fit comfortably into your schedule. If your child is preschool age, you might want to take the lead in choosing, and in the beginning select "mom and me" classes so that you and your child can attend together. If your child is older, it is important not to convey any fears you have about activities she chooses. For example, a child with a hearing aid *can* play contact sports, and so can a child who has finished outer ear reconstruction. A child with a repaired cleft lip *can* sing in a choir or act in a play. A child with hand anomalies *can* take dancing lessons.

Like any child, your child may decide that she really doesn't like an activity after she tries it. Some children may find that they don't enjoy an activity if they don't seem to have any natural abilities in it, or if it is too difficult for them. In any case, you should never force your child to try or continue an activity that she doesn't like.

Group activities will provide your child with opportunities for socialization. These opportunities may include children (and parents) that you and your child don't already know. As your child grows older, she may want to avoid these situations if she has had negative experiences with strangers. It is important for you to encourage your child to pursue activities that she enjoys and to provide the support and encouragement she needs to feel comfortable with the social side of these activities. This might mean that you will need to educate the adult in charge, your child's peers, and possibly their parents. In addition, you need to educate your child and supply her with a range of answers for questions and comments, so that she feels comfortable when you're not there. (See "Responding to Adults' Reactions" and "Responding to Children's Reactions" later in the chapter.)

Although it might seem easiest to give your child private lessons for her interests, this would deny her "her place" in community activities such as girl scouts, team sports, theater productions, etc. Sometimes, however, private classes or activities in your neighborhood may seem like the best option or a good place to start. You and your child will know when it is time to move to activities outside of the safety of your home or neighborhood. Sometimes both parent and child need to gain confidence before venturing into typical childhood activities.

As your child participates in activities with her peers and becomes known to them, she will be better accepted in her community and in the places where she spends much of her time, such as at school. Identifying activities that make her feel proud, talented, and capable will therefore keep her in the mainstream of life where she belongs, and will help her focus on her abilities rather than on her differences.

Educating Peers

The more your child's peers understand about her facial difference, her experiences (such as surgery), and any assistive technology such as hearing aids, the more likely they are to accept her. In some families, a parent accompanies the child to school at the beginning of every school year to help educate classmates. With the help of the child and teacher, the parent talks to the class about the child's differences, similarities, and assistive devices.

If you choose to educate peers, your child should ideally be present and participate in some way. Take care that she feels comfortable with what is being said and proud of who she is. Use simple language and focus on information about your child that will increase her acceptance by peers.

Looking at Differences Objectively

Another method of coping is for your child to be able to step outside herself—that is, to create a comfortable emotional distance between herself and her condition. This allows your child to talk about her differences in an "objective," rather than overly emotional way.

If your child is unable to be objective, she might refuse to talk about her facial difference, or talk about it only with an outpouring of tears, shame, or other emotions.

Being able to objectify is something children generally learn over time for themselves. It helps, though, if parents can model this behavior. If parents are usually low-key about their child's facial difference, the child will probably also learn to be low-key.

Social Skills

Your child should not have to feel like a victim of facial difference, or be ashamed to show her face. She will need to learn how to rebound from being teased or stared at and still maintain her sense of integrity and humor in social situations. Supporting her and helping her learn to recognize her strengths, as described under "Discovering Talents and Abilities" will help. But your child must also have a repertoire of social responses available to her so that she feels secure and proud of who she is. She should know how and whether to respond to hostile, curious, and ignorant questions from both children and adults. The section on "Community Life" later in the chapter offers guidance on this important subject.

Making Choices/Taking Risks

Another important key to building self-esteem is allowing your child to make choices and take risks and then learn from her mistakes. Any child who is overprotected and not allowed to do things for herself gets the message that she isn't capable of doing these things.

Although you may think you are doing your child a favor by shielding her from staring or the like, this can actually do more harm than good in the long run. You will not always be there to protect your child. Therefore, she needs to learn how to handle situations on her own. She has a right to do and be anything anybody else does—to walk to the grocery store by herself, to play in a soccer league, to shovel neighbors' walks to earn some pocket money, to act in a school play. But she needs the confidence to follow through with the "doing" and "being." It is largely up to you to give her this confidence by letting her see your confidence in her.

Reconstructive Plastic Surgery

Some parents and their children look upon reconstructive plastic surgery as the miracle that will "take away" the child's facial differences. Reconstructive plastic surgery is certainly a scientific miracle. It will not, however, take away your child's condition. It is only one part, albeit an important part, to the enhancement of self-esteem in your child.

Although operations may make a difference in your child's appearance and how she feels about herself, it "does not guarantee a 'new' or normal face, but rather a transformation from less presentable to more presentable" (1990, p. 256). As a parent, you need to understand and anticipate, and help your child understand and anticipate, that there are realistic limits to plastic surgery. These limits include how much of a physical difference the surgeries can make in your child's appearance, and at what point surgery may no longer be possible or make a difference.

There are several ways to help your child understand what to expect from surgery. As you and your child discuss an operation with the surgeon and craniofacial team, ask them to give you an idea of what to expect. Looking at before and after photos of other children will help you and your child know what to expect, but bear in mind that surgeons always show photos of their most successful surgeries! In addition each child is unique—is affected to a different degree and may respond differently to surgeries. Again, be prepared to discuss any and all issues related to upcoming operations as many times as your child needs. As a parent, it is your job to understand what the surgeon is really saying if he says some-

thing like "This surgery will make her appearance more acceptable, but she won't look like a fashion model." Then you must explain your understanding of things to your child. The team
psychologist can help you understand and share this knowledge
with your child.

Some parents go "surgeon hopping" to find the one who will offer the best prognosis. This is dangerous. Although a second or
third opinion is always a good idea, you should be cautious about
any surgeon who offers miracles—especially instantly.

At the point when surgery may no longer be possible or make a
difference, you need to help your child understand that things may
change in the future. New technology and surgical techniques are
always being developed, so it is possible that what is impossible today may be possible in ten years. You should never let your child
feel as if she is at the end of the road—there should always be a
glimmer of hope.

Sometimes parents are reluctant for their child to have surgeries that would only enhance her appearance, not improve how she
functions. They may feel that they are losing the child they love by
changing her appearance. Or they may not feel that their child has
any significant facial differences, and is accepted 100 percent by
everyone. Or they may not want their child to miss more school for
surgeries. Or they may feel as if the surgeon views their child as an
experiment on which to try out what he's been reading in journals
or learning at conferences.

While it is always important to include your child when planning surgeries, in this situation it is especially important. Your interest in surgeries for your child needs to mesh with your child's
desires. Listen to what she says about what pleases her or bothers
her about her appearance. Then try to reconcile it with what the reconstructive plastic surgeon and psychologist say about your child's
need for surgeries and the importance of enhancing her physical appearance.

Seeking Professional Help

One father of a child with microtic ears would always request a
table by the wall when he took his toddler son to a restaurant. He
would then position the child so that his less complete ear faced
the wall. Each time this occurred, the mother, who was the primary
caretaker of their son, would comment that she was so used to be-

ing in public with him that she never thought to hide his ears. As time went on, the father began "hiding" his son's ears more frequently and in more situations. Finally, the father realized that he needed outside help accepting his son's facial differences.

There may come a time when you, too, realize that you or your child is feeling overwhelmed by the impact of your child's condition. Your child in particular may have a harder time coping as she grows older—perhaps as early as seven or eight years of age, or by adolescence. Feeling overwhelmed is nothing to be ashamed of, and does not point to any inadequacy in you, your child, or your family. To recognize that something is not working the way you would like it to, and to want to change it, is a strength.

If anyone in your family is having trouble coping with issues related to your child's facial differences, you might want to start by taking an inventory of everything that you have already tried: your own common sense, contacting a support organization and networking with others, contacting your child's craniofacial team, talking with professionals who are involved in your child's treatment, education, etc.

If none of these strategies has helped appreciably, you, your child, or your family may need on-going support from a mental health professional. This is especially advisable if one or more family members is depressed.

Commonly recognized symptoms of depression include:

1) poor appetite or overeating;
2) sleeping too little (insomnia) or too much (hypersomnia);
3) low energy or fatigue;
4) low self-esteem;
5) poor concentration or difficulty making decisions;
6) feelings of hopelessness.

Locating an Appropriate Mental Health Professional. Your child's craniofacial center should be able to refer you to a mental health professional in your area. You can also ask for referrals from other families, support organizations, your child's early intervention program or school, therapists, a local mental health agency, or a local professional organization for psychologists, social workers, or counselors. Each discipline might offer a slightly different perspective on coping, and all could be equally helpful.

It may be difficult to find a mental health professional in your community who has a background in facial difference issues. You can always teach the therapist what you think is important for her to know about facial differences. You can also suggest that your therapist contact the National Foundation for Facial Reconstruction or the American Cleft Palate - Craniofacial Association at the numbers listed in the Resource Guide. Acting as a clearinghouse, these organizations will then refer your therapist to a psychologist with the expertise to offer consultation about issues related to facial differences.

Make sure that the professional you choose has a thorough understanding of your family's situation, is willing to learn about facial differences, shows respect and empathy, makes you feel comfortable, and gives the impression that she will find answers for you, your child, and your family.

Family Life

When your child is born with facial difference, her medical needs may be immediate and the focus of your attention until her physical condition becomes stable. Each time an operation or other medical intervention occurs, concerns about your child's well-being may again overshadow all others. With this seesawing of concerns, you may feel as if you are alternately over-involved or too detached from parenting. Each time your child with facial difference reaches a new developmental stage or an important transition, such as starting school, these feelings may be reawakened. It might feel like an impossible balancing act to give each of your children the care and attention they need and deserve, and for you and your spouse to give one another the support and attention important to your marriage.

Each family adapts differently. Some families come together and grow stronger when a child with facial differences is born. In other families, the bonds holding them together weaken and the family falls apart. In still other families, time is the determining factor. Although it is impossible to predict which families will be successful at coping together, one thing is clear. Families that do well are *dynamic*—that is, they change as a reflection of what is happening with their family. This is because the challenges a family faces change over the coming years: children grow and pass through developmental stages; treatment plans begin or draw to an end. Any of these changes can change the balance in the way a family functions.

All families encounter problems, and most families find solutions for their problems. The solutions that work for your family's problems will not necessarily be solutions that would work for another's. What matters is that you honestly work to identify and verbalize the problem. The more honestly you can approach the problem, the easier it will be to work on the solution.

The next sections discuss some common problems often encountered by families of children with facial differences, as well as some solutions that frequently help. Use these ideas as a jumping off point to figure out the best solutions for your family.

Balancing Everyone's Needs

Even if family life is in an uproar due to an operation or the daily routine of school and therapy appointments, all children want their share of love, support, and attention. They also want and need to be treated equally and fairly.

Encourage Individuality. Just as your child with facial difference does, her siblings need your help and encouragement to discover and develop their own abilities and talents. This is especially crucial to helping them develop their own identity outside of the family. Siblings are often described as being caught between two worlds: the world at home, where they might have to compete with the child with facial difference for attention; and the world outside, where they want to fit in. If they do not receive enough support and attention, siblings may identify their role as being only the brother or sister of a child with facial difference, rather than as a unique individual who is special for the qualities and talents she possesses.

Limit Siblings' Child Care Responsibilities. Another potential pitfall is to allow your child's special needs to interfere with your other children's ordinary needs. Sometimes older brothers and sisters are expected to help care for the child with facial difference. They may feel as if the burden of their sibling's care rests on their shoulders. Consequently, they may feel as if they are forced to grow up too quickly in order to do what is expected of them.

Siblings can be asked to help in the care of the child with facial difference in ways appropriate to their age and ability level—for example, "Can you hand me the tape and scissors so I can rewrap Jamie's ear?" They shouldn't, however, be expected to shoulder the responsibility for the child's care, initiate the care, or make decisions about the care. If you are expecting an older sibling to be "too" responsible for the care of your child with facial difference, the family dynamics are unbalanced and need to be re-balanced.

Don't Neglect Siblings' Needs. Your other children may also get the message that their needs are not important when you are occupied with your child's surgeries. You might feel that you must center your energy on the needs of your child with facial difference and restrict the activities of your other children, or forget to tune in to their needs. At these times, it is critical to make sure that you try to help your other children feel special, so they do not feel rejected.

For some families, devising a plan that satisfies everyone's needs is helpful. The theme to this plan is to make sure that each child knows that you love and care about her and value being part of her world—even if it seems like you are concentrating your time and effort on only one child at a time.

Try to schedule a special time or activity once a week with each of your children to make sure they all receive the one-on-one attention they need. You might want to designate on your family calendar one day each week for each child. This special event doesn't need to take a lot of time or money. It could be as simple as taking a walk around the block together or having lunch with Dad at a fast food restaurant. Often "special" activities can be fit into even the busiest routine if you include your children in activities that would need to take place anyway. For example, you could share a snack, or bake cookies together, or take the car to the drive-through car wash. If carving out some special time is impossible to do some weeks, still ask your child what she would like to do when you have time so that you stay tuned in to her needs.

Having a Different Kind of Family

It is human nature to compare ourselves and our lot with others. Differences are noted and usually labeled as being good, bad, or neutral. Young children might notice, for example, that they have fewer toys than some of their friends (bad), that their mother packs a better school lunch than other kids' mothers (good), or that their house is white and the neighbor's house is green (neutral). If one of their siblings looks or talks or behaves differently from other children they know, they will inevitably notice that their family is different from others. How they come to regard this difference, however, is not inevitable. Depending on their experiences, they may decide that the difference is good, bad, neutral, or variable.

As a parent, you will naturally want to keep your children from regarding your family's difference as something bad. Sometimes this may be impossible—particularly if your children are at any age when they want to be exactly like everyone else. A teenager, for instance, may be humiliated to be seen in public with a parent who has a "bad" haircut or "unstylish" clothes, let alone to be seen with a sister with facial differences.

Typical Sources of Problems. Being aware of typical problems can help you deal with your children's emotions about coming from a family with differences. You should know, for example, that siblings may feel stigmatized by your child with facial difference as they try to fit into and participate in school, social, and community activities. They may feel ambivalent toward your child by wanting to protect her, yet also wanting to be in the mainstream of relationships, such as peer groups at school, which might shun that child.

Siblings might also react to differences by feeling that they must be "super kids." They may try to overachieve in academics, sports, or other activities to compensate for any difficulties their brother or sister with facial difference might have. Problems can arise if they feel ignored and unappreciated by you for their achievements. This is less likely to happen if you recognize, praise, and acknowledge all your children's achievements—large and small.

Help Your Children Feel Good about Your Family. It's probably unrealistic to expect *any* child to feel 100 percent positive about her family and her role in it, all the time. But your attitudes and behaviors can go a long way toward ensuring that your children feel basically OK about who they are. Some helpful points to keep in mind when deciding what attitudes to convey include:

1) Your child with facial differences is a child first; her medical condition does not define who she is.

2) Remember what it was like for children with differences when you were a child and let those experiences guide your thinking and behavior.

3) Try to maintain as typical a family life as you can, especially during crises.

4) Siblings aren't miniature adults and shouldn't be expected to behave like adults.

5) Help siblings comprehend the reasons for differences in your family. Information about your child's condition and her health care concerns should be openly explained to siblings who are old enough to understand.

Seek Outside Support. It may also help your other children to participate in a support group for siblings of children with facial differences. Here your children can share their feelings with other children who face the same family stresses and perhaps learn some new coping techniques. They may feel free to express emotions that they would never feel comfortable sharing with you. For example, they might wish for a brother or sister without a facial difference—one who would not make so many problems for them. Some support groups for parents include a siblings component. In many communities, special "Sibshops" are offered periodically. See the Resource Guide for more information.

Consider Professional Counseling. Sometimes siblings can benefit from professional counseling, as described under "Seeking Professional Help," above. This is especially true if siblings are depressed or feel as if they must continually attack their family life as abnormal.

Be aware that what might appear to be a sibling-centered problem could really be a total family problem. This may be the case if siblings feel that there is too little communication about their brother or sister with facial difference or if they feel a need to protect you and your child. Siblings may also perceive and be bothered by problems between you and your spouse, such as financial difficulties, uneven division of responsibilities, or disagreements about parenting.

Usually the "identified patient" (such as the sibling with disruptive behavior) ends up in counseling first. At that time, the real problem may be diagnosed as a family problem. That is, the counselor may determine that the child's behavior is a reflection of what is happening in the family.

Surgical Crises

When your family is anticipating or experiencing a surgical procedure or other intervention, your family is thrown into a state of crisis. Whether it is the first surgery or the sixteenth, family life is disrupted and this cannot be ignored. Acknowledging what is taking place and how it will change everyone's routine is the first step in stabilizing your family. Provide your family with a "plan" for what is to take place, when, and how. This does not mean you have to explain events in technical language. You should, however, describe what you and your child will experience during surgery and in recovery, where everyone will be during these times, and how everyone might feel.

It is important to keep your other children updated on the progress of surgery, especially if siblings can't visit the hospital themselves. You should devise a system for maintaining communication —by calling on the telephone, sending postcards, taking a video of your family that your other children can watch during the separation. It is also important to brief siblings about what to say and what not to say the first time they see their brother or sister after surgery, so they don't undermine her self-esteem. Let them know that their sibling's face may be swollen and discolored, and the results of surgery may not be apparent for some time.

Your coping plan should also cover how your family will recover from this crisis. For example, some families plan a celebration after the child has completely recovered from surgery. Every family celebrates in different ways. When operations are frequent or family finances are tight, the dreamed-about trip to Disneyland might need to be put on hold, and family members may need to come up with some creative ideas. What is important is to choose something fun that everyone can participate in.

Marital Stresses

As children with facial differences emerge from the cuteness of infancy and toddlerhood, their physical differences may become more apparent. The number and extent of surgeries or other interventions that will be necessary may also be more apparent, and parents will have a better understanding of the drain on their finances, time, and energy that lies ahead. All of these factors can be stressful not only for your family as a whole, but also for your marriage.

Every marriage is different. How (and whether) stress creates problems within a marriage differs widely from couple to couple. This section touches on problems that *may* crop up in your marriage because you have a child with facial difference.

Differences of Opinion about Treatment. Ideally, you and your spouse will agree on your child's treatment plan—extent and timing of surgeries; how closely you should work with professionals in planning treatment; obtaining second or third opinions; how far you are willing to travel for the best care; whether to sign up for Medicaid or SSI if your insurance won't pay for some or all expenses; how much surgery is enough. If you each feel strongly about following a different approach, especially regarding timing, you need to meet together on some common ground so that you are working together as a team and not struggling against each other. It will certainly not help your marriage to struggle with each other, nor will it help your child to get caught in the middle.

If you and your spouse disagree on your child's treatment, you might be able to start resolving your disagreement by getting as much information as you can find about the suggested treatment. Sources include: your child's health care professional, a support organization for your child's condition (they usually have a lending library or access to current information from professional publications), or your public library. A reference librarian may be able to refer you to helpful publications, such as *The Encyclopedia of Associations* or *Index Medicus,* or tell you how to get access to databases such as Medline, the National Library of Medicine's database. Other parents of children who have successfully or unsuccessfully had the treatment or decided against it can be a gold mine of information.

If you have a hard time understanding information you uncover (especially "medicalese"), share it with a health care professional you trust. This person can help you sort through the pros and cons of treatment. Then, approach your spouse with your information and the conclusions you've drawn and start a dialog. If you still cannot agree on a treatment plan, go back to the health care professional and ask her to become involved. She may be able to set up an appointment with you and your spouse, call or meet with your spouse alone, or take your concerns back to the craniofacial team or to specific team members, such as the psychologist.

A key question to bear in mind when you and your spouse disagree is "What is in the best interest of our child?" Ultimately—unless there is a life-threatening situation—treatment decisions are the parents'. In theory, joint decision making and parent/professional collaboration should be part of the process, but it's not as simple as deciding about a new haircut. Treatment planning is a complex process, laden with a variety of factors which can move it along smoothly, with stops and jolts along the way, or stop it completely. Parental disagreements can hinder the process, create opportunities for growth in the marriage, or cause further decay in a relationship that is already crumbling. And in the end, someone still needs to make decisions about the treatment plan.

Different Coping Styles and Schedules. Chapter 2 discussed the emotions parents often feel shortly after the birth of their child with facial difference. Unfortunately, these are not just feelings that can be wrestled with early on, and then never be faced again. Emotions such as shock, denial, sadness, anger, and anxiety may resurface many times during your child's life. An upcoming surgery or a major life event often re-triggers these feelings. As an individual, you may find that past ways of coping with these emotions may continue to work for you, or you may need to learn new methods of coping from others.

Sometimes the emotions you are coping with and the way you are coping with them can lead to marital stress. This may be the case if one spouse feels as if the other has been "stuck" in one emotion too long; feels isolated from the other because he doesn't seem to understand what she's feeling; thinks the other is coping inappropriately, such as by working extra hours to avoid their child; thinks the child is getting attention from the other spouse that he or she should be getting; denies that their child has any problems; refuses to go out in public with their child; refuses to come to the hospital for operations or visits with the craniofacial team; doesn't participate in decision making.

Here is an example of a couple whose emotions were continually "out of sync":

Shortly after birth, the obstetrician spoke to the mother about her son's facial differences using the term "birth defect." The mother relayed this information to her husband using the same term. He immediately responded by saying that their son did not have a birth defect, and instructed her to never use the term again.

For the next several years, this father was attentive to his son's medical needs. It was not until his son faced his first surgical procedure at age six, however, that he was able to fully accept his child's facial difference. In the meantime, the mother had begun educating herself about her son's condition, and became as knowledgeable, if not more so, than many of the health care professionals. Her husband recognized this and began to look to her for information. As the husband learned about his son's condition, he began to realize that his son's future wasn't as bleak as he had thought it was at birth. Over the course of several years, Dad was able to see his son as a fun, able little boy rather than a label ("birth defect").

In the example above, Mom was very patient with Dad, and sought out other sources of support. She developed strong friendships with other mothers of children with facial differences to get the support she needed. Sometimes a spouse needs to wait for the other spouse to catch up. When this happens, it's important for that spouse not to feel isolated, but to seek out the support he or she needs. It really doesn't matter where the support comes from, as long as you feel satisfied—that you're being heard, responded to, and respected.

Unfortunately, conflicts in coping styles can recur many times during the course of your child's life. You are changing individually, and as a couple, and both you and your spouse should be prepared to accommodate for these changes. Often, these changes become apparent when your child starts school. You and your spouse may feel as if you're reliving your child's birth. You must suddenly deal with a system of professionals who usually do *not* have experience working with children with facial differences. You may be confronted with a barrage of questions, concerns, and anxieties; forms to fill out; unaccepting attitudes; and countless meetings.

Just as when your child was born, one parent may try to take control, while the other stays in the background. Now, however, this arrangement may not work. Both parents may really want to be involved in sending their child off to kindergarten so they can share all the knowledge and skills they have learned since their child's birth. They need to recognize that they have each changed individually, as a couple, and as a family, and the old way of doing things needs to be changed. Maybe each parent might feel comfortable taking on a different task that can be worked on individually (educating classmates, attending Individualized Education Program meetings), or you may feel more comfortable working as a team with your spouse. What is important is that you are both satisfied with what is taking place and how it is taking place.

Uneven Division of Responsibilities. Sometimes parents feel as if they have to bear more than their share of the child-care responsibilities. Perhaps the mother always winds up taking her child to the doctor, hospital, therapist, audiologist; makes all the decisions about treatment; and meets with school personnel about educational accommodations, while the father feels his only job is to make money to pay for treatments. The father, for his part, may be working twelve-hour days to make the money he thinks his family needs, thereby adding to his wife's child care burden. Before too long, either parent may begin to resent the other for "forcing" a particular role—whether it be sole breadwinner or primary parent—upon them. They may yearn to have parenting responsibilities divided up more fairly, but feel as if they are "stuck" where they are.

Although it would be nice to avoid these problems, what usually happens is that the situation worsens until at least one parent can no longer stand it. At this point, you and your spouse need to be able to communicate and come up with some mutually agreeable solutions. Your spouse truly may not know that you are unhappy because he works twelve hours a day. If you can identify what is and is not working for you, you may be able to figure out how to make the situation more workable. It may help if you jointly and individually define your personal and family values: Do we really need a new car this year? Am I afraid of making decisions that will affect my child's' education? Why *can't* my wife go back to work?

No Time to Be a Couple. Some couples find that family life seems to move along at such a fast clip that there is little time for the two of them to do things alone as a couple. If this happens to you, you may need to deliberately create the time to be a couple. Recognize that it is okay to hire a babysitter and go out for a quiet, romantic dinner with your spouse, enjoy a movie without the company of children, or socialize with other adults. It is also necessary and healthy to talk together about issues other than your child's facial difference and special needs.

Some parents are reluctant to leave their child with facial difference with a babysitter because they think that they alone can give her the special care and attention she needs. Others are afraid that a babysitter might act negatively toward their child. Parents may also think they can't afford the expense of a babysitter on top of everything else.

If your child does not have complex medical needs (such as a tracheostomy or feeding tube), neighborhood teens or family members truly *could* do a good job caring for her. Other sources of reliable babysitters include parents of other children with facial differences or special education students at a local university. You should, of course, educate the babysitter about any special issues that concern you before leaving him or her alone with your child.

If your child does have complex medical needs, you should seek someone (possibly a nurse) specially trained in caring for those needs. Respite care may be another option, depending on where you live and the eligibility criteria. Respite care is usually provided through a county or state agency or organization to give parents a break from the daily routines of caring for their child with special needs. Some respite programs send respite workers directly to your home; others provide the funding and require the parents to find the respite worker. Some programs train the workers in caring for children with special needs; others expect parents to educate the workers. For children with complex medical needs, the worker may need to have a certain level of education (such as R.N.) or certain certifications. In theory, respite is a great idea. In practice, however, it may be difficult for parents to obtain. This is because respite funds are usually limited and are used quickly. Often there is a waiting list. And your child may not qualify if eligibility criteria include developmental disability or intellectual impairment. It's worth checking out, though. To find out about respite care in your community, contact your child's early intervention program or therapists, or a parent support group for any disability (such as the ARC or UCP—United Cerebral Palsy).

Community Life

Every family lives in some type of community. Some families live in big cities, some in small towns, and some in isolated rural areas. Each community is different. Some communities are close knit and have formal and informal networking systems which support residents and help them feel like

part of the community; others merely provide services such as electricity, water, and waste disposal, and little human contact. Whatever kind of community you live in, you and your family are a part of it.

After your child with facial difference is born, you may be tempted not to go out into your community. You may fear reactions to your child's appearance or be unsure of your ability to handle the responses to your child's difference. It may feel safer to isolate yourself and your child from the world and the people in it. If you do this, however, you are performing a great disservice to yourself, your child, and family. Your child needs to learn how to accept her difference and adapt so that she can successfully function in the world. She must learn how to socialize with other children and other adults. You and your family need to learn these things also. You cannot learn them by isolating yourself inside your house.

Do not wait to enter your community until your child is required by law to start school. This would be a very harsh awakening for her and for you, and one which neither of you would be prepared for. (You also may want to think twice if you are considering home schooling solely to protect your child from others' reactions.)

In the beginning, your participation in your community may be limited by the fragility of your child's health or by your emotions about your child's appearance. Go as slowly as you need to. You will encounter a variety of people and a variety of responses. In time, you will learn what to say, how to say it, and what to do. The more you participate in your community and have the opportunity to practice your responses, the more comfortable these interactions will become.

You will be asked questions or overhear comments about yourself, your child's facial differences, or her other differences, such as a hearing impairment or webbed fingers. Some people may be polite and inquisitive, while others may be rude. Some people may just stare, while others will act as if "it" is contagious. You may be asked if you adopted your child, took drugs when you were pregnant, or were exposed to a harmful substance.

Sometimes you will feel sad and tired by these responses, other times you will be angry or outraged, and still other times you will be taken by surprise because you have forgotten that your child's face appears different. Some parents feel extra-sensitive to their child's difference when they take her to places or situations where they are unknown. While they may not consciously attend to every response, at some level they are noticing how people are reacting and deciding whether it would be helpful for them to say or do something.

Parents frequently ask the following questions: "How should I react to adults' reactions? How should I react to children's reactions? What responses should I teach my child and her siblings?" While there are no right or wrong answers to these questions, there are strategies to use that are more helpful and less helpful. Focusing on the strategies that are more helpful is a way of viewing the situation from a positive rather than a negative perspective.

Your child will be influenced not only by the perspective you choose, but also by your responses and your ability not to overprotect her. She will hear what you say and how you say it. If you find that responding to questions makes you so anxious that you would just like to melt away, keep in mind that you are modeling behavior for your child, as well as communicating your acceptance of her facial differences.

Don't be too hard on yourself if you don't always know the best way to respond. You will have plenty of opportunities to try again. You can try a different response the next time someone asks a similar question (and the next time, and the next time. . . .).

Responding to Adults' Reactions

When dealing with adult strangers, listen to what they are asking or commenting on before you respond. Their inquisitiveness may be triggered by their fear or anxiety about seeing a child with a condition they have never encountered before, or possibly by empathy because they know someone with a similar condition. Less often, people are just rude or insensitive. It is also quite possible that they have been caught off-guard by the unexpected appearance of your child's face. As Jeanne McDermott, the mother of a child with Apert syndrome has observed, "Staring, in its pure and simple essence, is the time required by the brain to make sense of the unexpected."

You may want to tailor your response to a stranger's questions or stares based on what you think his motivation is for asking about your child. If you think a stranger's questions are basically well-intentioned, you can provide a variety of factual information in response. It is usually helpful to mention that your child was born that way. No one is to blame; it just happened. Ask if they know anyone who was born with some type of difference.

Frequently people will want to know if your child's condition is painful or "fixable" by surgery. What they are tapping into is their anxiety about your child's appearance, and hoping it will decrease if the condition is "fixable" and your child is pain-free. By offering a clear answer and not getting into the specifics you are answering their questions and lessening their anxiety. In answering these questions, there is terminology that is psychologically more and less helpful. For example, it is OK for your child to hear you say that she will look more "typical," but not "normal." Likewise, you can talk about how operations might "enhance" your child's appearance, rather than "improve" it. Spend some time thinking about the amount of information you are willing to give out and your limits on privacy. Many people consider genetic information confidential, so you might not want to mention that.

Other aspects that people frequently want to know about include your child's intellectual functioning, her development, and her ability to speak, hear, and see. It is important to reassure them—and your child—that your child is able to do the things (tailor this to your child) that any other child her age is able to do.

If your child requires medical technology assistance, such as a hearing aid, tracheostomy, feeding tube, apnea monitor, or respirator, be prepared to mention what the equipment is used for and how it helps your child. Some assistance may be time-limited, such as a tracheostomy, so you might want to mention that your child needs the extra help right now to breathe, but will be able to breathe on her own sometime soon.

Questions about medical technology may become especially relevant if your child wants to join some type of community club or athletic activity. In these situations, your child might be seen as a financial liability. The question presented to you might be: "What will happen to her face or her hearing aid if she gets knocked over or is hurt during the activity? Who is responsible?" The underlying question might really be: "A child with a facial difference has never before wanted to participate in this activity. We do not know how to include your child. Can you help us?"

Decide in advance how you will answer this question. You might want to start by describing your child's enthusiasm for participating, and how your child will be an asset to the activity. It will probably help to directly address any physical limitations or difficulties your child has, and your expectations for financial liability (who *will* pay for repairs to the hearing aid if it gets damaged?). Be prepared to cooperate and volunteer to help with the activity. Help your child to blend in rather than stick out. The guide below [or on next page, etc.], "Including Children with Facial Differences" may be helpful to offer when you introduce your child and yourself.

If people persist in asking questions you would rather not answer, you have a perfect right to end the conversation. Try asking them, "Why are you asking these questions?" Or say, "Thank you for your interest, but we need to go." You can also let people know at the start that you don't mind educating them a little, but you aren't prepared to play twenty questions. At the beginning of the conversation, you might say, "My daughter and I are happy to answer a few of your questions, but this is our time to be together and enjoy ourselves."

Responding to Children's Reactions

Children will often notice a child's facial differences, and will usually ask questions. Their questions may be very direct. Their intent in asking questions is not to be rude, but to have their curiosity satisfied. In responding to their questions, it is important to keep in mind that they may not be able to articulate well what it is they want to know. Often children may use language that might be interpreted as hurtful without intending to *be* hurtful. For exam-

INCLUDING CHILDREN WITH FACIAL DIFFERENCES

This guide is being provided to you because there is a child in your classroom, school, or activity who has a facial difference. Through your professional or personal experiences you may never before have met a person, child or adult with a facial difference. The purpose of this guide is to provide you with:

- basic information
- to clarify misconceptions
- to facilitate peer acceptance
- to provide resources for additional information

What is Facial Difference?

The term "facial difference" is used to describe a person whose face appears different due to under or over development of the bones and tissue of the face and head, because of a condition present at birth, disease, or injury. Some conditions occur only in the face and others include additional areas of the body, such as the hands and feet. Facial difference does not hurt and is not contagious.

Some people with a facial difference are mildly affected, and some more severely affected. Children who are more severely affected may need special equipment to help them breathe or eat. Some children will need to use a hearing aid, or utilize the services of a speech and language therapist to help them speak clearly.

Typical Children

Without regard to how mildly or severely a child is affected, most children who have a facial difference have normal intelligence and development, attend regular schools, and participate in activities in their communities as children without facial differences. That is, children with facial difference are usually typical children who have a facial difference. They have strengths and weaknesses, artistic talents, athletic abilities, sense of humor, etc.

Health Care Concerns

Most children with facial difference will be followed by a team of health care professionals who specialize in treating a person's head and face. During the "growing up" years, one or more surgeries to rebuild the structures of the head or face are usually scheduled. The child's facial appearance may change as the result of these surgeries.

In Your Community

All children want to be included and supported in their efforts, without exception. Children with facial differences can actively participate—and should be encouraged to do so—in school and community activities. This includes physical education, music, art, foreign language classes, sports, scouting, etc.

Resources

The following resources can provide you with additional information on facial differences:

AboutFace
Alliance of Genetic Support Groups
Let's Face It
National Foundations for Facial Reconstruction

ple, they might say "What's *wrong* with her? Why does her lip look
so funny?"

Rather than getting angry at a child's lack of subtlety, it is better to reassure both the questioner and your child that she really is
all right. You might say something like, "When Julie was born, her
lip wasn't fully formed. Pretty soon she will have an operation to
close her lip. Julie is a really fun girl. She likes to . . . . (age appropriate activities). Do you like to do these things?"

Often, children's questions will be aimed at understanding
how your child is like them and different from them. Simple and
direct answers are usually the most helpful: "Joey was born this
way." "We all look different. Christy looks the way she looks, you
look the way you look, and I look the way I look. And we are all
shopping at the same store!"

Teasing or Avoidance of Your Child. Neighborhood children can provide your child with facial difference a safe social situation, since they will probably know her from play. However, you
will need to be alert for times when your child is teased or avoided.
When children tease or avoid other children, they usually do so because, at some level, they have been taught to do this by adults or
older siblings.

Before you jump into a situation to "save" your child, observe
what is happening, if possible, and try to understand the interactions that are taking place. Wait to see how your child responds.
She may have an explanation, deny any differences, pretend nothing was said, or come to you then or later. Of course, if your child is
in physical danger—someone is trying to touch or pull on a surgical
site or equipment such as a tracheostomy—you need to intervene
immediately.

If you feel that your child needs support in responding to comments, you can intervene or ask her about it later. "I heard you and
Joey talking today. I heard him ask you about the scar on your lip.
Would you like to talk about it? How did you feel when he asked
you about it? Do other kids ask questions about the scar on your
lip? What do you think they want to know? What do you want
them to know?" To help your child learn a range responses, you
may want to role play with her. Take turns pretending you are
either your child or someone else, and create a scenario in which
your child is questioned about her facial difference. Give your child
the opportunity to experiment with different strategies and saying
different things.

Sometimes children with facial difference are continually assigned the role of "monster" or "bad guy" in play because of their appearance. They then may assume that this is what they are supposed to do when they play because of how they look. Teach your child and her playmates that this is not true, and that everyone takes their turn in different roles. Stress that it will be fun for each child to have the opportunity to act out different roles. Your goal is to model for your child and her playmates that facial differences does not define who your child is.

Teaching Your Child to Respond to Strangers

Your child will need to know how to respond to stares, comments, questions, and unwanted attention from adults and children. That is, she will need to have a variety of responses so that she can hold her head high and feel proud of who she is.

It is usually helpful to teach your child to say that she was born with her differences, and to focus on what she can do and the things that she has in common with other children. She may also want to let others know that her physical differences are not anyone's fault and that she is not responsible for it having happened.

In guiding your child to develop her responses, be sure to ask her what she thinks is important to tell others and what is important to keep private. For example, she may not want to talk to others about the genetic basis (if any) of her condition and how that might affect her own decision to have children. She may be more motivated to prove to others that she does not have mental retardation simply because she has a facial difference and possibly a hearing impairment. She may want to show that she can speak, hear, think, be funny, participate in typical activities, etc. Be careful to respect your child's wishes, and keep that information in mind as you develop your own responses.

To help your child learn to respond to questions, you can try directing questions her way when you think she is capable of handling them. For example, if a stranger asks you a straightforward question such as how old she is, you could turn to your child and say, "How old are you, Michelle?"

Your child should also learn that she doesn't have to stay in a situation that is hurtful. Children who tease and are intentionally hurtful do so because of their own insecurities, so to respond with name calling and rudeness might just add fuel to the fire. Your child can ignore the teaser or walk away. If she's with other kids, they will ideally defend her and help her feel part of an accepted group. ("She's my friend; leave her alone.") If your child is alone, she can respond by saying, "This is the way I was born. If you would like to know about me, I'll answer your questions." For more information on handling teasing, see Chapter 6.

Teaching Siblings to Respond to Strangers

Your child's brothers and sisters also need to know how to react to stares and comments. Keep in mind that your other children will follow your lead and model your behavior. If you try to hide your child with facial difference, they will do the same. Focusing too much on your child with facial difference, however, is not the solution. You should encourage your other children to be proud of having a brother or sister in the same way any child is proud of having a sibling. Talk to your children about what makes your family special. This conversation does not need to focus on your child with facial difference, but she should certainly be mentioned as one reason your family is special.

Although siblings should be educated about how to respond to strangers and peers, remember that they are children. They won't always have answers for strangers, or know the "right" thing to say or do. In addition, they may have to deal with added stresses from peers to tease or stay away from certain kids. It's unrealistic for you to expect that your other children won't be influenced by these factors. When they make mistakes (we all do!), they need explanations as to why their response wasn't helpful and how it could be more helpful the next time.

Conclusion

During our first few visits to the craniofacial center, professionals repeatedly told my husband and me that our son's intellectual potential and development should be normal, and he could be expected to go to college and have a profession, if he so desired. Although this information was certainly reassuring, I soon began to think about questions that the professionals were not addressing and that had no answers: Would he be happy? Would he have girlfriends, go on dates, and go to the prom? Would he find a spouse to love him? Would he have a family?

Seven years later I still do not have the answers to these questions, but no other parent does, either. What I do know, however, is that there is no reason these events cannot be part of his life if he so chooses. I have met a variety of adults with facial differences who are happy, have loving spouses and families, and went to the prom! While the road was not always easy for them, they were successful in getting what they wanted in their lives. Provided you nurture your child's self-esteem and make sure she receives plenty of support from family and friends, there is no reason to believe that she, too, cannot succeed.

REFERENCES

Macgregor, Frances Cooke (1979). *After Plastic Surgery: Adaptation and Adjustment.* Westport, CT: Praeger Special Studies, Greenwood Press Publishing Group.

Macgregor, Frances Cooke (1990). "Facial Disfigurement: Problems and Management of Social Interaction and Implication for Mental Health." *Aesthetic Plastic Surgery.* 14:249–57.

Parent Statements

Justine is quite smart and understands when someone is making fun of her. Up to now her social life has been very good. She has a lot of neighborhood friends. One reason, I think, is that we have told the kids and adults exactly what she has and what it means. I know I won't be able to follow her around with an explanation her whole life, so I hope I have armed her with the ability to do this for herself. I hope she doesn't lose the self-confidence she has, due to a few cruel remarks from people who shouldn't matter as much as her family and friends.

✼

We've told our son he may look different to others and they may stare because they don't understand or know what happened to him. We just tell him to explain it to them if they ask. We've talked about how everyone is different, in that some kids have glasses, hearing aids, wheelchairs, etc.

✼

What's nice right now is that Lisa doesn't realize why she's being stared at or even that she is being stared at. It will bother me more when she knows.

✼

I have always tried to teach Emma that appearance is far less impor-tant than what a person is like, but it's hard to believe that when you're a child beginning to be influenced by peers. She has just reached the stage where other people have become more impor-tant, and being different is decidedly not what anyone wants.

✼

Our son is only three, but he tends to avoid mirrors.

✼

My daughter's psychologist is guiding her to accept her differences and deal with her anger about being different. We probably didn't take the best approach in letting Emma know what she had: we al-ways told her stories about being in the hospital and what she had specifically (surgery on her foot, her eye, etc.), but gave her no overall name for her condition until she was nine. One doctor had told us he didn't like children being labelled, and identifying them-selves as a person with a syndrome. We should have told her a lot earlier, probably around the age of six. She now tells me that she thought her condition had no name and that worried her. She also worried that she had something she knew about, like cerebral palsy.

✼

We really want her to feel good about herself as a person, to de-velop her talents, and to grow up believing she can do anything she wants to do in life. We want her to feel so secure about herself that she will be able to tolerate the inevitable negative comments and teasing and deflect them with ease. And, with time, we hope she will come to realize that the true beauty of a person is radiated from the inside out, and that she will appreciate differences in others just as she accepts herself.

✖

I think now that she's twelve and a half and going to dances at school, she's beginning to notice that all her friends are asked to dance and she's not. I'm hoping that her academic skills will help her deal with missing out on the social aspect of her early teenage years.

✖

We tell him he's very cute and special and we love him lots and lots. He doesn't realize he's different yet. My biggest suggestion: build their self-esteem and they'll handle the rest!

✖

It used to be very difficult for me to be in public with my son. Strangers stared; children pointed at him. It hurt me severely. I try to tell myself and my children that people react this way because they see something "different." Children can be cruel, but they don't know any better.

✖

Once at a conference, a ten-year-old boy was walking toward us. When he say Katherine, he made a face and said "ugh" quite loudly. My husband told us to keep going (fortunately Katherine didn't notice the boy) and he caught up with the boy and asked why he did that. The boy, probably feeling slightly scared and intimidated, said he didn't know. Brian then asked him how he thought Katherine would feel when he made a face and said "ugh." I don't think the boy said much, but Brian felt he got the point.

✖

Out in the community, there are always bridges of understanding to build, and I am the one who has to facilitate that by being open and forthright and vulnerable. It is a constant drain of my emotional storehouse! Sometimes you want to hide.

✖

People seem to notice her glasses and comment on them more than anything else. The stares come most when we are in the pool and her glasses are off and her hair is wet. Then it is usually children who follow us around and just stare. I am not consistent about how I react—sometimes I don't care; sometimes it bothers me.

❋

People tend to ignore Craig, but he often approaches them and starts a conversation. Most often then they see that he's "normal," and warm up.

❋

Strangers usually notice his bubbly personality and his club feet first. Most say, "I never even noticed his face" or "He's really cute, anyhow." Occasionally a five-year-old will say something like, "Why is your face so flat?" He answers, "Because I have Freeman-Sheldon syndrome, but the doctors are fixing it."

❋

When my daughter was an infant, I was on the receiving end of several thoughtless comments by strangers we encountered in stores or while going for walks. Now her hair has started to grow over her small ear so it is less noticeable. Most new people we meet either don't notice the facial difference or are too "polite" to mention it. Frankly, we wish people *would* ask us, in a concerned or curious way, about her condition. We welcome the opportunity to discuss it. What bothers us most is when people stare at her and give us sympathetic looks.

❋

Our daughter is definitely sad and angry that she has facial and speech differences. My biggest concern now is that her self-esteem doesn't further erode, but improve. She still has her spunk and optimism, but I see that life is harder for her now than it was just a year or two ago.

❋

People assume that facial difference must have accompanying mental retardation. I tell them to ask him his age or other questions so they can see that he has "normal" intelligence.

❋

If strangers are genuinely concerned, I think it's only polite to be courteous towards them and answer their questions. I try to teach my children not to be annoyed at people's stares.

※

The enormous amount of stress and guilt split our marriage apart. We each mourned our loss alone. We were separated less than one year after the birth of our son. We had been married sixteen years.

※

Because of Michael, my husband and I have gone through a lot of ups and downs. We have had more arguments because of the added stress, but we have grown through our experiences and are now closer than ever. We are dedicated to each other and our children.

※

My husband's strength and determination that our daughter would survive as a normal child has carried me through the heartache of people staring at her.

※

My husband and I have a common problem we have to deal with together. While certainly not our choice, the facial difference has made us stronger.

※

We both have a faith that we have been able to draw spiritual support from. This has helped us every step of the way and has given us the necessary hope to endure.

※

I'll never forget the nurse who said, "It'll either make or break your marriage." Well, we've been separated for a year now and have started divorce proceedings. We had a bad marriage already, though.

※

I put a lot of time and energy into my daughter. I work to make her speech better or to reassure her she'll be accepted. My other kids and husband sometimes have to wait for what they need.

※

My kids argue just like other teenagers do.

✖

Jenny is accepted by her two brothers as a normal, regular sister. They fight and squabble like any other brothers and sisters, but are very protective of her in public.

✖

One day when my mother had had our son overnight and mended his teddy bear's ear for him, he asked her on the drive home, "Grandma, why don't you fix Lisa's eye for her?"

✖

My other children have certainly resented some of Jamie's demands on my time. His older brother is very protective of him outside the house, but at home they have a normal sibling rivalry.

✖

Our older daughter just gets a little disgusted when milk comes through Anna's nose.

✖

We have not had other children. However, I'm very close to my sisters, and Emma has numerous cousins, all of whom treat her like anyone else, and clearly love her. People used to ask Emma if she had any brothers or sisters, and she would answer, "No, but I have four cousins." I loved her optimism.

✖

Our other daughter was three and a half when Brittany had her operation. She seemed to be too young to understand or be afraid of what her sister was going through. I wasn't quite sure how she was going to react, so I was very worried about her too.

✖

His youngest sister has become his "Junior Mother." His oldest sister thinks he's a spoiled brat but is also amused by him sometimes. She loves to bug him!

✖

We live in a small community and there are not any real friends for my daughter. People say "hi" and are nice, but she is not included and is very lonely. She just wants to have friends like her sister does. She doesn't talk about her differences, but knows it's probably why she doesn't have friends. It hurts so bad knowing how lonely she is.

✖

Our daughter has been in play groups since birth and has always been accepted as part of the group.

✖

I'm afraid that all her friends will have boyfriends and not include her in their lives or social activities and Jenny will suddenly feel alienated. She sets great store on having lots of friends and wants to be part of them.

✖

When she is on good terms with her close friend, she's on top of the world. When she has no one to play with, she is depressed. The depression makes me very, very sad, but this is a difficult stage and I know I can't solve it all for her. I'm hoping continued psychotherapy will help her through the next difficult years.

✖

One little friend who is six and has known Lisa since she was born asked her mother, "Why does everyone talk about Lisa?" (like, what's the big deal?).

✖

My five-year-old son's friends *love* playing with Cory. I have *never* had a problem. Cory also has lots of two-year-old friends, but they are too young to notice.

✖

Chapter 5

❖

Speech, Language, and Hearing Needs

My son received his bone conduction hearing aid when he was five months old. This was the first time he was able to consistently hear speech and environmental sounds within normal ranges. As his communication skills began to emerge and develop over the next months, his receptive language skills always tested beyond his age. His expressive language skills, however, continually tested as five months delayed.

I anxiously asked the mother of an older child with Treacher Collins syndrome about her daughter's speech development. She recounted a story that paralleled ours, but with a happy ending: her daughter's speech not only caught up, but at three years old the child was so delighted with talking that she talked, and talked, and talked! (This is a typical developmental sign for that age.) The mother even felt she needed a break from her daughter's talking. To me, this seemed like an enviable position and one I could only dream about. So, my husband and I breathed a big sigh of relief when my son's speech skills finally caught up to his chronological age when he was two. As he grew older, he too talked, and talked, and talked! To this day, I cannot think of any sweeter music to my ears than my son's talking.

Introduction

Children with the conditions of facial difference described in this book often have difficulties with hearing, speech, and language. This is because fluid in the ear or structural problems of the ear canal or middle ear are common. These problems can result in hearing loss, which can in turn result in delays in speech or language development. (If a child cannot hear speech sounds accurately and consistently, he will have trouble learning to produce and understand speech sounds and difficulty learning proper language usage.) The atypical structures of the head and face associated with these conditions may also make speech more difficult.

Because of the potential for both oral and aural (hearing) problems, it is essential that your child's hearing, speech, and language be regularly assessed and monitored. This chapter will provide you with enough basic information so that you can understand your child's hearing, speech, and language needs and thoughtfully choose the professionals who will evaluate and work with your child. Your awareness of what your child does or does not hear and how to provide him with the extra help he might need will increase as he grows older.

HEARING

Hearing enables us to bring in information about the world by attending to sounds, loud and quiet, near and far. We rely on hearing to provide us with information that we need to know—whether it be the ringing of a telephone, the warning sound of a horn, or spoken words.

When a child cannot hear, or cannot hear clearly, he can use sight or another sense to try to understand the world around him. But he will have trouble learning to speak, since learning to speak is dependent on being able to hear and imitate others. He will also have difficulty learning to understand and use spoken language, since he cannot hear which words correspond to which objects and actions. He may, for example, be slower to learn concepts such as color, size, or number if he cannot hear his parents talk about the red ball or the three little butterflies in a picture. And he will have trouble learning about his environment if he cannot ask about things that puzzle him.

In the past, most physicians did not realize it was necessary to test and treat hearing problems of infants with facial differences. Now, however, physicians know how important it is for infants to hear their mother's voice and other sounds, and to be comforted by these sounds. Consequently, consultations about your baby's hearing should begin at birth. His hearing can easily be tested as soon as he is medically stable.

The following sections explain how hearing is tested and what the results of hearing tests mean.

The Ear and Sound

To understand how hearing problems are diagnosed, caused, and treated, you need to understand how the ear works and how we perceive sound.

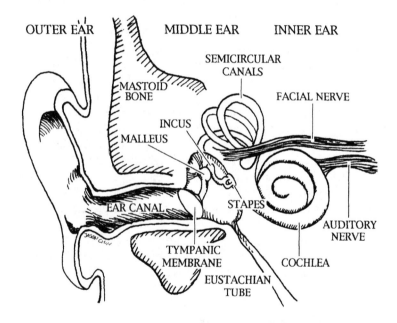

OUTER EAR   MIDDLE EAR   INNER EAR

SEMICIRCULAR CANALS

MASTOID BONE

FACIAL NERVE

INCUS

MALLEUS

EAR CANAL

STAPES

AUDITORY NERVE

TYMPANIC MEMBRANE

COCHLEA

EUSTACHIAN TUBE

The ear is divided into three main parts: 1) the outer ear; 2) the middle ear; and 3) the inner ear.

The **outer ear** includes the part of the ear that is visible outside the head (the *pinna* or *auricle*), as well as the external ear canal (auditory canal), which connects the outside ear to the inside ear. The outer ear collects sound waves and directs them through the ear canal to the eardrum. The eardrum (*tympanic membrane*) separates the outer ear from the middle ear.

The **middle ear** is an air-filled cavity that contains three tiny bones: the *malleus, incus,* and *stapes.* These bones are collectively called the *ossicles.* The ossicles pass on sound vibrations from the eardrum to the fluid in the inner ear.

The **inner ear** includes the *cochlea,* a snail-shaped organ that contains nerve endings necessary for the transmission of sounds via the *auditory nerve* to the brain. The inner ear also contains the semi-circular (*vestibular*) canals, which are responsible for balance.

When sound causes the fluid in the inner ear to vibrate, it forms a pattern that looks like a circle of waves. The loudness and pitch of a sound depends on the speed and height of these waves.

The pitch (high or low) of a sound depends on the *frequency* of the sound wave—that is, on how many times per second it causes the fluid to vibrate. Frequency is measured in Hertz (Hz), or cycles per second. Each Hz is equal to one cycle per second. People with normal hearing can hear frequencies from a low of 20 to a high of 20,000 Hz. Sounds with a frequency of 500 Hz or below are perceived as low-pitched, while sounds of 2,000 Hz or higher are perceived as high-pitched. A window air conditioner registers about 125 Hz and a power table saw registers 3,500 to 6,000 Hz.

The intensity or loudness of a sound depends on the height of the sound wave. Intensity is measured in decibels (dB). Normal conversations are usually carried on in the range of 45–60 dB, while a whisper registers about 30 dB. Sounds which measure 100 dB or more, such as those produced at a rock music concert, can damage the ear.

When one or more parts of the ear do not function in the way they are supposed to, a hearing loss may result. The hearing loss may make it impossible to hear sounds at certain pitches or degrees of loudness, or both.

Types of Hearing Losses

Not all hearing losses are alike. Some can be treated so that normal or near-normal hearing is restored. Others cause permanent hearing impairments, but can be minimized to some extent with hearing aids. Most children with hearing losses have at least some hearing.

How much hearing can be restored depends on the cause of the hearing loss. When the problem originates with the outer ear, or middle ear, hearing may be improved with treatment. (Sometimes, however, the loss may be permanent.) This type of hearing loss is known as a *conductive hearing loss.* When the problem is with the inner ear or auditory nerve, hearing loss is usually permanent. This type of loss is known as a *sensorineural hearing loss.* If a conductive hearing loss occurs in combination with a sensorineural loss, it is known as a *mixed hearing loss.* Children with facial difference are most likely to have conductive hearing losses.

Conductive Hearing Loss

A conductive hearing loss is caused by a problem in conducting the sound from the outer and middle ears to the inner ear. The problem may be caused by a blockage, either partial or complete, in the outer or middle ear. This blockage can result from a missing or narrow ear canal or a malformed pinna.

In addition, conductive hearing losses are frequently caused by *otitis media,* an inflammation of the middle ear often accompanied by a buildup of fluid in the space which is normally filled with air. Fluid accumulates when the eustachian tube that runs from the middle ear cavity down into the throat cannot open and close properly. When this tube cannot do its job, a normal amount of air cannot be maintained in the middle ear. Instead, some of the air is absorbed by the lining of the middle ear cavity and fluid starts to build up. The extra fluid prevents sound vibrations from being transmitted efficiently, and can muffle sound. If not properly treated, repeated episodes of otitis media can cause permanent damage to the ear.

If your child has a conductive hearing loss and you want to understand what hearing is like for him, try thinking of a radio. When the volume switch is on low or your child is not using a hearing aid, it is hard for him to hear the music clearly, although he may hear some sounds. When the volume switch is turned up louder or your child is using a hearing aid, the music is clear and loud enough so that he can understand the words and hear the music.

If your child has a conductive hearing loss, especially one that is unilateral (on one side), he may have trouble localizing sound. That is, he will have difficulty in identifying the direction a sound is coming from. Over time and with some training, he will gradually learn the clues in his environment that will help him figure out where sounds come from. However, each time he is in a new setting, he will need to learn how to navigate the sounds of the environment.

Sensorineural and Mixed Hearing Loss

A sensorineural hearing loss, or nerve loss, is caused by damage to the cochlea, auditory nerve, or both. This damage may be hereditary or it may be caused by high fever, meningitis, a tumor, complications of prematurity, or certain antibiotics. Sensorineural hearing losses are permanent, and can get progressively worse over time. This type of hearing loss is much less common in children in general than are conductive losses. Sensorineural losses are also relatively rare in most conditions of facial difference.

A mixed hearing loss is partly conductive and partly sensorineural. Sometimes a child who has sensorineural loss can also develop a conductive loss due to recurrent middle ear infections. Mixed hearing loss is less common than conductive loss among children with facial difference.

Facial Difference and Hearing Loss

Understanding the reason your child may have a hearing loss can help you communicate with professionals and understand treatment options. Below are descriptions of the ways the conditions described in this book most often affect hearing.

Apert Syndrome and Crouzon Syndrome. Children with Apert and Crouzon syndromes are very likely to have conductive hearing loss, primarily because of fluid build-up in the middle ear. This happens because the eustachian tube and the structures around its lower end (in the throat) are usually not well formed. Children with these syndromes may also have congenitally abnormal external ear canals (small or completely closed) or abnormally formed ossicles. This further interferes with efficient transmission of sound waves. A small percentage of children with Apert or Crouzon syndrome have sensorineural problems in addition to the more common conductive hearing loss.

Cleft Palate. Up to 94 percent of children with this condition experience repeated fluid in the middle ear. This fluid buildup often causes a conductive hearing loss. This problem decreases as the child grows older, but does not always go away completely.

Hemifacial Microsomia. At least 50 percent of children with hemifacial microsomia have a conductive hearing loss because the outside ear is not fully formed and the ear canal is narrow or absent. The hearing loss may affect only the ear that is visibly abnormal, or it may affect both ears. Although it may look as though only one ear is abnormal, many children with this condition also have smaller, harder-to-detect abnormalities on the other side of the face which can affect hearing. In addition, recent studies have shown that some children with hemifacial microsomia may have a sensorineural component to their hearing loss.

Treacher Collins Syndrome. In 85 percent of children with Treacher Collins syndrome, the outside ear is underdeveloped. One third have no ear canals. Consequently, most children with Treacher Collins syndrome have a conductive hearing loss in both ears.

Hearing Tests

Testing of your child's hearing may be done shortly after birth. Hearing tests are generally divided into two categories: objective and behavioral. Objective tests are those in which it is not necessary for your child to show any awareness of sounds. This means they can be done in early infancy. Behavioral tests are those in which your child indicates an awareness of sound by making an obvious response. All hearing tests (*audiologic assessments*) are performed by a certified audiologist, a professional who specializes in evaluating hearing and in hearing aids.

Objective Hearing Tests

One of the newest types of objective tests is the *Otoacoustic Emissions Test.* This is a screening test that can be used in early infancy to determine whether or not the cochlea is vibrating normally to sound stimulation and whether the middle ear is normal. This test cannot determine the reason for a hearing loss or precisely measure the degree of hearing loss, if any. It does, however, indicate whether or not there is a need for further testing.

The most popular and frequently used objective test used to assess hearing in very young child is the *auditory brainstem response (ABR)*, also called *evoked response audiometry (ERA)*. ABR is conducted while your baby is sleeping. Your baby does not need to have an outer ear to be administered this test. Your baby may be given a light sedative to help him fall asleep, or you may be asked to make sure he is sleepy when you bring him in so that he will fall asleep on his own. This is important because movement interferes with the test.

The audiologist will attach electrodes to your baby's forehead and on or behind each ear with tape or a gel. These electrodes are connected by wires to a computer. The computer produces sounds that are transmitted through the electrodes to each ear. Every time the child hears a sound, there is a slight change in the brain wave pattern. The audiologist can tell which sounds your baby is able to hear based on the way his brain responds to the electrical activity produced by the sounds.

The sounds are presented at different intensities to determine the weakest level at which your child responds. Different pitches are also presented to determine whether your child has better hearing for tones in the middle or high range. Each ear is tested separately. The audiologist will be able to identify those sounds your baby is able to hear based on the way his brain responds to the electrical activity evoked by the sounds.

Behavioral Hearing Tests

An audiologist may use several different types of behavioral testing to follow up after the ABR. These tests take place in a sound booth—a small room where the audiologist can close the door and regulate sound without interference from outside noises.

When your child is an infant or toddler, the audiologist will produce sounds and watch your child's response to the sounds. Your child may see a toy light up or move if he looks for the sound in the correct place, or if he responds in some way such as widening his eyes. This method is called conditioned orientation reflex (COR). Since your child is not wearing headphones, his ears cannot be tested separately. The responses that are obtained are for the better ear only.

At around age three or four, your child may be able to wear headphones and be tested through play audiometry. With this method, the audiologist will instruct your child to respond to sounds using a specific action, such as putting a peg in a hole. The audiologist will note the softest sound which your child hears and responds to. The audiologist will also test his auditory word discrimination—his ability to hear sounds within words correctly and clearly. The audiologist will make a sound or say a word or words, then ask your child to point to one of a group of pictures that sound similar or repeat back what was said. Judging by your child's pronunciation of the sound(s) (and factoring in his anatomical ability to make the sound), the audiologist will determine if he is hearing the sound clearly.

If your child uses a hearing aid, he will be tested with the hearing aid on to determine how well he is hearing with this device. The ABR will not be used for this testing. Instead, some type of behavioral play testing will be used, or you will be asked to observe how well your child respond to sounds and words in the environment. The audiologist will want to routinely and frequently test your child's hearing to make sure the hearing aid(s) is working right and that your child is benefiting from it. This means that his hearing should be tested by an audiologist at least every six months until he turns three or four.

Determining Hearing Loss

What your child hears or does not hear is measured in decibels (the units that measure loudness of sound). The lowest decibel level at which your child's brain starts to respond to sound is called his hearing threshold. For example, if your child can only hear sounds that are at least 40 decibels (dB), his hearing threshold is 40 dB. Sometimes parents mistake dB for percentages and think, for example, that their child has a 60 percent hearing loss, rather than a hearing threshold of 60 dB. There is no such thing as a percentage of hearing loss.

The results of your child's hearing test will be plotted on a graph called an audiogram. (See next page) This graph shows what your baby's hearing threshold is at different frequencies or pitches in each ear. The numbers across the top indicate whether the pitch or frequency is low (on the left) or high (on the right). The numbers going from top to bottom on the left side of the audiogram indicate the level of loudness (decibel level). Your child might, for example, hear sounds better at lower frequencies than at higher frequencies. If your child's hearing threshold is higher than normal, then you will be told that your child has a hearing loss. You should also be told what degree of hearing loss your child has at dif-

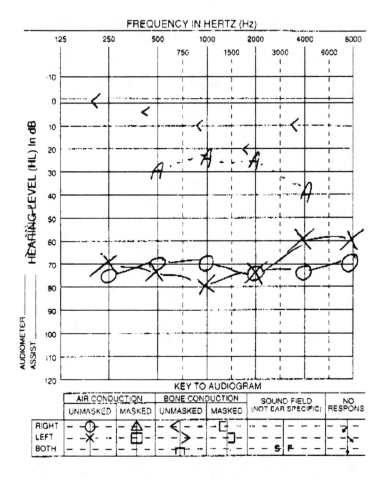

ferent frequencies. The following classifications or similar classifications may be used by your child's audiologist:

normal hearing: 0–15 dB hearing level (HL)
slight hearing loss: 16–25 dB HL
mild hearing loss: 26–30 dB HL
moderate hearing loss: 31–50 dB HL
moderately severe hearing loss: 51–70 dB HL
severe hearing loss: 71–90 dB HL
profound hearing loss: 91 dB (or greater) HL

Until your child is three or four, his hearing should be retested at least every six months. You should also request a hearing test any time you notice signs that his hearing might be changing. Signs you should be alert to in older children include: watching your mouth closely as he listens to you; saying "huh?" or "what?" a lot; turning up the volume on the TV or radio. In babies, batting at the ears or pulling on them may indicate an ear infection.

If the results of a hearing test indicate that your child has a hearing loss, your first step is to find out as much about the loss as possible. Some questions to ask the audiologist are:

- What is my child's hearing threshold? That is, at what decibel level does he start responding to sound? Is this in one or both ears?
- What type of hearing loss does my child have?
- If he isn't hearing within normal limits in one or both ears, what is the recommended treatment? How quickly can he be treated?
- Would an appointment with an ENT (ear, nose and throat specialist or otolaryngologist) be helpful? If so, what types of questions should I ask? What will the ENT be looking for? (See below.)

Treatment of Hearing Loss

Hearing can usually be treated and improved in children with facial difference and associated hearing loss. If the results of hearing tests indicate that your child has a conductive hearing loss, the first step is usually to contact an ear, nose and throat specialist (*otolaryngologist*) or an *otologist* (a medical doctor who diagnoses and treats disorders of the ear). This doctor can attempt to improve blockages or other physical problems that are impeding your child's hearing. Procedures the ENT or otologist may perform include:

- removing ear wax.
- prescribing antibiotics or other medications in an attempt to clear up otitis media.
- repairing damaged eardrums.
- surgically inserting tiny ventilating tubes (also known as pressure equalization or P.E. tubes) in children with repeated build-up of middle ear fluid. These tubes, which are inserted in the eardrum, equalize the pressure of the

middle ear by helping the eustachian tubes function better, and can reduce fluid build-up and the number of infections.
- replacing damaged ossicles with artificial implants.
- surgically attempting to enlarge or create external ear canals. Opening ear canals, however, will improve hearing only by about 20 dB. For children who have multiple ear anomalies, opening the canals is not very efficient, unless doing so makes it easier to fit a hearing aid.

Depending on your health plan, you may need to consult an ENT or otologist even if your child is not a candidate for one of these procedures. Some insurance plans require "medical clearance" before a hearing aid can be fitted. In general, even if your child has not been diagnosed with a hearing loss, it is a good idea to consult with an ENT. At a minimum, he can help monitor and treat problems that could lead to a hearing loss.

After consulting the ENT (or perhaps simultaneously), you will likely be referred to a pediatric audiologist. If your child's outer ears are underdeveloped, this audiologist should also have experience fitting hearing aids on children with microtic (underdeveloped) outer ears. The audiologist on your child's craniofacial team should have this experience.

If hearing tests indicate that your child has a nerve or mixed loss, the audiologist and ENT/otologist will consult with one another about the best type of amplification and any indications for medical treatment.

As your child grows and his hearing continues to be evaluated, you may learn that he has a fluctuating hearing loss. That is, sometimes his hearing may be better than other times. This may be the case if he has intermittent ear infections and fluid in the ear. If so, he will need to see an ENT for medications or P.E. tubes to reduce the fluid build-up and number of infections.

Hearing Aids

The audiologist will recommend hearing aids for your child if he has a loss that is significant enough to impair his development of speech and language. If hearing in one ear is within normal limits and hearing is mildly or even moderately impaired in the other, your child may be able to hear adequately unaided. However, if both ears have a moderate or greater hearing loss, it is likely that your child will need hearing aids to bring his hearing within normal limits. If your child is five or younger, he might also be prescribed hearing aids as an interim measure while he is awaiting surgery to open up his ear canals.

The job of a hearing aid is to pick up sound and amplify it (make it louder). Most hearing aids can raise the range a child can hear by 30 to 50 dB. For example, a child who cannot hear sounds softer than 60 dB unaided may be able to hear sounds as soft as 10 to 30 dB with a hearing aid.

The hearing aid cannot tell the difference between conversations and background noise, so it amplifies all sounds. As a result, children with hearing aids hear all sounds, including noise, equally loudly. Over time, your child will need to learn how to listen and discriminate between sounds that are more and less important to him. This is hard work and can be very exhausting, especially in noisy environments, such as at a children's museum. Often children (and adults, too) who wear hearing aids do not enjoy being in loud, boisterous environments, because the sounds they hear can be quite confusing, indecipherable, and, over a long period of time, irritating and frustrating.

The hearing aid will need to be adjusted by the audiologist so that sounds are not too loud or distorted for your child. The sound your child hears by using his hearing aid will complement and build upon his residual hearing—that is, the degree of hearing he was born with. Residual hearing can be damaged by a hearing aid whose volume switch is turned up too loudly.

The type of hearing aid your child wears will depend on the type of his hearing loss, conductive or sensorineural. Children with conductive losses use bone conduction or air conduction hearing aids. Children with sensorineural hearing losses use air conduction hearing aids.

A bone conduction hearing aid works by sending vibrations or sound waves from a vibrator (called the oscillator) through the bone of the skull. The sound bypasses the outer and middle ears, which is where the blockage is when there is a conductive loss. In air conduction hearing aids, sound is transmitted through an earmold inserted in the outer ear.

In both bone conduction and air conduction hearing aids, sound waves enter the hearing aid through the microphone, are amplified, and are then received by the wearer. Sound is picked up by the microphone as sound waves, changed into electrical signals which the amplifier strengthens, and are changed back into amplified sound waves in the receiver. All this activity is powered by a battery.

A body aid

Types of Hearing Aids

Hearing aids can be worn at body-level or ear-level (also called behind-the-ear or post-auricular aids). Children may wear one hearing aid (monaural) or two hearing aids (binaural). If a child with a conductive hearing loss wears a bone conduction aid, only one hearing aid is necessary. This is because the sound is transmitted through the bone of your child's skull.

The body-level aid is so-called because it is worn on the child's body in a specially made vest or is clipped onto his clothing. In the past, this type of aid was frequently prescribed for young children and for those with severe to profound hearing losses. This is because body-level aids used to be more powerful than behind-the-ear models. Now, however, some behind-the-ear models are as powerful as body-level aids, and are preferred by most audiologists. For some children, though, a body-level aid is still the best choice. Only the audiologist can determine which type of hearing aid is the most appropriate for your child.

The body aid is a small box which contains a microphone and amplifier. When the aid is used for bone conduction (for a conductive hearing loss), a cord connects the box to the receiver, which is an oscillator (vibrator). The oscillator is worn snugly against the child's mastoid bone (directly behind the outside ear). When the aid is used for air conduction (for a sensorineural loss), a cord connects the box to the receiver, which is an earmold in this case. The earmold goes directly into the child's ear.

The behind-the-ear (bte) aid is much smaller than the body aid. It contains the microphone, amplifier, and receiver. When a child has developed outer ears, the hearing aid curls around the back of the outer ear. The receiver, an earmold, is connected to one end of the bte and goes di-

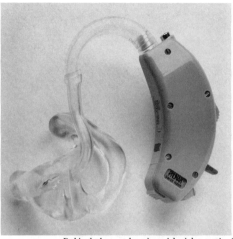

Behind-the-ear hearing aid with a typical earmold attached.

rectly into the child's ear. For a conductive hearing loss, the bte can be modified. A bte that houses the microphone and amplifier can be worn in a headband or clipped to the child's clothing. The receiver, or oscillator, is connected by a cord to the bte and worn snugly against the child's mastoid bone.

If your child has underdeveloped (microtic) outer ears, as some children with Treacher Collins syndrome or hemifacial microsomia do, he can still wear a hearing aid. Frequently children with microtic ears have a conductive hearing loss and need a bone conduction hearing aid. In this case, they have several choices of hearing aids: 1) a body aid with an oscillator held in place by a sweatband, an elastic band, or a headband made of plastic or plastic-coated metal which extends from ear to ear; 2) a bte and oscillator placed in pockets in a cloth headband called a HUGGIE HEAD™ ; or 3) a bte and oscillator situated at opposite ends of a sweatband or plastic-coated metal headband. Many parents of girls decorate the bands with ribbons, frills, etc. to match outfits. Often, the decorations are so beautiful that the public just thinks the child is wearing a girl's fashion headband bought at a clothing store.

Recently, a new way of wearing hearing aids was devised by Peter Keller, a hearing aid dispenser in Toronto, Canada, and is used by the audiologists on the craniofacial team at the Hospital for Sick Children there. He modified the traditional bte/oscillator set-up by using dou-

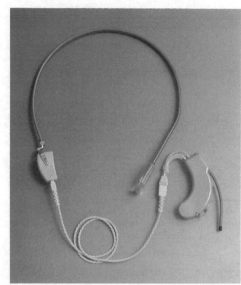

Behind-the-ear hearing aid modified for bone conduction. The bone conductor and hearing aid are shown attached to a headband.

ble-stick tape to adhere the oscillator to the child's head. He cautions, however, that double-stick tape cannot be used with just any oscillator, but only with this specially modified version. Parents or audiologists interested in learning how to make the modifications can request a reprint of "Modification of the Traditional Bone Conduction Hearing Aid" by Debbie Ross and colleagues, published in the *Cleft Palate-Craniofacial Journal,* Vol. 30 (1993), p. 328.

If your child uses a bone conduction hearing aid, the oscillator must press against his head with constant firm pressure to obtain the best quality of sound. This pressure can be obtained from a snug elastic sweatband, plastic-coated metal headband, HUGGIE HEAD™ band, or double-stick tape when used with the specially modified aid. If the pressure is not constant and firm enough, your child will not receive strong enough vibrations from the oscillator, and the sound will not be loud enough. (My son uses sweatbands that I buy in packages of three at the drugstore. They are 93 percent cotton and made by Goody, Inc.)

Your child's audiologist will likely select a specific type or brand of aid for your child based on its flexibility—its ability to be modified as your child's hearing needs change and as those needs become clearer. In talking with other parents, however, you may hear about other types and brands of hearing aids and wonder whether they might be better for your child. For example, you may wonder if smaller in-the-ear or in-the-canal hearing aids might benefit your child. As your child grows older, he will be able to provide you with reliable information about how much he hears and how clearly he hears it. Before that time, you and the audiologist will need to rely upon the results of your child's audiological testing to determine how much he hears and how clearly he hears it. This should not stop you, however, from learning about other brands and types of hearing aids.

Getting the Maximum Benefit from a Hearing Aid

Some babies receive hearing aids at an early age, and their speech and language are still delayed. This may be because of structural limitations caused by the anatomy of the child's face and head. For example, a malocclusion caused by abnormal growth of the jaws can affect speech. The surgeries or devices that are needed to correct these anatomical problems can also contribute to delays, at least temporarily. For example, some orthodontic appliances can cause temporary "slushiness" in articulation.

Sometimes a structural limitation may be suspected when the hearing aid is actually at fault. A child might be fitted with a hearing aid that doesn't provide adequate amplification, so his speech and language development may be hindered. Sometimes surgery to improve hearing might be proposed on the grounds that anatomical differences may be inhibiting development. If you encounter this situation, you may want to ask some questions before agreeing to the operation: 1) Is the hearing aid providing adequate amplification? Would another brand or style offer better results? 2) Are the health care professionals involved in treating your child's hearing loss truly experienced in treating his condition? That is, is surgery being proposed prematurely as a dramatic answer to a problem that is not really as big as it seems or that could be remedied via other means?

Parents can also unintentionally limit the benefits of a hearing aid by not ensuring that their child wears his aid(s) all day, everyday. For sound to be meaningful to a child with a hearing impairment, he needs to wear his hearing aid consistently. Your child needs to be able to experience the sounds of the world—conversations, speech, music, noise—all day long, not just at selected times. His hearing aids should not restrict his ability to participate in childhood activities such as ball playing, dancing lessons, gymnastics, learning a musical instrument, and ice skating. If you feel that your child's hearing evaluation did not truly reflect his hearing abilities, do not decide on your own to reduce the amount of time he wears his hearing aid. Contact the audiologist or ENT with your concerns.

The key to ensuring that your child wears his hearing aid consistently is to give him a lot of positive support. When he is young, it is important to help him enjoy listening to sounds. Some ways to do this include: directing your child's attention to sounds he might be especially interested in, such as the "choo choo" of a toy train; singing songs with animal sounds; pretending to be an animal and making animal sounds; going on an outing and paying attention to environmental sounds you know he can hear, such as squeaky doors, bells, and sirens.

After you have started your child on the path to learning about the sounds around him, these sounds will gradually become more important to him. As this happens, he will want to wear his hearing aid to make sure he doesn't miss out on anything. If, for some reason, he doesn't want to wear it, do not try to force him to wear it with punishments. Instead, find out why he doesn't want to wear the aid and have it checked by an audiologist to make sure it is working properly.

Most hearing aids have a life of five to seven years. If the hearing aid becomes wet, gets food particles inside, or is thrown or dropped, it may need to be replaced sooner. If your young child wears a hearing aid, these events will likely happen from time to time. Every day you will need to: 1) check the battery to make sure it is strong enough, and replace it if it is not; 2) check the tubing for cracks or blockage and replace or clean if necessary; and 3) listen to the aid at the same level of loudness as your child uses it. With daily monitoring of your child's hearing aid, you will know fairly quickly if the sound has become distorted, the aid has stopped working, or the aid is damaged. If any of these things happen, call your child's audiologist. If your child's aid needs to be returned to the manufacturer for repair, she may have a loaner available.

Auditory Trainers or FM Systems

Some children may benefit from using a device called an auditory trainer or FM system in addition to a hearing aid. An auditory trainer is not a substitute for a hearing aid.

Like a hearing aid, an auditory trainer amplifies sound, but has some additional capabilities. When your child uses his auditory

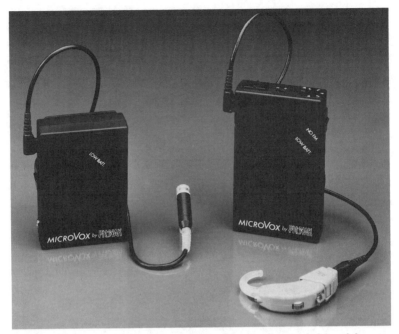

A traditional FM system, showing the transmitter with microphone on the left and the receiver on the right.

trainer, he wears a receiver and someone else, such as a teacher, holds or wears a microphone that transmits sound directly to your child's receiver. In newer versions of auditory trainers (such as the Phonic Ear - Free Ear™ and the Extend-Ear™ system), the receiver is built right into a hearing aid and is activated by merely flicking a switch. In other models still used today, the receiver is housed in a box your child wears like a body-aid. If your child has a bte-FM model, he has the opportunity to hear: 1) only the teacher's voice through the microphone; 2) the teacher's voice and background sounds; or 3) a combination of these two. In any case, the teacher's voice sounds like it is no more than six inches away from your child.

An auditory trainer can be particularly useful during speech therapy or in the classroom, where your child may be concentrating on discriminating sounds that are similar (such as "p" and "b" or "pin" and "bin"). If the teacher wears the microphone in a classroom setting, your child will always be tuned in to what the

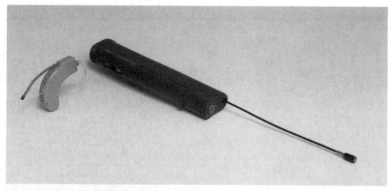

The Extend-Ear™ system.

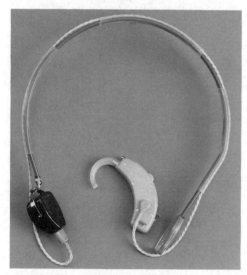

The Extend-Ear modified for bone conduction.

teacher is saying, no matter where in the room your child and the teacher are or what the noise or activity level of the other children.

Your child's audiologist and teacher will jointly determine whether your child could benefit from an auditory trainer.

Implantable Hearing Aids

In recent years, scientists have developed an implantable hearing aid for people with a conductive hearing loss. At the time of this writing, the Audiant Bone Conductor™, manufactured by Xomed-Treace, Inc., is the only brand available in the U.S. Another device, the Bone Anchored Hearing System, manufactured by NobelPharma, a Swedish company, is being reviewed by the Food and Drug Administration (FDA) of the U.S. Government for approval.

The Audiant Bone Conductor was designed for people with a conductive hearing loss who are not able to use a regular air or bone conduction hearing aid or have their hearing loss corrected through surgery. This situation is common in children with Treacher Collins syndrome whose middle ear structures are not developed enough that ear canals can be surgically reconstructed. Other criteria must also be evaluated by the surgeon, audiologist, and child himself to determine if he is a good candidate for this device. The Audiant Bone Conductor is not used with children under the age of three.

With the Audiant Bone Conductor, a tiny magnetic disc is surgically implanted onto the surface of the skull behind the ear. When this heals, the child returns to the audiologist for a small transmitter that is magnetically placed on the skin over the implant. He is also fitted with an external sound processor, which holds the microphone and amplifier. The sound processor delivers sound vibrations (through the transmitter) directly to the temporal bone, which contains the inner ear.

Some advantages of implantable hearing aids over external hearing aids include:

- There is no need for a headband or other means to keep the hearing aid on your child's head.
- Concerns about whether there is adequate pressure to drive the oscillator are reduced.
- The quality of amplified sound may be better than with a traditional hearing aid.
- The aid is less cumbersome and less obvious to others.

Some disadvantages are:

- Repairs are more difficult than with a traditional hearing aid, and loaners are usually not available.
- The wearer must be motivated, mature, and responsible.
- It is a fragile device that can't be dropped or mishandled.
- A sound processor must still be used, which for bone conduction is housed in a body-style aid the size of a small cigarette box.
- When using a telephone, all sound is amplified, including background noise.

To obtain more information about this device, contact your child's ENT or audiologist. They can help you evaluate your child's hearing needs and determine if implantable hearing aids are appropriate for him.

Reconstructive Surgery

Reconstructive surgery can sometimes improve hearing by correcting structural problems in the ear. An otologic surgeon—a physician who specializes in the anatomy and disorders of the ear—can tell you whether your child has a problem that might be surgically corrected. For example, abnormal ossicles can be replaced by prosthetic devices—tiny artificial structures that function like ossicles, but don't look like them. And an eardrum can be constructed if the ear canal is large enough.

One of the more delicate procedures is reconstructive ear canal surgery. This operation might improve your child's hearing if he has a bilateral (both sides) hearing impairment due to underdevelopment of the outer and/or middle ear (missing ear canal and/or underdeveloped middle ear bones). When your child is quite young, you may begin discussing this operation with your otologist or ENT. The earliest that the actual surgical procedure should be scheduled, however, is age four or five. This is because the head grows so rapidly in the first six years or so that it would "outgrow" the reconstructed ear canal.

Before proceeding to reconstructive ear canal surgery, other less invasive methods of improving your child's hearing should be carefully evaluated. It is not recommended to hop from reconstructive ear canal surgery to implantable hearing aid surgery if the first procedure is not successful.

If your child's outside ears (pinnas) are also underdeveloped, it is important to coordinate reconstructive ear canal operations with the outside ear reconstructions. You and your child must discuss the timing of these operations with the otologic surgeon and reconstructive plastic surgeon prior to beginning any of these operations. Currently, the preferred order is to complete the outside ear reconstructions before beginning any operations on the ear canals and middle ear structures.

Before ear canal reconstruction can even be considered, your child needs to have an ABR performed along with a high-resolution CT scan. A CT scan or CAT scan is a diagnostic procedure in which a computerized machine takes x-ray pictures of cross sections of the body. In this case, the x-rays are taken of the outer, middle, and inner ear. These cross sections may be on "slices" as small as one millimeter thick. Before your child can be considered for surgery, the CT scan must show that your child has an inner ear. The ABR must show evidence of cochlear functioning—that it is capable of transmitting sound to the auditory nerves. If the cochlea (or large portions of it) is not functional, opening up a pathway to it is useless.

Ear canal reconstruction and middle ear reconstruction are very delicate procedures. For more information about what is involved, see the Reading List.

During surgery, complications can lead to facial nerve injury and damage to the cochlea. Therefore, be very careful to choose only an otologist who has had a great deal of experience with this surgery *and* has had highly successful results. If your child's surgery goes well, his hearing threshold may be increased by 15 to 25 dB.

Otologic surgery on children with Treacher Collins syndrome is especially complicated. The atypical configurations of their middle ears make this delicate surgery very difficult, if not impossible. Their facial nerve is frequently located in a position that makes the risk of facial paralysis too great when evaluating the risks of the surgery. Also, restoring hearing in children with this condition can be unpredictable. Sometimes the surgery restores hearing in a child with Treacher Collins syndrome, but within several months his hearing threshold may have returned to the preoperative level. If your child has Treacher Collins syndrome, it is therefore especially important to consult with the craniofacial team about the otologists who have been most successful in restoring hearing in children with this condition.

COMMUNICATION

Parents of children with facial differences often wonder whether their children will have trouble developing speech and language. If your child has a hearing impairment in addition to a facial difference, the odds may seem stacked against him. How hearing loss affects speech and language development, however, will be different for each child.

If your child's hearing loss is conductive, as is most often the case among children with facial difference, there may be few effects on his speech skills. A conductive loss is usually correctable within normal ranges with a hearing aid if the child is taught to make sense of what he hears. Children with conductive losses hear clearly, but softly. Hearing aids will increase the volume. There-

fore, unless there are other factors which might interfere with speech development, you can expect that your child will probably develop adequate speech and language over time and with speech therapy.

Even if there are other complications, such as structural differences with your child's palate, he may still be able to develop adequate speech and language. It might not be as easy, however. He might need extra support and therapy. He may also need surgical interventions or special devices such as an *obturator*—a device placed in the mouth to decrease nasal air flow during speech. Alternative forms of communication, such as sign language, are also an option if your child is unable to develop adequate speech and language.

If your child has sensorineural or mixed loss, he will not always understand speech sounds, even when using his hearing aid(s). And it might not be as easy for him to hear and reproduce sounds as it is for a child with a conductive hearing loss. But that is not to say that he cannot develop adequate speech and language. Like a child who has structural differences that affect speech, he will likely benefit from extra support, therapy, patience, and time, and perhaps from careful surgery and devices such as an auditory trainer. Again, sign language or another alternative form of communication may be an option, depending on the degree of hearing loss.

In thinking about how your child's hearing and facial differences may affect communication, it is important to remember that speech and hearing are not the only prerequisites for communication. All children—with and without hearing impairments—use a variety of abilities to communicate, not just speech and hearing. Your child probably attends to spoken language, expressions on people's faces, and their body movements, body language, and actions. For example, when he sees you getting his coat out of the closet, he may conclude that you are getting ready to take him outside. Or when he sees steam rising from his oatmeal, he knows that it is hot. From birth onward, children naturally absorb these ways to communicate.

When your child has a hearing impairment, he may rely more on sight than hearing to learn about his environment. He learns language by observing activities, the time when events occur, and how things such as cause and effect work. As people are talking, he is probably also watching their lips and beginning to acquire speech. Many people with and without hearing impairments find it helpful to be able to read lips. So, with little effort he is attending to his surroundings. When others make special efforts to point his surroundings out to him, speech, language, and the activities he observes and participates in can become even more meaningful.

For your child to learn how to talk, he will need to watch and listen to other people talk, in addition to hearing himself talk. The people involved in his daily activities and routines will provide him with role models for learning the sounds of speech, and the meaning of language, body positions, and facial expressions. You can help your child learn by speaking directly to him, at his eye level, from not more than a few feet away, and by speaking at an average rate of speed and using short and complete phrases. It may be harder for him if you speak to him while smiling, eating, chewing gum, smoking, or moving around.

The following sections explore the typical problems children with facial differences can encounter in both speech and language, and discuss what can be done to minimize them.

Language

Technically speaking, language refers to any set of gestures, written symbols, or spoken words people use to communicate with one another. For example, English, Japanese, and German are spoken and written languages, American Sign Language is a language made up entirely of gestures, and braille is a written language. In learning to use a language, a child must understand the *content* of the language (what the words mean). He must also understand the *form*, or how words change according to their meaning in a sentence ("He walk*s* to the store vs. "He walk*ed* to the store") and how they are put in order to make sense ("I see the dog," not "See the dog I.").

As children develop language skills, they learn how to understand language that others are using, as well as how to use language to make their own wants and needs known. The ability to understand others' language is known as *receptive language*, while the ability to express oneself to others is known as *expressive language*.

Many children with hearing impairments have stronger abilities in receptive than expressive language. First, children learn receptive language before expressive language, so they spend more time practicing it. This is especially the case for children who have recently been fitted with hearing aids. They have to learn about the sounds around them before they can start trying to express their wants, needs, and opinions. In addition, children with many of the conditions discussed in this book have structural abnormalities of the face which can affect their ability to make themselves understood.

Too often, parents whose children have delays in expressive language development make the mistake of assuring themselves (and others) that "He understands *everything.*" It is very easy to overestimate how well a child really understands spoken language. For example, you might think that your child understands two- or three-step commands. In reality, however, you may be accompanying each of these steps with gestures. Only a fully qualified speech-language pathologist can accurately assess your child's receptive language.

The following sections explain how therapy can help your child improve both receptive and expressive language (speech).

Speech

Speech is one way of communicating language. It is the process of producing sounds and combining them into words. A child's speech can be described in terms of a number of characteristics, including articulation, fluency, and voice.

Articulation. Articulation refers to the ability to move and control the lips, tongue, jaw, and palate to produce the sounds of a language. With good articulation, a child produces sounds clearly and accurately. To articulate well, a child must pass through developmental speech milestones—that is, he must learn to pronounce easier sounds (like "d," "g," "b," "m,") before he can master more difficult sounds (like "f," "s," "sh").

Fluency. Fluency is the way speech flows. Stuttering is one of the better-known fluency problems. When a child stutters, he may hesitate, repeat sounds or whole words, or seem to "block" a sound or word for several seconds at a time.

Voice Production. Voice refers to the speech sounds coming from the larynx (voice box, vocal folds). If there is a structural abnormality of the vocal folds, or if the child uses his vocal folds inappropriately, his voice may sound hoarse, breathy, squeaky, high pitched, low pitched, or just too soft. Voice quality is also affected by the resonance characteristics of the mouth, nose, and upper part of the throat. If there is an abnormality of resonance, the child's voice may sound *hyponasal* ("plugged up" as if he has a cold) or *hypernasal* (too nasal). Hypernasality may occur in children with repaired cleft palates if the surgical repair did not provide a palate long enough to close off the nose from the mouth during speech.

Children with facial difference, with or without a hearing impairment, are more likely to need assistance in developing speech sounds on time and correctly. The most common speech problem among children with facial difference is with articulation. Due to the anatomical structure of a child's mouth, he may not be able to produce certain sounds. In time, he may outgrow this problem, or it might be corrected as the result of surgery. In the meanwhile, he may learn to substitute sounds made in the throat or the back of the mouth for sounds that should be made in the front of the mouth.

Children who have hearing impairments in addition to facial difference often have problems with speech production. Certain facial differences, including cleft palate and Treacher Collins syndrome, can also lead to *hypernasality*—a twangy, talking-through-the-nose voice quality.

Children with the following problems are more likely to have speech problems:

- problems with swallowing and chewing of food (more common in children who have used feeding tubes);
- nasal regurgitation of food and liquid;
- nasal air emission (partial loss of the vocal airstream through the nose due to inadequate functioning of the palate);

- abnormal position of teeth and malocclusion or severe anterior open bite—misalignment which prevents teeth on upper and lower jaws from meeting when the mouth is closed (common in conditions where the lower jaw is receded);
- underdevelopment of the jaw (common in most facial difference syndromes); and
- a short or immobile palate (often found in Treacher Collins syndrome and some other craniofacial syndromes, even when there is no actual cleft of the palate).

Evaluating Your Child's Speech

The first step to improving your child's speech is to pinpoint what difficulties he has in speaking, as well as what causes those difficulties. While you will certainly have a feel for how much your child understands and expresses, it is important to have your child evaluated by a *speech-language pathologist*—a professional who specializes in analyzing speech patterns and improving speech and language skills. This professional will test your child and compare his language development and speech abilities with the average for a typical child of his age. Based on the results, he will recommend a treatment plan for speech therapy that he or another speech therapist will carry out.

Depending upon your child's age and history, the speech and language evaluation will likely include some naming tasks (pictures, objects); identification tasks (pointing to pictures of objects or activities); some activities where your child follows a series of instructions; "description" tasks, where your child tells the speech-language pathologist about what he sees; and a variety of activities designed to get a feel for your child's conversation skills. If your child is very young, the speech-language pathologist will spend a lot of time observing him playing with you, his parents, preferably at home. Evaluation often takes several sessions, and many times the sessions are videotaped (or at least audiotaped) for later analysis.

After the evaluation, the speech-language pathologist will write a report which will include information about your child's history, articulation, voice, language development, and the structure and function of the speech mechanism (lips, teeth, tongue, palate). The report will specify your parental concerns—so that other professionals reading the report will know what those concerns are—and offer a list of recommendations. The speech pathologist should be willing to explain everything in the report to you. If you do not agree with the results—if, for example, you think your child's speech and language is better or worse than the report indicates—be sure to mention this to the speech-language pathologist. He might suggest waiting three months and then re-evaluating, or contacting another speech-language pathologist for a second opinion.

Ideally, your child's communication skills should be evaluated by the speech-language pathologist on your child's craniofacial team. He will know how your child's condition of facial difference affects his hearing and his ability to acquire and develop speech and language. He will also have an understanding of child development in relation to speech and language acquisition.

If you want your child to qualify for no-cost speech therapy through an early intervention or preschool program, your child may have to be evaluated by a speech-language pathologist employed by the program. Before the evaluation, try to meet with this speech-language pathologist and explain your child's condition of facial difference. More than likely, he has never before worked with a child with that condition. While it would be helpful if you could provide him some background on your child's anatomical structures that affect speech and language, it would be especially helpful to refer him to the speech-language pathologist on your child's craniofacial team. That professional can provide your local speech-language pathologist with background on your child's condition and how it affects communication, information from tests previously administered, tips on what to look for during the evaluation, and ideas about treatment plans.

Although the local therapist may be able to gather this information using his own research methods, he may not have easy access to the professional literature which describes the speech and language aspects of your child's condition and treatment. The craniofacial team speech-language pathologist can usually provide this information easily over the phone and through the mail. He can also be available for on-going consultation during treatment. See Chapters 6 and 7 for more information on services available through early intervention or special education programs.

Speech Therapy

If the speech-language pathologist who evaluates your child recommends speech therapy for him, he can often receive it without charge. As Chapter 7 explains, infants and toddlers with facial difference frequently qualify for free educational or therapeutic services provided by publicly funded early intervention programs. And children 3 and older can often receive speech therapy through the school if they need it to benefit from their educational program.

If your child does not qualify for free services, even though you feel he would benefit from them, or if you are not satisfied with the speech therapy provided by the early intervention program, you may wish to use a private speech pathologist. First, however, you should check whether your health insurance will pay for any services and whether any pre-authorizations are required. Some insurance policies will pay for speech and language evaluations and some will not. The same is true for therapy. Some will pay if the therapist has a Ph.D., but not an M.A. or M.S. Others will pay for either educational degree. Some will pay only if therapy is ordered by a physician (M.D.). Some insurance companies will not pay if the same service is offered by the school district. Some also have restrictions regarding therapy before vs. after surgery. Also, some policies may require you to use *only* certain speech pathologists.

In general, you can expect the speech-language pathologist to work with your child regularly to increase awareness of sounds and discrimination between sounds that are similar, to help your child correctly pronounce sounds, and to encourage and monitor your child's ability to acquire language.

The precise skills the pathologist works on will depend on the speech difficulties identified during your child's evaluation. You and the pathologist will set goals aimed at overcoming those difficulties. For example, your child might have trouble articulating the "f" sound. A goal might be for your child to pronounce this sound accurately when it occurs at the beginning of a word 80 percent of the time. For a language-delayed two-year-old, the goal might be to increase his vocabulary up to 200 words or to get him to a level where he is consistently using two-word "sentences" (saying "Daddy work" to mean "Daddy went to work"). For an older child, the goal might be to improve his use of verb forms or possessives.

For each goal, there will also be a timetable for meeting that goal. For example, your child might be expected to meet a specific goal by January 1, or by the end of the school year. If your child is anticipating surgery that might affect speech, the timetable should be worked into the pre- and post-surgical plan.

How often your child meets with the speech-language pathologist may depend upon the restrictions of the program he is involved in, the cost of private services, or your child's age. Younger children might have speech therapy two or three times a week; older children, once a week. A session may range from half an hour to an hour. Your child may be seen alone, with another child or group of children, or with you. In some school-type settings (often encountered in preschool special education programs), the speech pathologist may be in the classroom at all times. He then works with individual children as the need arises.

Speech-language pathologists work with children in a variety of ways. Sometimes they use drills such as practicing the correct production of "s" in different word positions. The current trend, however, is to spend less time on drills and more time working speech practice into daily activities, based on a child's interests. For example, when my son was four, he loved rhyming. He and the speech-language pathologist would make up games with rhyming words. Often, speech-language pathologists use a mirror to help children see what their lips, tongue, and teeth should look like when pronouncing certain sounds. Games including the mirror can be created.

Some speech-language pathologists encourage parents to repeat therapeutic activities at home with their child. Others feel that the child will have enough therapists in his life for those activities and that the parents' job is to be supportive and understanding of their child's needs and to have fun with him. As a parent, you need to decide which approach feels most comfortable to you. Whichever way you decide, keep in mind that every activity with your child is an opportunity for speech and language growth. Your child will learn about the world through play and the routines of living in a household with others. For example, when you take him to the grocery store with you, he gets practice using words for numbers, colors, and sizes when you ask him to "Pick out two onions" or "Get the big orange box of detergent on the bottom shelf." With your daily support, his speech and language development will give him the tools to learn how to solve problems, build social relationships, sequence events, think for himself, and remember.

Some speech-language pathologists automatically teach sign language to any child with a hearing impairment. Sign language is a system in which people communicate by using their hands to make formalized gestures that other people see and can interpret. The two forms of sign language most often used in the U.S. are American Sign Language and Signed English. With American Sign, people use their hands to make signs that represent ideas. In a sentence, these ideas are not usually arranged in the same order as they would be in a sentence of spoken English. Words can also be spelled out letter by letter. Signed English, on the other hand, simply translates spoken English into gestures. People use their hands to make signs that represent words or to spell words. Sentences are communicated word for word.

Sometimes people with hearing impairments who are not deaf learn sign language in addition to speech so they feel more comfortable communicating when they are unable to wear their hearing aids, such as in the hospital after surgery. This, however, may introduce a new problem for them. Unless they participate in a community of people who sign, they still may not be able to communicate with others.

You should be aware that teaching sign language to children who have both facial differences and hearing impairments is a controversial practice. Rarely is speech "out of the question" for children with facial differences. One exception may be children who have severe *dyspraxia*—difficulty planning the movements needed to pronounce sounds. Children with dyspraxia may need to use sign language or another alternative method of communication for a long time.

Rather than teaching sign language, many speech-language pathologists prefer a *total communication* approach. Total communication refers to using a variety of methods to communicate, including speech, sign language, fingerspelling (using the hands to spell out words), lipreading, and anything else that might be helpful. Using this method, a child is encouraged to approximate the speech sound as best he can while simultaneously signing the word. The use of signs is then gradually phased out as articulation gets clearer.

Although parents often worry that learning sign language or total communication may interfere with the development of speech skills, this worry is unfounded. When children are ready and able to speak, they automatically begin using speech as their main means of communication. Until that day comes, however, sign language and total communication can help eliminate the frustration a child might otherwise feel if he can't make himself understood.

As the parent, you will need to decide whether sign language or total communication would be preferable and more appropriate for your child to learn. If you decide that your child will learn to sign, you will also need to learn to sign. So, too, should other important people in your child's life: siblings, grandparents, other family members; teachers or classroom aides; babysitters; friends; health care providers such as nurses who may frequently interact with your child. You may learn the signs along with your child as he is learning, or there may be classes available in your community. Ask your child's speech pathologist for information about classes that would be helpful. Funding might be available through your child's programs to teach sign language to your child's family and other significant people.

Most parents of older children with facial difference who have hearing impairments believe that their children function adequately with speech alone. Consequently, many may not ever use sign language with their child, or use it only until their child develops age-appropriate speech and language. If your child has a severe or profound hearing impairment, however, sign language may be the best method of communication for him.

For a variety of reasons, usually anatomical, some children are unable to speak or to speak clearly enough to feel comfortable using speech to communicate. When this occurs, alternative methods of communication need to be considered. The most common method is sign language. Other methods include language boards (with symbols, words, or pictures to point to) or various forms of computer-assisted communication. Your child's speech-language pathologist and/or special education teacher can work with you to help determine the best communication system for your child. In deciding on a system, you will want to bear in mind cost, ease of maintenance, flexibility (whether the system travels easily, for instance), and whether the system can keep pace with your child's needs as he matures. For additional guidance, your child's speech-language pathologist should be able to help you locate one of the many university-based centers for assistive or alternative communication methods.

Finding the Right Therapist

Not all speech-language pathologists have a background in working with children with facial difference. If yours does not, take care to educate him about your child's true abilities. This will help him adapt his teaching methods appropriately. As mentioned previously, it is also helpful to connect your therapist with the speech-language pathologist on your child's craniofacial team.

Usually it is a good idea for you to consult at least occasionally with a speech-language pathologist who has a thorough understanding of your child's speech and language needs. But depending on where you live, you might have trouble finding a speech-language pathologist experienced in working with children with facial difference. For referrals to a speech-language pathologist in your area, you can start by asking the speech professional on your child's craniofacial team. The American Speech-Language-Hearing Association also offers referrals. Many families find it helpful to network with other families and exchange information about the expertise and personality of different speech-language pathologists.

If there are no experienced speech-language pathologists in your community, you may be able to set up a system of long-distance assignments and check-ins with the craniofacial team speech-language pathologist to evaluate your child's progress. Or, you might consider enrolling your family in the Correspondence Course for Parents of Young Deaf Children (age birth through 5) available through the John Tracy Clinic in Los Angeles, California. This program, which focuses on language, is provided at no cost to the family, and is available to families around the world. For a more detailed description, see the Resource Guide.

The Impact of Reconstructive Plastic Surgeries on Speech

As Chapter 3 explains, children with facial difference may have reconstructive plastic surgery either to improve function (to make breathing or eating easier) or to improve the appearance of the face. As an added benefit, some of these surgeries also improve speech. The surgeries that are more likely to improve speech include closure of a cleft lip and/or palate; repositioning the upper and lower jaws so they are directly over each other with a corrected bite; and removing or repositioning teeth.

Sometimes speech improves dramatically after surgery. Other times, speech problems that need to be worked on with a speech-language pathologist may persist. Still other times, speech may temporarily (or permanently) get *worse*. Immediately after surgery, it may be difficult to tell exactly what effect the operation will have on speech. No judgements should be made until healing is complete and all swelling is gone.

It is important for the craniofacial team to consider how any planned surgery might affect your child's speech. Indeed, in planning an operation, the team must consider its possible effects from all perspectives. For example, a surgery might enhance your child's appearance, but temporarily worsen his speech. If the speech problems are likely to be temporary or correctable through a second procedure, it might be desirable to proceed with the surgery.

Conclusion

Sometimes when a baby is born with a facial difference, professional attention is channeled mainly into medical issues, and concerns about hearing fall by the wayside. Correcting breathing and feeding problems is certainly important. But the sooner your baby can be evaluated for a hearing loss and treated, if need be, the sooner your baby will hear your voice and begin to become accustomed to the sounds of the world.

Although you have many years ahead of you to work with hearing, speech, and language professionals, having positive contacts with them when your child is a baby are important to his development. Your child lives in a world where having adequate hearing and speech and language skills is often taken for granted. The sooner he adjusts to the world of sound, the sooner he will begin to develop the skills he needs to function in the world. With your support and the good work of professionals, I hope that one day your child, too, will talk, and talk, and talk, until you need a break!

Parent Statements

She has to have frequent hearing tests to find out how the cleft is affecting her. She has lost minimal hearing, but the doctors say we should have no problem once her surgery is done, because she learned some language before the loss.

※

My son was four months old the first time we met with the audiologist. She put a hearing aid on his head and we spoke to him. It was the first time he was *really* able to hear our voices. His world had been so quiet up until then. Hearing the voices and other sounds, he started to scream and cry. I cried, too. My tears were for his future.

※

We were told by more than one ENT specialist that the ear on Lisa's normal-looking side did not have an eardrum (the other side has no canal at all). When she was three and a half, an eardrum was sighted in her narrow, convoluted canal!

※

After successfully wearing his hearing aid for six months or so, Pete suddenly decided it made a terrific toy. He would whip it off his head, sail it across the room until it smacked into the wall, and watch me run to pick it up. All the while, he was laughing and cheering. When I told his teacher about this behavior, she encouraged me to punish him. I refused. I felt that would be a sure way to get him to dislike his hearing aid. As with most childhood stages, he outgrew the behavior and stopped doing it on his own.

※

One day when Pete was three, he decided to go swimming in his kiddie pool—clothes and all. He got into the pool and lay down on his belly. Unfortunately, his hearing aid was in a pocket on the front of his overalls. The aid spent the next three months at the manufacturer's factory drying out. Boys will be boys!

※

The first local audiologist we took our daughter to insisted that we take off her hearing aid in the car. (She said it was too much auditory stimulation for our daughter.) Whenever we took the hearing aid off in the car, though, she would scream for the duration of the ride. One day I decided to leave her hearing aid on. Not only didn't she scream, but she was happy.

�

Our insurance company wouldn't pay for the audiologist because she had an M.A. and not a doctorate, which was ridiculous.

✖

We have an annual fight with our insurance company about paying for hearing tests.

✖

The audiologist at our daughter's craniofacial center recommended a new hearing aid. I called the local audiologist and asked him about it. He explained that the aid wasn't appropriate for bone conduction. So I called back the audiologist at the craniofacial center. She referred me to the distributor, who referred me to an audiologist in Georgia. I called him and he told me a success story. He referred me to another audiologist in New Jersey. I called her and she told me she was unsuccessful in fitting the aid for bone conduction. By this time I was totally confused, but decided to try the aid anyway. It is the *best* aid our daughter has ever had.

✖

Pete was introduced to an auditory trainer during speech therapy. He was OK about wearing the box on his chest in the therapy room of the elementary school. However, he refused to walk out of the room with it on. Even at the age of three, he realized that the equipment drew attention to him in a way that he didn't want.

✖

Our son's first hearing aid was a body aid. It used one AA battery. When batteries went on sale, I would buy ten or twelve packages at a time, since I changed the battery at least once a week (wanting him always to have optimum sound). The clerk would usually ask why I was buying so many batteries. It took a *very* long time for me to feel comfortable answering that question. I associated hearing aids with elderly people, not children.

✖

Justine's speech is coming along quite well. She has the most trouble with "b" and "p" sounds.

✖

What strangers usually notice is how Kevin's condition affects his speech. We explain that Kevin can understand what they say but is still learning to talk.

Tyler, now four, has had speech therapy since age two. He recently had a pharyngeal flap operation. He has improved some, but is still very hard to understand. He drops beginning consonants and can't say "t's" or "d's." He's very stubborn and conscious of his speech problems. Frustration over speech sometimes affects his behavior.

Lyle has had speech therapy since he was two. We are working on articulation. His expressive language, however, is quite extensive.

Theresa has had to repeat her words *often* to others all her life. She is very patient with those who don't understand her.

When Lawrence was 22 months old, he could speak only about seven words. His speech therapist wanted to teach him sign language. I researched it and believed it wasn't appropriate for him. I believed that what he needed was more time and effort put into his speech therapy. I fought to have him retested for the early intervention program. This time he qualified, we switched therapists, and by two and a half he was saying 50 words.

My biggest concern is finding ways to overcome the sensory impairments so he can absorb knowledge.

Our insurance doesn't pay for speech therapy, but Medicaid does.

Because of his cleft, my son is over a year delayed in language. I worry that he may never speak correctly.

Clare has been in speech therapy since she was 22 months old. She is now almost three. She was slow to start speaking, and even now isn't real easy to understand. We can definitely see great improvement, though. She is now a non-stop talker. What really helped, I think, was putting her in preschool two days a week so she could be with other children. She has really picked up a lot at school.

❌

I feel that he is diagnosed as having "delayed speech" only because he was evaluated for such. His playmates who have "no conditions" are no more advanced than he is in speech.

❌

Emma has a very serious speech disorder connected with the paralysis of facial muscles (speech dysarthria). When people hear her speak, they stare. At three we began to teach her to express feelings with body language and words, since her ability for expression is extremely limited.

❌

I don't think the school provides the right kind of speech therapy for children with clefts. They really need individual attention and a speech therapist who really knows the difficulties a child with a cleft can have.

❌

My number one concern is that when she is in school she will be speaking well enough that she is not made fun of. We all know how critical children are.

❌

Although Kelly's speech is delayed, she focuses well on people's lips, works well with speech therapists, and will work for an hour without a break.

❌

Chapter 6

✻

Your Child's Education
By David M. Drazin, Ph.D.*

"You can't judge a book by its cover." This adage applies to people as well. A very good book with a plain cover may go unnoticed for years on the bookshelf. Likewise, people with less attractive physical appearances are often overlooked or prejudged negatively. This is especially tragic when it happens to children, who have difficulty expressing profound feelings of rejection, concerns about self-image, and other troubling emotions. Children with facial difference in particular may be tempted to hide their faces or may be unable to express certain emotions due to muscle weaknesses, missing bone structure, or different facial proportions.

Obviously, if a child with facial difference has negative feelings about her appearance or encounters negative reactions from classmates or teachers, it can make it harder for her to have a successful school experience. Other potential hurdles include hearing impairments, speech impairments, mental retardation (in some children with Apert syndrome), and frequent or lengthy absences due to surgeries.

Because of these possible stumbling blocks, many children with facial differences need at least some extra help to do their best at school. As Chapter 7 explains, many qualify for bona fide

---

* David M. Drazin is a licensed clinical psychologist. He received his doctorate from the California School of Professional Psychology, San Diego. Dr. Drazin provides evaluations and treatment of children, adolescents, and adults. He specializes in school consultations, ADHD, learning disabilities, couples and family therapy, and issues related to self-esteem. He is also the President of the Treacher Collins Foundation.

"special education" services under federal laws. Others may not need special education, but could benefit from minor changes to the learning environment, teaching styles, or curriculum.

Since the facial differences covered in this book are rare, you will probably have to educate school staff about your child's needs. Even though federal law may require that the school provide an "appropriate" education for your child, school staff may not know what is appropriate unless *you* tell them. This chapter will therefore help you understand what to look for in a classroom for your child, whether you are "shopping around" for a new school, or are trying to make her existing classroom more conducive to learning. It also offers suggestions on building acceptance of your child's differences.

The Right Classroom for Your Child

Several ingredients are essential to the success of *any* child at school. These include the staff, the curriculum, the makeup of the class, and the physical setup of the classroom and school. If any of these ingredients is not right for a particular student, she can have trouble making progress. For example, a student could have an outstanding, caring teacher, but still flounder at school if the course of studies was too advanced for her. Or a student might be intellectually capable of mastering the subjects taught, but still have trouble learning if she cannot hear what the teacher is saying or is seated too far from the blackboard to see. This section explains how to make sure the mix of ingredients in your child's classroom is right for her educational and emotional needs.

Who Teaches Your Child?

Having the right school staff on your child's side is perhaps *the* key to her success in school. If your child has experienced, caring teachers, therapists, counselors, and administrators, you can work together with them to overcome any obstacles that stand in the way of your child's progress.

Types of Professionals. Your child may need services from a variety of educational professionals, depending on her special needs. Your child's school should either have appropriate professionals on staff, or arrange to have these professionals visit the school as needed. The types of professionals children with facial differences may encounter at school include:

- *Speech-Language Pathologists:* If your child has a hearing impairment or speech problems, a speech-language pathologist can help her improve her communication skills. As a parent, it is important that you make sure the speech-language pathologist at school knows the cause of your child's speech impairment. Is it a result of a hearing impairment? Is it related to some physical problem with the structure of your child's face? If the therapist knows the cause, he or she should not try to make your child do things that are not effective or even possible. For example, the structure of your child's jaw or mouth may make it impossible for her to make the "s" sound until further growth or surgery occurs. See Chapter 5 for more information on speech therapy.

- *Occupational Therapists:* Children with motor difficulties due to webbed fingers or to underdeveloped thumbs or forearms may need the assistance of an occupational therapist (OT). An OT works to help children overcome difficulties with motor skills and with the activities of daily living, including self-help skills and play skills. The OT may use exercises to strengthen muscles or improve dexterity or eye-hand coordination. He or she may also suggest adaptations to utensils or other objects to make them easier for the child to manipulate. For example, the handle of a spoon or fork might be built up to make it easier to grasp. By improving a child's functioning in her environment, the OT helps promotes the child's independence, mastery, and self-worth.

- *Special Education Teachers or Learning Specialists:* There are a variety of reasons that children with facial differences may work with a special education teacher—a teacher trained in instructional techniques for children with special learning needs. Although most children with facial differences learn reading, math, spelling, and other academic subjects at the same time as other children, they may require special teaching techniques in some subjects because of hearing, speech, or motor impairments. And children with Apert syndrome and mental retardation may require special education in all or most subjects.

The special education teacher may provide instruction in your child's regular classroom, or in a separate classroom known as the Resource Room or Learning Center. For many children with facial difference, the main role of the special education teacher is to advise the regular classroom teacher about helpful techniques. For a child with hearing difficulties, the special education teacher might advise using visual aids, such as instructions written on the blackboard, and ensure that the child is seated where she can best hear the teacher. If your child's awareness of sounds is significantly affected by a hearing impairment, she may need specialized instruction in reading, spelling, and writing skills. For a child with speech difficulties, the special educator might suggest giving extra time to respond to questions, or allowing the child to communicate ideas through writing, a computer, or sign language. A child who has trouble with handwriting due to motor difficulties might need shortened assignments or technical assistance such as the use of a computer.

Some children with facial difference benefit from participating in social skills groups led by a special education teacher. Often, children with facial differences benefit when the special education teacher serves as a bridge for communication between the student, teachers, and parents. The special educator can be vital to a student's success in school.

- *School Psychologists.* The school psychologist may help plan and manage a program of psychological or educational services for a student and her parents. School psychologists often consult with teachers about the best ways to manage classroom behavior and strategies for dealing with emotional or behavior problems within the classroom. In addition, they administer psychological and educational tests.

- *Guidance Counselors:* Guidance counselors often have a variety of responsibilities, including counseling students and consulting with staff and parents. A guidance counselor can help your child learn strategies for dealing with problems with teachers or students. Often, guidance counselors step in and try to help resolve disputes. For example, if a particular child was constantly teasing your child, the counselor might bring the two children together and help them try to work out their differences. One middle school guidance counselor I know sets up class meetings with children with disabilities and their parents to convey information about the child's disability and ways of dealing with potential problems.

Whether your child is receiving services from one, many, or all of the professionals described above, they should all work as a team with the classroom teacher. Each needs to keep the others updated about what they are doing with your child, and consult with one another as appropriate. For example, your child might receive assistance from a speech and language pathologist, guidance counselor, and special educator for problems related to poor articulation of speech, hesitation to talk in class, and poor self-esteem. If so, it would be important to be clear about what each is supposed to do. All these professionals can help with your child's self-esteem, but the speech and language pathologist will need to tell the special educator, guidance counselor, and classroom teacher what makes speech difficult for your child and what speech goals your child is working on. Each of these professionals needs to know how he or she can help your child reach these speech goals, thereby reinforcing her self-esteem.

Staff Attitudes and Experience. It is not enough just to have the right kinds of teachers and therapists involved in your child's program. For your child to succeed at school, educators need to know how best to interact with your child and with one another. They must also either know how to meet your child's special needs, or be willing to find out.

The quality of a school is often directly related to how the teachers and administrators within that school treat each other and respect each other. How easily and efficiently they communicate with one another determines how productive and positive the environment is for students. You can begin to assess the climate of the school by interviewing the principal. He or she is the primary person who sets the atmosphere of the school. A principal who feels that it is important to include all children and looks at children's differences as an opportunity for everyone to learn and benefit would likely create a good atmosphere for your child.

In looking for the right teacher, you would ideally be able to choose from among several teachers with previous experience teaching students with your child's condition. Since this is unlikely to happen, you will need to focus instead on finding a teacher who is open to learning about your child and how best to meet her educational and social needs. A good place to start might be with questions such as: Have you previously had students with facial difference or appearance issues? If not, have you had children with disabilities in your classroom? Have you worked with hearing impaired children, and if not, are you interested in learning about hearing impairments? How do you feel about having my child in your classroom?

Some people might consider such questions as overly bold or as something you should be "hushed" about. But if said in a straightforward and caring way, you can learn a great deal that will help you evaluate whether the teacher is a good match for you and your child. For example, does the teacher truly seem interested in your child? Is the teacher open to your questions, or does he or she quickly dismiss them? Does the teacher seem anxious about answering your questions? Try your best to convey that your questioning is basically to learn more about how you and the teacher can help your child benefit the most from the classroom experience. If the teacher seems to perceive your questions as a challenge to his or her competence, this is likely not the best teacher for your child.

Although asking questions *is* essential, try not to overdo it. Choose your questions wisely, or you may be seen as a parent who is overly concerned or anxious. Most teachers want to help their students to the best of their ability, so ask your questions in a sensitive manner.

If possible, you may want to observe the teacher in action. Whether you will be permitted to do so depends on the particular teacher and school system. By observing, you can get a good idea of how the teacher responds to each child's needs and what the classroom atmosphere is like. The teacher's responsiveness may be especially important if your child needs classroom modifications that you need to negotiate with the teacher. For example, if your child tells you that the computers in the classroom that click bother her because of her hearing impairment, you may need to persuade the teacher to find computers that don't click. Or your child may tell you that she doesn't like to speak out in class because she is embarrassed by her speech impairment. The teacher might allow her to respond in writing or by using some other method.

If a teacher does not have much training and experience in teaching children with a hearing loss, it doesn't necessarily mean that she can't be a good teacher for your child. It is vital, however, that someone who understands your child's particular hearing problems assess her language abilities and make recommendations for teaching. This is because children with hearing loss may have difficulties reading and writing that are different than those of other children. These difficulties can look like a learning disability. If the teacher does not have much experience, she may be confused whether problems are due to hearing impairment or to a true learning disability (problems with memory, attending, sequencing, etc.). Mishearing or not hearing information is very different from hearing accurately but processing information incorrectly. Children can write only as well as they can think or speak. Thus, if they have a faulty language system which is largely based on what they hear, then the output (writing) becomes "faulty."

If you decide to request a certain teacher in the school system, be clear to the principal or other appropriate personnel about why you think this teacher is the best match for your child. For example, say "I like teacher A because he has some experience with children with special needs"; or, "I like teacher B because she is open to learning about my child's special issues."

What Will Your Child Learn?

Unless your child has a cognitive impairment, she should learn the same academic subjects at the same time as other students in her class. On top of everything else, however, she may also have special instruction in communication skills, motor skills, social skills, or in any other area where she has delays or difficulties related to her facial difference.

As Chapter 7 explains, if your child qualifies for special education under federal laws, her curriculum will be individually tailored to her special needs. The educational goals she will work on and the professionals who will work on them with her will be specified in a document called an Individualized Education Program (IEP).*

(If she is under three years of age, the document is called an Individualized Family Service Plan, or IFSP.) For example, speech and language goals might be: "Susie will add twenty new words to her vocabulary in the categories of home, family, toys, household items, and transportation." "Susie will learn to pronounce the "s" and "z" sounds correctly at the beginnings of words." To help Susie meet these goals, the speech and language pathologist would work directly with her and consult with teachers.

An example of a social or behavioral goal might be: "Matt will participate in group discussions, and eventually lead a group discussion." To help Matt reach this long-term goal, the IEP might specify short-term goals such as: "Matt will participate in class by raising his hand and asking questions." "Matt will make eye contact when speaking."

Besides listing goals, the IEP also specifies the amount of time your child will spend with the designated person for instruction in a specific subject. For example, she will meet with the speech therapist two times a week for one hour each time in a room outside the regular classroom.

If your child has an IEP, don't assume that the school is carrying out everything on the plan the way you might expect it to be. First, schools may fail to follow a child's IEP due to philosophical differences of school boards and school administration, budgetary pressures, and climate of the school. Second, under the law, staff are supposed to read the IEP and know what is in it. When a child goes into the next grade, however, this does not always happen. Make sure you meet with the new teacher before school begins so that the teacher will understand your child's educational needs. If the teacher has not had a chance to read the IEP, explain the most important features of it. For example, point out that the IEP stipulates that your child should be given preferential seating and be allowed to tape record lessons to help in reviewing the material later. If you have trouble understanding all the features of your child's IEP, ask the learning specialist, an advocate, or someone else who understands your child's needs to accompany you to this meeting. For more information about IEPs, see Chapter 7.

One other important consideration to keep in mind when evaluating your child's curriculum is whether it includes a unit on

---

**The exact name given this document may vary from place to place; for instance, you may hear it called an Individualized Education Plan.

disabilities. This unit should focus not just on your child or other classmates, but be broad in scope. Ideally, students at your child's school should be taught that everyone is different and that differences are an acceptable and valued part of this world. If students are not routinely taught about differences, you might suggest to the classroom teacher that she consider teaching about this topic. See the section on "Building Acceptance in the Classroom," below, for suggestions on helping children learn about differences.

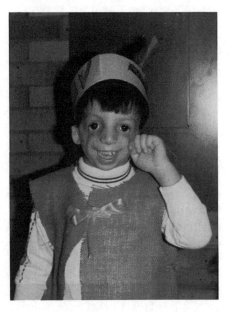

Who Is in Your Child's Class?

Your child's classmates can have a powerful impact on her progress and happiness at school. Ideally, classmates will be supportive and accepting of individual differences. Hopefully, a few of them will have similar interests and abilities as your child and will want to become friends.

For a child with facial difference, having supportive classmates is a big issue. For example, if your child feels absolutely tormented in class because she is constantly being teased, she may have sleeping problems and difficulty concentrating. She may be reluctant to speak up in class, especially if she has a speech impairment. Her social skills may suffer, and in extreme cases, she may develop a school phobia—a fear or avoidance of attending school.

Being in a classroom with children with similar academic abilities is also important. Obviously, if the majority of students in the class learn at a much faster or slower rate than your child, she will feel frustrated and may feel as if she does not have much in common with her classmates. In any classroom, it helps if the teacher uses a variety of teaching methods that enable all children to find their strengths and build on them. For example, some children learn better when information is presented orally, others when it is presented visually, and still others when they can have hands-on experience.

Thinking about these issues leads naturally to the question: should your child be mainstreamed? (Mainstreaming, also referred to as integration or inclusion, refers to the practice of including children with disabilities in classes with nondisabled children for at least part of the day.) There are degrees of mainstreaming. At one end of the continuum, a child might spend almost all her time with normally developing students, leaving them only for a short time to receive specialized instruction, such as occupational therapy, in a different room. At the opposite end of the continuum, a child might spend the majority of the school day in a classroom with children with disabilities, mingling with other students only during lunch and recess.

There are differences of opinion as to when it is best for a child to be in the regular school setting. Today it is generally agreed, however, that all efforts should be made to meet the child's needs within the regular school setting before trying a less mainstreamed setting. As Chapter 7 discusses, federal law actually requires that an education be provided in the "least restrictive environment"—that is, the setting that permits maximum contact with nondisabled students.

Usually, there is no reason for a child to go outside the mainstream simply because she has a facial difference. A child with a very significant hearing loss, however, might require instruction in a separate classroom for students with hearing impairments, or possibly in a school for deaf children. Rarely, a child whose behavior is out of control due to emotional or behavioral problems might also be placed in a separate classroom or school.

What Is the Actual Classroom or School Like?

If your child had a physical disability, there would be very obvious concerns about the layout and accessibility of her classroom and school. She would need ramps or elevators to go up stairs, and low sinks in the rest rooms. The need for adaptations to the school environment may be just as great, although not as obvious, for children with facial differences. For example, if your child has a hearing impairment, it may be a problem for her to be in a school where there are many metal lockers banging shut. Likewise, it would be better for her to be assigned to a classroom that has carpeting, to reduce the noise from desks and chairs scraping against the floor. Sometimes, of course, physical changes to the classroom or school may not be financially possible, or staff may balk at making them. As the next section discusses, however, you may be able to persuade the school to make changes that will benefit your child.

Requesting Accommodations

An accommodation is any change made to the regular school program that will help a child succeed. Accommodations might include changes in teaching or testing methods; services provided by a professional other than a classroom teacher; special technology or equipment; or changes to the physical classroom. As Chapter 7 explains, if your child qualifies for special education, her IEP will include accommodations she is supposed to receive. If your child is not receiving special education, or if you feel she needs accommodations not noted in her IEP, you should still feel free to request accommodations.

Accommodations for Hearing Impairment. Consider the case of eight-year-old Timmy. Timmy wears a hearing aid, but cannot localize sound (tell where the sound is coming from). Because of his hearing aid, he can't shut out background noise—he hears all sounds with the same degree of loudness. On the first day of third grade, he comes home from school and complains to his mother that he can't hear the teacher because "the classroom is noisy."

Because Timmy can't get all the information, he wonders what is being said or even whether others could be talking about him. Obviously, this could impair his self-confidence. In addition, some children can develop inappropriate ways of responding to other children if they must constantly wonder what has been said. They may act as if they understand, when they don't, or misbehave. They can also become self-conscious if they do not "get" a joke or worry that they aren't responding appropriately to what has been said.

When Timmy's mother arranges to meet with the teacher, she finds that there is no carpeting on the floor as in Timmy's earlier classrooms. She would like to request carpeting, but knows that it would take time before the basic staffing team, which recommends services and accommodations for students, could meet. Timmy's mother is concerned that time will pass and he will continue to be frustrated by missing information. After some discussion, she and the teacher think of putting rubber casters on the chair and table legs. This reduces background noise when other students move their chairs and desks. Timmy is also moved to the front row and the teacher writes important information on the board. The teacher makes sure she looks at Timmy when giving or repeating instructions, and makes sure that he understands the directions. She and Timmy agree on a signal (raising a hand) if he doesn't understand.

Timmy's story is an example of accommodations that can and should be made for a child with a hearing impairment. If Timmy resisted wearing his hearing aid, the teacher could make still other accommodations to help. For example, his mother could set up a time with the teacher to discuss having him present a "show and tell" about his hearing aid, as described in the section on "Building Acceptance in the Classroom," below. The teacher could also work with parents and other professionals to help Timmy understand why it is important to use the hearing aid, even though it may be uncomfortable and interfere with sports activities.

Do not expect the teacher to come up with needed accommodations on her own. First, your child's teacher may have little or no experience dealing with students with your child's condition. Second, the teacher probably has twenty or more children to supervise. It would be impossible for her to keep everyone's needs in mind all the time. As a psychologist and father of an eight-year-old who wears a bone conduction hearing aid, even I can't always remember how to handle his hearing problems. For instance, I know he can't localize sounds. Yet often when he calls out, "Dad, where are you?" I just say "over here," giving him no clue as to where I am.

The localizing issue comes up often at school, particularly in open places (on the playground, in the gym, on class trips). It is therefore a good idea to remind the teacher about localizing problems every once in a while. Do it in a nice way by letting the teacher know that you remind yourself frequently as well. Or ask the speech and language pathologist to talk to the teacher about your child's difficulties.

Accommodations for Speech Impairments. Children who know that their speech is less sophisticated than other children's tend to be inhibited about speaking up in school. They raise their hands less, use avoidance techniques such as lowering their head or averting their eyes so they won't be called on, and use shorter responses if they need to speak.

Depending on the age of your child, the teacher or speech and language pathologist could lead a class discussion about speech issues in general. The teacher or therapist could explain that some children have a hard time producing sounds and describe ways to communicate with someone who is having difficulty speaking. If your child is older, the teacher might prearrange a signal (such as touching her nose or putting her hand on her head) that would let your child know that she is about to be called on to answer in class. Or the teacher might always ask your child question number 7. These strategies would help your child prepare what she needs to say, plus she would not have to spend the rest of the time in class worrying about when she will be called on.

Another strategy is to set up cooperative learning activities with classmates who are more open and willing to work at understanding difficult speech. In cooperative learning, students work in small groups and cooperate on a common goal or task. This way, students get to know your child better, which speeds acceptance and the development of friendships. This, in turn, can lessen your child's anxiety about speaking.

Accommodations for Absences. Children with facial difference may miss a lot of school due to numerous operations. Your child should have an educational plan that takes these absences into account. It may make sense, for example, to devise a plan that allows your child to keep up with lessons through tutoring or closed circuit television. It is also a good idea to plan how you and the school can handle your child's anxiety about her absences. If she has several surgical procedures scheduled, she may be worrying about what she will miss, even if these things aren't that essential. It will probably help if you ask the teacher to talk to her and reassure her that she will be able to make up any important work she misses, and that some things will not need to be made up. If your child is older, she may want to tell the class what will be happening. If she is younger, you may want to come to class and help her explain what is going on. It all depends on your child's needs and how comfortable she is in calling attention to herself.

Accommodations for Motor Difficulties. As mentioned earlier, some children with Apert syndrome have webbed fingers, while some children with hemifacial microsomia or Nager syndrome have underdeveloped thumbs or forearms. Either of these

problems may contribute to fine motor problems, especially with handwriting. If your child can't write quickly or legibly enough to finish all her class work or to keep up with the teacher when taking notes, a variety of accommodations can help. These include: assigning your child fewer problems to complete in class; allowing her to use a computer with or without a specialized keyboard for writing assignments; allowing her to respond orally to test questions rather than writing the answer; letting her take notes by tape recording lectures, photocopying another student's notes, or having the teacher provide her with lecture notes.

In addition, the occupational therapist and special educator should work with your child to help her improve her motor skills and to suggest other helpful accommodations.

In thinking about accommodations, ask your child to tell you what specific problems she is having in the classroom and what she thinks might help. Try to get this input without first telling her what *you* think it would make sense to do. One of the mistakes parents, teachers, and other adults often make is to assume what a child may be feeling or thinking. Your child is living her life and you and her teachers need to understand *her* needs.

Whatever your child's hearing, speech, or other needs may be, be sure to educate school staff about them. Explain your child's special needs clearly and discuss how they may affect her social and academic performance. Let them know that just because your child has facial or other physical differences, she does not necessarily have a learning disability or mental retardation. Usually it is best if you can sit down and talk with the teaching staff about these issues. That way you can answer their questions and concerns on the spot. If you have trouble scheduling time for a meeting or feel more comfortable writing a note or letter, this is also an acceptable way to communicate. Ideally, you should try to talk with the teachers before the beginning of the school year, or as soon as possible after school starts.

Some teachers and staff will probably be very responsive and eager to work with you to find solutions to problems. Others may show little interest. If you simply cannot convince school staff to make needed accommodations, your first option may be to go to the principal or school superintendent and ask for their assistance. If they are unable to help, your next step depends on whether your child is eligible for special education under the Individuals with Disabilities Education Act (IDEA). If she is, you can initiate a due process hearing, as described in Chapter 7.

If your child is not eligible under IDEA, you can pursue her rights to an appropriate education under Section 504 of the Rehabilitation Act of 1973. This law prohibits discrimination against persons with disabilities by any agency (including schools) that receives federal funding. Under the law, a person with disabilities is someone with an impairment that substantially limits one or more "major life activities," which include "caring for one's self, performing manual tasks, walking, seeing, hearing, speaking, breathing, learning, and working." Chapter 7 provides more information about using Section 504 to obtain needed accommodations.

Building Acceptance in the Classroom

Most children are occasionally teased at school, whether in fun or maliciously. Obviously, children with facial difference are much more vulnerable to teasing than usual. We live in a world where everyone is judged by how they look, where the media and publications glorify people with "good looks."

For parents and teachers to deal with teasing, they need to first accept that it is a very difficult issue. There is no easy solution. We often ask children to ignore what people say, or walk away. We tell children that if they do so, eventually the teasing will stop. Sometimes it does, and sometimes it doesn't. We tell children that the kids who are teasing them have their own set of problems and feel insecure or whatever, but this still doesn't always take the hurt away from their comments.

Don't feel that you have to come up with an instant solution to teasing or to arm your child with some great strategy. If your seven-year-old comes home in tears because some kids at school were poking fun at her face, the best thing you can do at that point is to be supportive and loving. Your child needs to know first that you love her unconditionally and completely. After your child has calmed down, you should try to understand what happened. If your child doesn't want to talk about it in detail, don't force her to do so. You may want to tell your child that you are going to discuss the incident with the teacher or some other school staff so they can be aware of the problem and make sure it doesn't continue to happen.

When you are not facing a crisis situation, you can discuss various ways of dealing with teasing with your child. Make sure you let her know, however, that these strategies might or might not work, and that she should let you know afterwards how things turned out. Otherwise, if you tell your child to react a certain way and it doesn't work, she may feel even more upset and helpless. Strategies you may want to suggest include ignoring the teasing, walking away, being assertive with the other person, or asking an adult at school to let the bullying child know that this is unacceptable behavior. See Chapter 4 for more information on responding to questions and comments.

The best way to control teasing at school is for staff to make sure that the school is as free from bullying as possible. If teasing is a problem at your child's school, you may want to suggest that staff participate in training that will help them create a better atmosphere at school. Teachers should know and convey the belief that differences are part of our world and are OK. They should also let students know that teasing or hurtful comments are unacceptable. Students should treat one another with respect.

To help students learn to respect one another, teachers should make sure that every child in the class gets to know one another on a one-to-one or small group basis. This is because studies have found that children are rejected more often when others base their impression on visual appearance alone, and don't see the child as a whole person. When a child gets to know another child on a more intimate basis, the notion of what that child must be like based on what she looks like changes.

In preschool and early elementary school grades, teachers may want to formally teach their students about differences. Key ingredients for teaching children of this age about differences include:

1. Fostering a trusting relationship between teacher and students. This trusting relationship can only thrive if the

teacher treats every student with respect and encourages their endeavors.

2. Using picture books or puppet shows that deal with the theme of difference. Some useful books are included in the Reading List.

3. Encouraging the use of non-sexist language in the classroom. For example, terms such as mail carrier, fire fighter, and police officer should be used. Animals should be referred to as "she" as well as "he." The word "she" can be added to songs in which only "he" is mentioned.

4. If dolls are used in the classroom, making sure that there are a variety of types of dolls.

5. For younger children, learning songs that address differences. "The World Is a Rainbow," from the album *We All Live Together*, Vol. 2 (Little House Music) is a good example of such a song. You may also encounter appropriate songs on television shows such as *Barney* and *Sesame Street*.

6. Talking about the idea that all families are different.

You or your child may also want to give a short presentation to familiarize her class with facial differences. Kids love this kind of information and are eager and interested listeners and learners. Often, they ask very perceptive questions. You should only suggest this type of presentation, however, if your child feels comfortable with the idea. If she is resistant to getting up in front of the class and talking about herself, respect her wishes.

When a problem situation arises, teachers should intervene constructively. For example, if a teacher overhears another student asking a classmate about her "funny lip," the teacher should first listen to determine whether the remark was made in a curious or hurtful manner. If the other student was simply curious, the teacher may not need to intervene if the child with facial difference can explain her difference without feeling hurt. Or the teacher could help with an explanation in a matter-of-fact way. Handling curious questions in a matter-of-fact way helps children learn that differences are a part of life and questions about differences are OK.

If teachers notice hurtful teasing or insensitive questioning going on, they should intervene. A teacher might tell the student that if she is curious about Kathy's differences, she can ask the question in a more appropriate way. The teacher could then model a better way of asking the question. The teacher might also ask a guidance counselor or other staff member to speak to the class about why teasing can be hurtful. In addition, teachers should let all students know that there are clear rules and consequences for mean-spirited teasing. Repeat offenders might have privileges taken away and be sent to the principal's office for a discussion with the principal and their parents. Teachers should also let peers know that it is not OK to encourage or ignore bullying behavior.

Although the goal is to end teasing by teaching the children who are teasing to stop, this goal is not always met. In spite of the best efforts of parents and teachers, some children may continue to say hurtful or mean things. We must remember that all children learn perceptions from their families and communities, and these perceptions may be difficult to change. In these situations, you might ask that your child or the children who are the main abusers be placed in a different class. You and the school staff could also help your child avoid being alone during less supervised times such as during recess or walking to and from school.

Early Intervention, Day Care, and Preschool

As Chapter 7 explains, many children with facial difference are eligible for *early intervention*—special therapies and other services for children under the age of three that are aimed at minimizing delays from hearing impairments or other potentially disabling conditions. If your child is in an early intervention program, you might not have to worry about many of the issues discussed in this chapter. Your child may or may not encounter teasing, depending on your child's age, the quality of the program, and the other children and families participating in the program. Staff should be willing to provide most accommodations you request, as their job *is* to provide accommodations and special services to infants and toddlers. If you have a choice of programs, however, you may want to shop around for teachers and therapists with the experience and attitudes described above.

Finding a child care setting that you feel comfortable with may be another matter. Indeed, finding good daycare is a difficult dilemma for many parents, including those whose children do not have any special needs. We all want to find daycare that will provide a safe and nurturing environment—which can be easier said than done.

To find a good daycare setting, you can follow many of the same steps that other parents do. You can meet with the daycare director or staff and ask to observe staff and kids during a typical day. Asking other parents their experiences at the daycare can be helpful as well. Because the way the daycare staff responds to differences will be critical, it will be important to find out as much as you can about how they would handle questions that come up about your child. You can get a good feel for this from the questions they ask you, their responses to your questions, and their experience and willingness to work with children with differences.

If your child uses a feeding tube, apnea monitor, or other technology, you will obviously need to look harder to identify a daycare setting suited for your child. Some daycare centers might have a nurse on staff. More often, however, the daycare may accept your child into their program but request that a full-time aide, health nurse, or a feeding specialist come to their facility to help in the areas that they do not feel trained to do. A child with a feeding tube may need someone to come during scheduled feeding times, or a child with a tracheostomy may need someone to be there throughout the day. In some cases, the local school system or early intervention program may provide this service free of charge. Contact your early intervention program or state department of education to find out whether funding for this type of assistance is available.

Once you have found an appropriate daycare program for your child, you might worry about whether your child will be accepted by other children or their parents. The good news is that young children are often very accepting. If any social difficulties arise, consultation from a psychologist or other counselor may help. As usual, good communication between your daycare providers and yourself will be important.

As your child moves on to preschool, the issues you encounter may depend on why and where your child is going to preschool. For example, she might receive speech therapy, assistance from a full-time aide, or other special services if she qualifies for special education. She may go to a school or other center, attending "class" with other preschoolers with disabilities. If so, things may go as smoothly as in an early intervention program. Some children with facial difference may go to a typical public or private preschool instead of, or in addition to, receiving special education services in a segregated setting. If so, the problems they run into may be similar to those encountered in day care.

Conclusion

You probably have many concerns about your child's school experience. You may worry that she will have trouble being accepted, or worse, teased or socially isolated. You may wonder how hearing, speech, or other impairments may affect her ability to keep up with her class. And it is true that your child may face special challenges. Just like all children, however, children with facial differences can have very positive experiences in school as well as extremely negative ones.

Fortunately, there are many things that you as a parent can do that can and will make a difference. Right from the start, you can help your child develop a healthy self-esteem by loving her completely. You can treat her like any child, setting appropriate limits and being available to her when she has questions about the world and herself.

If your child has good self-esteem, there is no reason your child cannot make good progress in school and find joy in both learning and friendships. My eight-year-old son, for instance, has had five operations to recreate his ears. He often tells me that other children at school ask him about his ears. He matter-of-factly tells them he was born with small ears and that he had operations to make these new ones. When they ask about his hearing aid, he simply states that he wears it because he needs help with hearing. Thus far, he seems to be able to handle questions matter-of-factly—not surprising, as he has a healthy self-esteem. You, too, can help your child feel good about herself, and, in the process, contribute to her academic and social progress at school.

Parent Statements

Early intervention has been a lifesaver. I needed the coaching, especially in the area of feeding and oral-motor therapy. We had home visits from school teachers from age six months, and she started going to school in a hearing impaired program when she was eighteen months old. It was overwhelming for me to know where to start, so having the different specialists to consult was wonderful. I did have to remind myself I was doing the best I could and had to set priorities, because it would have been impossible to accomplish all the treatments, therapies, exercises, etc. that were recommended.

✖

David received home intervention for his speech and language. We never had any problems with the program, except that they had a big overload of children with special needs and it was hard to reach goals in a timely manner.

✖

Michael is involved with Easter Seals's Infant Development Program, a speech and hearing center, physical therapy, and occupational therapy. We have found these programs enlightening and encouraging.

✖

The most valuable thing about early intervention was that it connected me as a parent with professionals and other parents.

✖

Early intervention was a safe, secure environment where other special-needs families shared their fears and worked together for their child.

✖

Early intervention helps our son open up to new activities. He learns so much through playing with other children and adults. Most of all, he loves every minute of it.

✖

Laura saw a PT, OT, and infant educator for two years. They were wonderful with her and with us. I did get frustrated with some of the testing, though. For example, the infant educator would give

Laura a manipulative test. The test required Laura to stack blocks—which she could do! But she never passed the test, because the test required her to do it with one hand. Laura used two because she didn't have a wide enough space between her fingers and thumb to grasp the block. The test just was not adaptable to kids with Apert syndrome.

�֍

When he started preschool, we brought in a skull from our local dentist and photos of David before his surgery. We told the children what the doctors did and why he has scars on his head. The children accepted it all very innocently and he's had no problems at school.

✖

Laura is now in kindergarten. She is starting to read, can write legibly, can use scissors, and can run, walk, hop on one foot, and balance on one foot. She has problems coloring in lines and tying shoes. We work with her shoulder and finger restrictions, but we expect her to do everything her sister and brother do. How is up to her, but we insist that she try. We don't allow "I can't," but emphasize "try."

✖

Because of our son's looks and his vision, hearing, and speech problems, the school greatly underestimates his intelligence and under-challenges him. Some teachers catch on quick, but others never do "get it." I home-schooled him one year for this reason and would do it again.

✖

We placed Henry in an alternative class (grades one-three) this year. It took the first three-quarters of the year for him to become part of the class, but he was in pain because of muscle contractions and using a wheelchair because of his club feet. It's better now that he has had an operation and is out of the wheelchair! He mostly plays with first-grade girls. He's intimidated by the size and strength of kids his own age. His only same-age friend has muscular dystrophy and is in a wheelchair.

✖

School is getting more difficult to deal with. She will be in eighth grade this year. Last year her IEP goals were not met by school officials as they should have been. We got a lot of run-around.

✖

We have broken ground in our district by pushing them to the wall on the issue of including our child in regular education.

✖

Jenny's school has been great to her. She is just another student to them, and is doing very well. In most subjects, she is getting A's or B's. I find athletic coaches and teachers tend to have a "soft spot" for her.

✖

Special education has been limited to speech therapy and OT. Both have been acceptable, as we live in an area with a very small school district and ample school budget. However, this last month we had psychoeducational testing completed because Emma has begun to be unhappy at school. She is losing friendships and feels very alone. The testing found her to be depressed, so we worked out a plan to improve her school experience next year, within the regular classroom. Her educational testing reflected a good student, but her mental state isn't allowing her to work to her fullest. In fourth grade, she tested at eighth grade in reading, tenth grade in writing, and eleventh grade in knowledge of music, art, and literature!

✖

Two years in a row, the school system called upon my husband and me to appear before the school principal and justify Robert's absences—even though we always notified the school and had letters from the physicians regarding his medical problems. They apologized, but said this was "their policy" on checking up on children with frequent absences. Give me a break!

✖

Every year we have written letters to the elementary school explaining our daughter's needs for the next year. Because she has hearing difficulties and uses two aids, she needs preferential seating and a quiet environment.

✖

Last year, several staff members taught a unit on differences, and included hearing impairments and learning disorders. The speech therapist also gave a presentation about Emma's differences, and the children asked questions. As hard as that was for Emma, I think it gave her a sense of relief.

�

My son is in special ed in a learning center. He is very well accepted there by his peers and by the teachers and other staff.

✖

When they get past the initial surprise, classmates accept my son for who he is. Therefore, his friendships are built on his personality and not his appearance.

✖

All children are laughed at school. But having a different facial appearance really makes you open to teasing.

✖

Jamie has been in the same regular school since preschool, so he has an accepting group of children who know and like him.

✖

Chapter 7

Legal Rights & Health Insurance

By Hope Charkins, M.S.W., and David M. Drazin, Ph.D.

"What is my child entitled to under the law?"

Most parents of young children probably give very little thought to this question. They assume that the same laws that apply to them will also apply to their children, and leave it at that.

When you have a child with a facial difference, however, learning the answers to this question is very important. One reason is that there are laws that may entitle your child and family to special services and assistance. It's unlikely, though, that anyone will seek you out to tell you about all these laws. Instead, it is up to you to find out what the laws say and then make sure that your child receives everything he is entitled to. Another reason to become educated about your child's legal rights is that he could possibly be denied some rights because of his facial difference. One good way to prevent this from happening is to know about the laws prohibiting discrimination. In addition, children with facial difference and their families may have a great deal of trouble getting and keeping health insurance. Learning whether there are any laws that can help with these problems is obviously a good idea.

As you read through this chapter, remember that laws, policies, and procedures change and the interpretation may differ from state to state. To keep abreast of these changes, it is wise to join or periodically contact support organizations that can keep you informed. The staff of the Parent Information and Training Centers are knowledgeable about anti-discrimination laws and government benefits in your state. The staff of the American Cleft Palate-Craniofacial Association maintains information about health insurance laws and regulations for conditions of facial difference. These and other organizations listed in the Resource Guide have fact sheets; can help you understand and interpret the laws, policies, and procedures; and welcome your interest, phone call, or letter.

YOUR CHILD'S EDUCATIONAL RIGHTS

As Chapter 6 explains, children with facial difference might need therapies or extra support to assist them in learning and attending school. They might also need extra assistance as infants and toddlers to help them optimize their early development. In addition, you and your family may need support and guidance to help you learn about your child's condition of facial difference, how it affects his learning, and what you can do to help him learn. If your child's condition impairs his ability to hear, to see, to breathe, to eat, to learn, or to acquire social skills, there are several federal laws that may help. Some children with facial difference qualify for assistance under The Individuals with Disabilities Education Act (IDEA), if their disability affects the acquisition of basic skills. Children who have fewer difficulties learning skills may need to use Section 504 of the Rehabilitation Act of 1973 to get the educational assistance they need.

The Individuals with Disabilities Education Act (IDEA)

In 1970, almost all 50 states had laws exempting children with disabling conditions from receiving public education. Then, in 1971, the PARC case (Pennsylvania Association for the Retarded vs. the Commonwealth of Pennsylvania) established the right of children with mental retardation in that state to a free public education. Many similar lawsuits were quickly filed in other states. By 1977, 49 states had laws requiring that public educations be provided for children with disabilities. What accounted for this change of the tide? It was the groundswell of public advocacy resulting in the 1975 enactment of Public Law 94–142, the Education for All Handicapped Children Act.

Since 1975, P.L. 94–142 has been re-authorized and amended several times. It is now known as the Individuals with Disabilities Education Act (IDEA), or Public Law 101–476. Section B of the law provides for educational services for children ages 3–21, while Section H provides for services for infants and toddlers from birth through 2 years of age.

Under IDEA, the federal government provides funding through the Department of Education to each state that meets a variety of federal standards for the education of children with disabilities. To qualify for these federal funds, the state must assure that all children with disabilities have access to and receive "a free appropriate public education." (This phrase is explained below.) Since all states want to receive federal funding, they all currently provide publicly funded special education.

It is important to understand that IDEA establishes only the minimum requirements for special education (and early intervention) programs. It does not require states to adopt an ideal educational program for your child with facial difference, or for any other child with a disabling condition. States can, however, create programs that exceed the minimum requirements of the federal law. The interpretation of the law varies from state to state, and sometimes from school district to school district within a state.

Some of the most important provisions of the law as it applies to children over 3 years of age are discussed in this section. The next section covers early intervention services for children under 3.

Coverage. To be eligible for special education services under IDEA, a child must have one or more of the disabilities specified in the law. Facial difference is not specifically listed as one of these disabling conditions. However, several disabilities that often accompany a facial difference *are* listed. These include hearing impairment, speech and/or language impairment or delay, and "other health impaired." Other health impaired means that your child has a documented medical condition that interferes with his ability to learn basic skills. It may apply, for example, if your child has a condition that interferes with breathing or eating. The section on "Qualifying for Services under IDEA" explains how children are evaluated to determine whether they are eligible.

"Free Appropriate Public Education." The requirement that children with disabling conditions receive a free appropriate public education is at the core of the law. Simply stated, it means that each child with a disabling condition is entitled to an education at public expense that takes into account his abilities and special needs. You should know, however, that exactly how "free" and "appropriate" are interpreted can vary from state to state and school to school.

A "free" public education means that your child receives every aspect of the educational program he needs at no cost to you. For most children with facial difference, this means they will attend a public school and receive any special services they need at this school. Occasionally, the only suitable school for a child with facial difference is a private school. This may be the case if the student also has another disabling condition such as a severe emotional or behavioral disturbance and needs specialized services to address the emotional/behavioral disturbance. If the school district approves this placement as being appropriate, it must pay the full cost of attending such a school. If the school district does not first approve the placement, however, the parents will be obligated to pay the costs if they enroll their child.

An "appropriate" education means that each child with a disabling condition has access to specialized educational services that are individually designed to benefit that child. It does *not*, however, guarantee that the education your child is offered is equal to that given to other children, or that it is the best quality education. This makes it critically important for you to monitor your child's education to make sure that it is appropriate to his needs. As explained below in the section on Individualized Education Programs (IEPs), the law allows you to have a great deal of input about what goes into your child's education plan.

"Special Education and Related Services." IDEA specifies that an appropriate education includes special education and related services. "Special education" means instruction that is specially designed to meet a child's unique needs and disabilities. It can be provided in a public or private school, at home, in the hospital, or some other appropriate setting. "Related services" are any supportive or therapeutic services a child needs to benefit from special education. Related services needed by a child with facial difference might include transportation to and from school, occupational therapy, speech and language therapy, nursing support, or psychological counseling. Related services do *not* include strictly medical services which can only be provided by a physician or hospital, unless they are needed for diagnostic purposes. For example, your child may need to have an audiological or neurological evaluation to determine how best to meet his educational needs.

"Least Restrictive Environment." IDEA specifies that children with disabilities must be educated "to the maximum extent appropriate" in the least restrictive environment (LRE)—that is, in the setting that allows them to spend the most time with children who do not have disabilities. This provision of the law is meant to keep children with disabling conditions from being isolated from their nondisabled peers, as frequently happened in the past.

If your child does not have severe mental retardation or severe learning disabilities, the least restrictive environment for him will probably be the regular neighborhood school in an age-appropriate classroom. To receive supplemental assistance with his special needs, such as speech and language therapy, he may stay in the classroom and receive services there, or briefly leave it to go to a therapy or resource room.

The idea of least restrictive environment is closely entwined with the concepts of mainstreaming, integration, and inclusion. These terms go in and out of favor and have had different meanings at different times. Basically, however, they all refer to the practice of including children with disabling conditions in at least some school activities with other children. At present, the terms "full inclusion" or "unified school" are generally used to mean that students with disabling conditions do everything in the same classroom with other students.

Individualized Education Program (IEP). The legislation for IDEA is uniquely worded to carefully spell out the rights of parents. The right of parents to contribute to their child's Individualized Education Program (IEP) is a notable feature. The IEP is a written document which describes:

- your child's present level of development;

- short- and long-term goals for your child in every academic or developmental area in which he is having difficulties (see below for examples of goals);
- the specific services (speech and language therapy, occupational therapy) your child will receive to help him meet his goals;
- the date services will begin and an anticipated ending date;
- what evaluation method(s) will be used to determine if goals are being met;

- the extent to which your child will participate in the activities of a regular classroom.

You and your child's teachers will jointly develop an IEP when your child is first determined to be eligible for special education. Thereafter, it will be updated at least once a year—or sooner, if you or your child's teachers request.

Before developing your child's IEP, it might be helpful to sit down with teachers and administrators from your child's school district to discuss his needs and to inquire about programs and services which are currently available. Then, ask if you can visit these programs and observe the services on a typical day. You might also request individual meetings with therapists and the school nurse to learn their background in working with children with your child's condition. Do not assume that school personnel will have an understanding of your child's facial difference and his needs. Be prepared to educate them. The more clearly they understand that your child is much more than a face, a hearing aid, or a shortened forearm, the easier it should be to obtain the services and programs your child might need.

Before you go to the first IEP meeting, prepare a list of the goals you think it is important for your child to work on. For example, a long-term goal for your child might be: "Joseph will improve his math skills." A short-term objective that could be specified to help him reach the long-term goal is: "Joseph will learn the multiplication tables 1–9." If your child needs help with social skills, a long-term goal might be: "Joseph will make a good friend at school." Short-term objectives leading up to that goal might be: "Joseph will make eye contact when speaking and listening"; "He will initiate conversation with peers"; "He will sit with others at lunch." It is certainly not up to you to come up with all the goals and objectives for your child or to figure out how to phrase them. If you have a general idea of the goals that are important for your child, however, you can ensure that your opinions are taken into account when the IEP is developed.

Another important step to take before attending the IEP meeting is to decide what services and programs you think your child should receive and your rationale for why this is important. Contact your child's craniofacial team to discuss what should and should not appear on your list and why. Some of the team professionals who might be especially helpful to you are the psychologist, speech-language pathologist, developmental experts, occupational or physical therapist, physicians, and others. Obtain copies of any evaluations which would support the items on your list. In compiling all of this information, you may find that you are learning more about your child and his condition of facial difference. So much the better. Many school personnel will have read the evaluations from your child's doctors, as well as the evaluations done by the school. However, the more clearly you understand this information, the more clearly you can explain it to school personnel at the IEP meeting, if needed.

Bear in mind that the services your child receives and the setting he receives them in should be determined based on his needs, not simply on what is currently available through the school district. So, don't limit your requests to services or programs you observed in local schools. For example, if you think your child needs skilled nursing services to assist with his tracheostomy or feeding tube, you should request that service even if no other student is presently receiving it. If an accommodation is required in your child's IEP or Section 504 plan, your school must provide it.

At the IEP meeting, you will ideally work as part of the team with the teachers and school officials. Once your child is older, he may also want to be part of this team, so he can provide his own input about his needs and goals. In the meantime, you will need to be your child's primary advocate. Do not feel intimidated by the IEP process or worry that you are taking up too much of the school personnel's time. It is especially important that you be prepared to explain your child's facial difference, associated problems such as syndactyly or vision impairments, assistive devices that he uses, and the relationship of his condition to his intellectual functioning.

If school staff have questions about your child's intellectual functioning that you feel you cannot adequately answer, contact the craniofacial center for support. If the school is not satisfied with the information provided by the craniofacial center, ask for an evaluation to determine your child's cognitive ability. Most likely, they will give your child an IQ (intelligence quotient) test to determine his cognitive strengths and weaknesses. It should satisfy any lingering questions as to whether your child has mental retardation.

Here are some tips to keep in mind when attending an IEP meeting:

1. Try not to attend IEP meetings alone, especially if you are concerned that you may miss some information or don't feel comfortable giving your input. A lot of information will be discussed, and you may not remember everything, or remember it accurately afterwards. Bring along someone who understands your child's needs and can help you make sure school personnel understand these needs so that he receives the services and programs he needs. You might want to bring your spouse, another parent, an advocate, or one of your child's health care professionals.

2. If your child will be receiving services from more than one school professional or more than one program, pay close attention to everyone's role in responding to your child's needs. Perhaps a speech-language pathologist will be focusing on your child's articulation, and a learning specialist (or special education teacher) will be assisting with writing skills. If more than one person is involved, there might be a mix-up as to who is doing what. Be clear about who will be your child's case manager or service coordinator—the person responsible for overseeing and coordinating all the services he receives. That way you can deal directly with the case manager if you have questions about who is working on what with your child.

3. If a service or program is not written on your child's IEP form, he may not receive it, even if it is discussed at the

meeting. Consequently, make sure the IEP addresses every service your child is to receive.

4. Be prepared to advocate for your child. Although many IEP meetings run smoothly and cordially, sometimes there is a difference of opinion between parents and school personnel. There may also be outside factors which affect the way school personnel respond to your child's needs. For example, there may be a shortage of occupational therapists in the school district, or a cut in the education budget for the coming year. You must therefore be clear about your expectations and be prepared to document your position. It is your right to do so.

It may take several meetings to work out all the details of your child's IEP. When the IEP is complete, school personnel will sign it, and you will be asked to do so also. If you are not satisfied with the IEP, you have the right to withhold consent by not signing it. In the event of this type of dispute, the easiest and least costly way to settle it is to go back to the IEP meeting and re-negotiate with school personnel. If you still can't agree about the contents of your child's IEP, you may wish to request mediation, or a due process hearing, as described below.

Mediation. Mediation refers to a discussion held before one or more neutral individuals in an attempt to resolve a dispute between the school system and a family. Many states provide the opportunity for parents and schools to seek mediation at no cost to either party. In fact, some states actually *require* mediation efforts before a due process hearing can occur. If changes currently proposed to the re-authorization of IDEA pass, all states will have mediation available.

Due Process Hearing. If mediation fails, or if your state does not offer mediation services, you may want to request a due process hearing to resolve a dispute with the school system. Under the law, parents have the right to formally appeal anything in the educational plan proposed by the school district that may result in their child receiving a less-than-appropriate education. For example, you may file an appeal if you and the school cannot agree on what your child's IEP should contain. Or you may challenge the school's decision not to fully include your child in an age-appropriate classroom.

Usually, to request mediation or a due process hearing, you can send a letter to the school district's director of special education or

240 • Legal Rights & Health Insurance

to the state department of education. In the letter, explain the nature of the dispute and request a "due process" hearing. Double check with a local advocacy group, such as the Parent Information and Training Center, to see if this is how a hearing is requested in your school district. If you are unable to obtain a copy from your local special education director, the advocacy group may also be able to give you an outline of the appeals process and a copy of IDEA. In addition, they may be able to refer you to an advocate or other parents who have participated in either mediation or due process hearings.

During a due process hearing, you have the right to a lawyer and to cross-examine and call witnesses (for example, a member of your child's craniofacial team or an independent psychologist). You and the school district's representatives will testify before an impartial hearing officer—someone who has no stake in the outcome of the case. He or she will listen to the evidence presented by each side, and then render a decision. If the hearing officer decides that you are right—that your child *would* receive an inappropriate education if the school district doesn't do as you ask—then the school will be ordered to do as you request. In addition, the school will have to pay for any attorney's fees you have incurred.

If you disagree with the results of the hearing, you can appeal, bringing a lawsuit in state or federal court. Since these options can be costly and time-consuming, however, it is definitely preferable to make every attempt to resolve disagreements by informal negotiations with the school personnel.

While you pursue a due process hearing or lawsuit, the law requires that your child remain in his last agreed-upon educational program. This may work to your advantage or disadvantage, depending on whether or not you are satisfied with this program. For example, you might request a hearing because you believe your child still needs speech therapy, but the school district no longer wants to provide the therapy your child is receiving in his present program. In this case, the school would have to continue providing speech therapy until the hearing officer renders a decision.

Early Intervention Services under IDEA

Children with facial difference and their families usually need some special coordinated support beginning at birth so they can start life on a positive and strong footing. The child himself may need speech and language, occupational, or other therapies to help minimize delays that could otherwise result from his condition. And the parents may need help obtaining equipment and devices, connecting with other families, or learning how to navigate the health care system. This whole package of support, generally provided until the child turns three, is known as early intervention.

Early intervention services are mandated by the same law that provides for the education of school-aged children with disabilities—the IDEA. The specifications regarding early intervention services, however, are found in Part H of the law, while those for special education services are found in Part B.

Most of the rights and safeguards established by IDEA for older children with disabilities also apply to infants and toddlers. For example, families of children in early intervention have the same right to due process. One major difference, however, is that states have more leeway in deciding how to implement their early intervention programs than they do with special education programs. This is because services for infants and toddlers often involve many more people than just school personnel—medical professionals, day care workers, parents, etc. Consequently, states have more say in determining who is eligible for early intervention, who is responsible for paying for the services, what services will be offered, and where the services will be provided.

Generally, staff in early intervention programs represent many different disciplines—education, health, mental health, and social services. Who sees your child will depend on his individual needs. Professionals who might be on the team of a child with facial difference include a nutritionist, audiologist, speech-language pathologist, occupational therapist, physical therapist, medical social worker, visiting nurse, teacher of children with hearing impairments, and psychologist. The team of professionals that works with your child may be referred to as a multidisciplinary, interdisciplinary, or transdisciplinary team.

States and individual school districts often have a great deal of latitude in deciding where services will be provided. Therapists and other professionals may visit the family's home to work with the child in his natural environment. Or parents may bring their child to a "center"—a school, hospital, office, or other building—to receive services. Who receives services where may be up to the school district. For example, medically fragile children, or children of a certain age, may generally receive services at home, while everyone else goes to a center. Or, parents may be given a choice of home-based or center-based services.

Individualized Family Service Plan (IFSP). Details about who will provide what services to your child and where are described in a document called the Individualized Family Service Plan (IFSP). This document is similar to the IEP used for older children. It lists long-term and short-term goals for the child, and specifies what services will be provided and how often to enable the child to reach his goals.

Like the IEP, the IFSP is developed by professionals and parents working together. If anything, parents often have more input

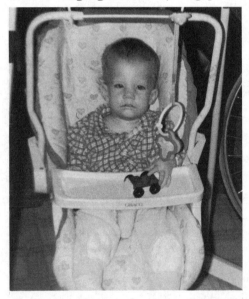

in creating the IFSP than they do with the IEP. This is because the IFSP emphasizes a family-centered philosophy for providing services. That is, the focus is on providing services for the family as a whole, rather than on addressing only the needs of the child, as the IEP does. For example, the IFSP might include family support or respite services for the parents, in addition to special therapy and instruction for the child.

In working together on the IFSP, families and professionals ideally come to see each other as partners. It is expected that, over time, the relationship will develop into a trusting and respectful partnership. To that end, the IFSP is supposed to:

- recognize and build on family strengths (for example, a family that has an extensive network of extended family members willing to help will probably not need as much help building their child's social skills as a socially isolated family);
- respect family beliefs and values;

- honor the family's choices and encourage and enable their hopes and aspirations.

IFSPs are updated or re-written at least twice a year, as changes in children's needs and development can occur very rapidly at this age. Like IEPs, IFSPs are developed during meetings between parents and professionals. These meetings may be planned, formal affairs with everyone who works with your child in attendance. Or, particularly if your child's needs have changed in only one area, they may be more informal and spontaneous. For instance, a speech problem that is not covered in your child's IFSP may become apparent during a speech and language therapy session at your home. You and the therapist may decide to hold an IFSP meeting as soon as possible in order to add a goal to his IFSP to address that problem.

The guidelines described under "IEP" can also help you in setting up an IFSP for your child.

Qualifying for Services under IDEA

Before your child can begin receiving early intervention or special education services under the IDEA, he must be determined to be eligible. The process for determining eligibility for children under age three and children over three is often somewhat different.

Early Intervention. There are no nationwide guidelines for determining which children are and are not eligible for early intervention services. Instead, states, counties, or school districts may establish their own criteria. For instance, the policy may be that any child with a diagnosed condition that could be reasonably expected to cause developmental delays is eligible. Under this policy, a child who has a cleft lip and palate might be eligible for services, as this condition can be expected to cause delays in speech and language skills. Or, the policy might be that children whose development is a certain number of months (or a certain percentage) delayed are eligible for early intervention. So, eligibility might be determined by evaluating a child's development and determining whether it is significantly delayed. Often, children can qualify under a variety of different criteria. Contact your local early intervention program through the local school district or state department of health to find out what the criteria are in your area.

Special Education. To be eligible for special education services under IDEA, a child must: 1) have one or more of the qualifying disabling conditions listed in the law; and 2) have significant difficulty functioning at school because of that condition. Some of the qualifying disabling conditions that children with facial difference may have include hearing impairment, speech or language impairment or both, mental retardation, a severe health impairment, visual impairment, or orthopedic impairment.

If you believe that your child needs special education services, you can ask that he be evaluated by the school. To do so, contact

the special education coordinator or director of your school or school district. A teacher or other school professional can also refer your child for an evaluation. In fact, the local school district has the responsibility to identify and evaluate all children who potentially have a disabling condition. This is often referred to as a "child-find" policy.

Once your child has been referred for special education, a special education team will define what information is needed to determine whether your child is educationally handicapped. This team may consist of your child's teacher(s), learning specialist(s), or other staff members.

To gather information about your child, an assessment or evaluation will then be conducted. Before the school can proceed with this evaluation, you or your child's guardian must sign a permission to test form. Once you have signed the form, the school has 45 calendar days to conduct its evaluation, which will be done at no cost to you.

Different professionals evaluate children suspected of having different disabilities. For example, if your child has a chronic health impairment that might qualify him for special education, he will likely be evaluated by a physician. If he has a hearing impairment, his hearing will be screened by the school nurse, audiologist, or other appropriate professional. If he has a suspected visually handicapping condition, he will likely be evaluated by the school nurse, an ophthalmologist, or optometrist. If he has a speech or language impairment, he will be assessed by a speech-language pathologist.

During the course of the evaluation, your child will be given intellectual and academic tests. Intelligence quotient (IQ) tests measure your child's cognitive ability and provide information as to what would be expected of him in school. Academic achievement tests assess what your child has actually learned in reading, writing, spelling, math, or other academic skills. The psychologist or other professional who gives your child these tests will look at the difference between your child's intellectual ability and where his academic skills presently are. This will provide insight as to whether your child's condition impairs his ability to learn at school.

Once the evaluation is complete, a meeting will be held to determine whether your child is eligible for special education services. If he is found to be eligible, the next step is to develop an IEP, as described above.

If your child is *not* found eligible for special education, and you disagree, there are several steps you can take. First, in most states, parents may request a second evaluation, which the school district is again responsible for completing without cost to the parents. Parents can also pay for a private evaluation, using professionals of their own choosing, and then ask the school to reconsider based on this information. Second, as described below, parents can see whether their child qualifies for services or accommodations under Section 504, rather than IDEA. As a last resort, parents can request mediation or a due process hearing and attempt to prove to the impartial hearing officer that their child needs special education.

Section 504 of the Rehabilitation Act of 1973

Section 504 of the Rehabilitation Act of 1973 may help you and your family if your child does not qualify for special education under IDEA. Section 504 is a civil rights law which prohibits any program or activity that receives federal funds from discriminating against people with disabling conditions. Since public schools receive federal funds, they must comply with the law.

Under Section 504, someone is considered disabled if he: "1) has a mental or physical impairment which substantially limits one or more of such person's major life activities, 2) has a record of such impairments, or 3) is regarded as having such an impairment." The term "major life activities" includes caring for oneself, performing manual tasks, walking, seeing, hearing, speaking, breathing, learning, and working.

Some children with facial difference would be considered to have an impairment that affects a major life activity. This impairment, however, might not be significant enough to qualify the child for services under IDEA. For example, suppose your child wears a hearing aid and can hear well enough with the aid to function reasonably well in the classroom. He does not have a learning disability or other speech difficulty. Academically, he is at grade level. Still, because he wears a hearing aid, he will have a harder time hearing the teacher and his classmates if there is a great deal of background noise from air conditioners, banging chairs, and so forth. He will also have difficulty hearing at school assemblies or large gatherings. He would not be eligible for services under IDEA since he is doing well academically. Under Section 504, however, he would be eligible for adaptations such as preferential seating and visual cues to help him understand verbal instructions.

Other reasons a child with facial difference might be eligible for accommodations under Section 504, but not services under IDEA:

- Although the child has a slight articulation problem, he doesn't need speech and language therapy and is doing well in school. Still, he could benefit from accommodations to make sure that teachers give him extra time to respond to oral questions.
- The student is making good grades, but will miss a great deal of school due to operations and hospitalization. He may need tutoring.

Many of the rights and safeguards established by Section 504 are the same as those in the IDEA. For example, Subpart D - Preschool, Elementary, and Secondary Education - guarantees "a free appropriate public education to each qualified person with a disability . . . regardless of the nature or severity of the person's disability." Section 504 also requires:

- Placement in the least restrictive environment (LRE);
- Nondiscrimination in assessment and evaluation;
- Periodic re-evaluations of students receiving related special education services;

- Opportunities to take part in extracurricular and non-academic activities.

Every local education agency is required to have a 504 Coordinator on staff to respond to families' questions and concerns. You can contact the 504 Coordinator at your child's school district for information about beginning the eligibility process for your child. Later, the Coordinator can answer your questions about rights and possibly help resolve problems in implementing your child's 504 plan. If you are not satisfied with the Coordinator's response, you may contact the State Department of Education or the regional Office of Civil Rights (a federal agency).

Even if your family does not need to use Section 504 to obtain needed educational services, you and your family may find it useful. Remember, Section 504 prohibits discrimination against persons with disabilities by *any* agency that receives federal funds. For example, day care centers that receive federal funds cannot discriminate against children with disabilities. Neither can federally funded recreation programs or summer job programs. As you will see below, the Americans with Disabilities Act (ADA) now also prohibits discrimination against individuals with disabilities. There may, however, be instances when it is more effective to challenge discrimination with one law than the other.

The Americans with Disabilities Act of 1990 (ADA)

Until recently, people with disabling conditions were subjected to many kinds of discrimination. It was permissible to shunt them into recreation programs or other activities designed solely for people with disabilities or to otherwise exclude them from activities with nondisabled peers. It was acceptable to erect buildings that were inaccessible to people with physical disabilities. It was standard practice for employers to refuse to hire workers just because they had disabling conditions. Today, at least in theory, all of these kinds of discrimination are prohibited by the Americans with Disabilities Act (ADA).

The ADA is a sweeping civil rights law designed to wipe out many forms of discrimination against individuals with disabilities. The ADA prohibits discrimination against people with disabilities by employers, by public and private services, by "public accommodations," and in the area of telecommunications. According to the ADA guidelines, failure to make "reasonable accommodation" for people with disabling conditions is defined as discrimination. "Reasonable accommodation" means making an effort to remove the obstacles that stand in the way of accessibility.

Public Accommodations. The ADA bans discrimination against people with disabilities at any place that is open to the public, including: hotels and motels; restaurants and bars; movie theaters, concert halls, bowling alleys, and other buildings for recreation and entertainment; stores, dry cleaners, and other retail businesses; doctors' and dentists' offices, travel agents, and other business and professional offices; schools and child care centers; transportation terminals. The law further requires that "reasonable accommodations" and physical alterations must be made to accommodate people with disabilities unless it is not physically or financially feasible to do so.

Public Services. The ADA prohibits discrimination by programs, activities, and services of state and local governments. For example, all public transportation, including buses, subways, and trains, must be accessible to people with disabling conditions. Public telephones must be hearing aid compatible, and emergency telephone systems such as 911 must be accessible to people who use a TDD or modem for telephone communication. In addition, all architectural barriers in government buildings must be removed or modified, and all new buildings must be constructed according to ADA guidelines.

Employment. Employers with 15 or more employees are prohibited from discriminating against people with disabilities when it comes to applying for a job, hiring, firing, promotion, compensation, training, and other aspects of employment. The ADA requires that employers make "reasonable accommodation"—that is, employers must make an effort to remove obstacles from a job, other terms and conditions of employment, or the work place which would prevent an otherwise qualified person with a disability from working. For example, someone with a facial difference could not be denied employment on the grounds that the job involves working with the public and his physical appearance might hurt business. And to enable an otherwise qualified person with a facial difference to work, a company might need to provide accommodations such as a speak phone or telephone equipment that amplifies sound.

Employers do not have to make an accommodation if it would cause the employer an "undue hardship." Under the law, an "undue hardship" is an "action requiring significant difficulty or expense." What an "undue hardship" is for a company is determined on a case-by-case basis. In general, larger companies with more financial resources are expected to spend more money and effort in making accommodations.

Because the ADA is still relatively new, it may take a while before persons with disabling conditions and their advocates learn how best to use it to their advantage. For the most current information about the interpretation of the ADA and the rights of people with disabilities, you can contact the Disability Rights Education and Defense Fund at 1–800–466–4ADA (weekdays 9 a.m. to 5 p.m., Pacific Coast Time).

Family and Medical Leave Act of 1993

At least in the early years, you and your child may spend a great deal of time in craniofacial centers, hospitals, and doctors', dentists', and audiologists' offices. Needless to say, if both you and your spouse are employed outside the home, one or both of you will miss a lot of work. If you work for a business which employs at least 50 people, you do not have to worry that these absences will jeopardize your job. Under the Family and Medical Leave Act of 1993 (Public Law 103–3), your employer must allow you to take up to twelve weeks of unpaid leave to care for a child with a serious health condition. This law also requires that you will be able to return to your original position, or an equivalent position, when you come back to work. In addition, your employer must continue your health benefits while you are on family and medical leave.

This law does not override state or local laws that provide greater protection to employees. It is therefore possible that in your community or state the name of the law and the eligibility rules may be different. To ask questions about the law that governs family and medical leave in your community, contact your state Attorney General, the county State's Attorney, the state Human Rights Commission, or the state Department of Labor and Industry.

Government Benefits

There are a variety of government-run programs and benefits for children with disabling conditions. Each has its own requirements for eligibility which can change yearly, depending on who is in office at the state and federal levels. For that reason, you need to check directly with the agency involved to find out specific eligibility guidelines and how to apply. In general, however, most of the programs described below are open only to children with limited financial resources.

Supplemental Security Income (SSI)

Supplemental Security Income (SSI) is a program administered by the Social Security Administration. It is designed to provide income for people who cannot work—not only for adults who worked and paid Social Security taxes before becoming disabled, but also for children who have disabilities that would prevent them from working. States may stipulate how SSI funds can be used; for example, to pay for expenses related to the child's condition that the family could not otherwise pay for. Eligibility criteria and maximum payments for SSI programs vary from state to state. Your local Social Security office can tell you what they are for your state.

In general, to qualify for SSI Benefits for Children, children under the age of 18 must meet several eligibility requirements. First, they must have limited income and resources, or come from a home with limited income and resources. Qualifying incomes vary from state to state and depend upon how many children are in the family and other factors. In 1995, for example, a family of four who lived in Vermont and earned less than about $33,000 could qualify for at least some SSI benefits for their child with a disabling condition. The other major requirement for receiving SSI is that the child's impairment is as severe as one that would prevent an adult with a comparable disability from working.

To determine whether your child is eligible on the basis of disability, a disability evaluation specialist checks for the disability or a condition equal to the disability in a listing of impairments that is contained in the Social Security regulations. These listings are descriptions of symptoms, signs, or laboratory findings of physical and mental problems that are severe enough to disable a child. If your child's disabling condition is on the list or is comparable to another condition on the list, Social Security considers your child to be disabled. If your child's disabling condition is not listed or cannot be established using the criteria on the list, the disability evaluation team then assesses your child's ability to function in everyday life. If your child's condition substantially reduces his ability to do things and behave in a way that children of a similar age normally do, he is considered disabled by Social Security.

Although many children with facial difference receive SSI benefits, parents in some states have had difficulty proving their child's eligibility based on the criteria described above. Most conditions of facial difference are not on the Social Security list of impairments. Hearing impairments *are* on the list, however, as are such catch-alls as "Catastrophic Congenital Abnormalities." In addition, babies who were born prematurely and weigh less than 2000 grams (about 4 pounds, 6 ounces) may meet Social Security's definition of "disabled" until at least the age of one. If your child has a more complex condition and is severely affected, your state evaluation team may be more likely to recognize him as eligible for SSI. For more information about whether your child may be eligible, call Social Security at 1–800–772–1213 and speak with an eligibility worker.

To begin the application process, contact your local Social Security office. Bring your child's Social Security number, his birth certificate, records that show your income and assets and those of your child, and thorough and detailed documentation of your child's disabling condition. As part of the application, you will be asked to provide names, addresses, and telephone numbers of all physicians, hospitals, clinics, and other specialists who have seen your child, as well as dates of appointments, account numbers, and any other information that will help the Social Security office obtain your child's medical records as soon as possible. You will be asked to provide school records, and the names of teachers, day care providers, and family members who can provide information about how your child functions in his day-to-day activities. You will also be asked how your child's disabling condition affects his ability to function as a child of similar age normally would.

All of the forms, documents, and evidence that you present to the local Social Security office is sent to the Disability Determination Service of your state Social Security office. There, a team composed of a disability evaluation specialist and doctor will review your child's case to decide whether he meets Social Security's definition of disability. If this team has any questions about your child's disabling condition, you may be asked to take your child to a special examination which Social Security will pay for.

Since the disability evaluation process can take several months, the law includes special provisions for people with severely disabling conditions. In these cases, SSI benefits can be paid for up to six months while the disability decision is being made. Call your local Social Security office for the conditions in your state that qualify for these immediate SSI payments. In addition, when an infant qualifies for SSI on the basis of prematurity, parental income and resources are not considered until the month following the month that the child comes home to live with his parents.

One final note: if your child was denied benefits, or had benefits terminated, between January 1, 1980 and February 27, 1990, it may be worthwhile to reapply. The criteria for determining children's eligibility has changed since that period. Your child could be among the half-million children found to have been wrongfully denied SSI in the 1990 Supreme Court ruling in Sullivan vs. Zebley.

Medicaid

Medicaid is a health insurance program for people with low income and limited assets. The application procedure and qualifications for eligibility differ from state to state. In most states, however, children who receive SSI benefits qualify for Medicaid. In some states, Medicaid coverage comes automatically with SSI eligibility; in other states, you must sign up for Medicaid separately from SSI. In some states, some children can qualify for Medicaid if their family's income and assets are too high to qualify for SSI. This eligibility is available through the Katie Beckett option, which provides Medicaid to children with disabilities regardless of their parents' income and resources. This option is usually available to families who choose to care for their child with a disability at home, even though he may need the same level of care that is provided in a hospital, nursing home, or intermediate care facility for the mentally retarded and mentally ill. The cost of caring for the child at home must be less than the cost of caring for him in an institutional setting in order for him to qualify for Medicaid under this option.

If your child is eligible to receive Medicaid, he will be assigned a case manager or case worker. You will probably need to explain your child's condition of facial difference and his health care needs to his case manager. Be sure to enlist your child's craniofacial team in helping to explain these things to the case manager.

All children who are eligible for Medicaid are also eligible for a program known as the Early and Periodic Screening, Diagnosis and Treatment program (EPSDT). This is a Medicaid-funded, comprehensive package of benefits designed to provide preventative health, mental health, and developmental care. Children in the EPSDT program receive periodic screenings to detect physical, mental, vision, hearing, and dental problems that require further treatment. If a problem is detected, the state is required to cover "necessary health care, diagnostic services, treatment and other measures . . . to correct or ameliorate defects and physical and mental conditions . . . whether or not such services are covered under the State plan." Services a state may be required to provide include: inpatient and outpatient hospital care; laboratory and x-ray services; physicians' services; private duty nursing; dental services; physical or speech therapy; services of optometrists, psychologists, or any other licensed practitioners recognized by state law (such as dieticians or nutritionists).

In some areas of the country, only certain health care professionals accept Medicaid payments, which can really limit access to professionals knowledgeable about facial differences. Craniofacial centers can, however, apply to a particular state to receive Medicaid benefits for a child, if they choose to do so. This is most likely to happen when a child requires operations.

For more information about Medicaid, call your local Social Security office or your state or county social services office.

Health Insurance

It's ironic that the very families who need health insurance the most often have the most trouble obtaining adequate coverage. Often, it seems as if insurance companies actually try to avoid providing coverage to people who are likely to file frequent or expensive claims. Unfortunately, children with facial difference often fall into this category.

In eight states, health insurance companies are required to cover "medically necessary" care and treatment of cleft lip and palate (but not necessarily other conditions of facial difference).

These states are: California, Colorado, Indiana, Louisiana, Maryland, Minnesota, North Carolina, and Wisconsin. The mandated coverage for cleft lip and palate varies among these eight states. According to a statement prepared by the Cleft Palate Foundation and AboutFace, "medically necessary care may include medical-surgical treatment; hearing and speech evaluation and management; psychological and psychiatric evaluation and care; dental and prosthetic appliances; and other services as prescribed by qualified health care providers. Care is medically necessary for the purposes of treating infection, pain, ulceration, bleeding, and disease; for the improvement of speech, sight, breathing, swallowing, chewing, hearing, emotional functioning, etc.; for restoration of facial function and form needed for a more normal appearance, and social acceptance."

In all other states, insurance companies are able to deny claims related to treating conditions of facial difference on a variety of grounds. Common reasons for denial include:

- **Pre-existing Condition.** Many health insurance companies refuse to cover the care and treatment of conditions of facial difference on the grounds that they are "pre-existing conditions." A pre-existing condition means simply that your child's medical condition existed before he was put onto the policy. Usually, if your child is added to the policy at birth, insurance companies do not deny coverage on the grounds of having a pre-existing condition. But if you change policies after your child's birth, the new health insurance company may exclude your child's facial difference as a pre-existing condition, or reduce coverage for it. The explanation is that the condition pre-existed the effective date of the new carrier's contract. If you are considering having other children, you should also be aware that some insurance companies may deny coverage of your newborn if prenatal genetic testing detects a medical condition. Talk with a genetics professional if you have concerns along these lines.

While there is currently no definitive genetic testing available for conditions of facial difference, that may change in coming years. Scientists involved with the Human Genome Project (HGP) are discovering the locations of genes which cause a variety of congenital conditions, diseases, etc. As the locations of these genes are discovered and definitive genetic testing becomes available, health insurance companies have started to re-evaluate coverage for health conditions that are genetic in origin. Their decisions about coverage vary depending upon the genetic condition and how much the insurance company estimates it will cost to insure individuals with that condition. Some insurance companies are refusing to cover certain genetic conditions or certain types of care or treatment for a genetic condition. The Ethical, Legal, and Social Implications Committee (ELSI) of HGP is in the early stages of discussion about health insurance issues, genetic discrimination, and other issues. If you or your child have been denied health insurance coverage or have been discriminated against based on genetic diagnosis, or if you would like more information about these issues, contact the Alliance of Genetic Support Groups (see Resource Guide).

- **Secondary Condition.** In the care and treatment of many conditions of facial difference, a secondary condition must be treated in conjunction with the primary condition. (A secondary condition is one that is affected by the primary condition, but is treated as a result of treatment of the primary condition, or in anticipation of treatment of the primary condition.) An example is: jaw reconstruction that is needed to properly treat cleft lip and palate. The insurance company can deny coverage or reduce coverage for the jaw reconstruction by claiming it is a secondary condition, and not part of the primary treatment for cleft lip and palate.
- **Cosmetic Surgery Exclusion.** Most insurance companies refuse to cover cosmetic surgery—surgery done primarily to enhance a normal structure in order to improve

the patient's appearance and self-esteem. The reconstructive plastic surgeries your child needs, however, are not cosmetic surgeries. If your insurance company balks at paying for these services because they are not knowledgeable about conditions of facial differences, be prepared to educate them. Make sure they understand that your child had bone and tissue deficiencies that were present at birth. Have photographs available and letters of recommended treatments from your child's health care professionals to back up your child's claims.

- **Not-a-Covered-Benefit Exclusion.** If you read the fine print of your insurance policy, you may find that many services essential to your child's treatment are not covered. For instance, your child may need the services of a speech-language pathologist, audiologist, psychologist, genetic counselor, and prosthetics specialist. Your insurance policy may not cover their services, perhaps on the grounds that they are not physicians. Your insurance company might also claim that the services of an oral surgeon, otologist, otolaryngologist, and prosthodontist (who are physicians) are not covered for your child's condition.

- **Dental Benefit Denial.** Health insurance companies may deny coverage for some dental procedures such as orthodontia or jaw surgery on the grounds that these procedures are for dental, not medical, problems. Payment for these procedures should not be denied, however. Conditions of facial difference are present at birth and have a medical origin.

- **Discrepancy on Inpatient and Outpatient Coverage.** Some supplemental insurance policies such as "accident and dismemberment" policies may exclude benefits for either inpatient or outpatient services. Thus, if you are counting on your supplemental policy to pay what your primary policy doesn't cover, it is a good idea to read the fine print. Most reconstructive plastic surgeries for conditions of facial difference require inpatient treatment, so an exclusion for inpatient treatment could leave you with substantial bills to pay on your own.

If you are shopping around for a health insurance policy for your family, you can start your research by reading the most current health insurance review in *Consumer Reports*. Also look for an insurance rating guide called *Best's* (listed in the Reading List), which rates companies based on their performance in paying claims, administrative costs, etc. Keep in mind the common denials listed above and be sure to ask the insurance company representative about each. After you ask about the pre-existing condition exclusion, you may find that all your alternatives have been eliminated. It may seem as if no company is willing to cover expenses related to the medical care and treatment of your child's condition of facial difference. However, you may be able to find a company that will cover your child's routine health care needs unrelated to his condition of facial difference. Contact your State Office of Insurance for information about this option.

In considering health insurance plans, be sure to ask whether there is a lifetime ceiling on benefits. Most policies have per person lifetime maximums, usually ranging from one to five million dollars. Some, however, have unlimited benefits. If your policy has a lifetime ceiling, find out if the insurance company employs a nurse manager to help their policyholders plan their care and treatment. With input from a nurse manager, an overview of your child's care and treatment can be planned so that your child's lifetime benefits will not be used up prematurely. This is particularly important if your child requires nursing care at home for his tracheostomy or has other high technology needs.

If you belong to, or are considering enrolling in an HMO (Health Maintenance Organization), there are special considerations to bear in mind. First, many of the HMO clinics that serve patients with facial difference may not have much experience with facial difference, especially the rarer conditions. Second, they may be unwilling to refer your child to a craniofacial center outside of the HMO, or to pay for services there. In fact, the newest trend is for HMOs to start their own cleft/craniofacial centers. This is because the principle behind HMOs is to provide all the health care services its members need within the HMO system. HMOs have their own physicians, therapists, mental health professionals, genetic counselors, audiologists, laboratories, and pharmacies. You should research the experience of the staff before signing up. If your HMO turns down your request to take your child to a non-HMO craniofacial center, be prepared to appeal the decision if you are committed to taking your child to a non-HMO craniofacial center. You may want to refer to the section on advocacy in Chapter 8 to help you navigate the HMO system and obtain care outside the system for your child.

If you are disputing a claim or coverage with your health insurance company or anticipate a struggle to have the care and treatment of your child's facial difference covered, there are several people or organizations to contact for information and possible assistance. They include: your state insurance commissioner, your AboutFace Insurance Advocate (see Resource Guide for address of AboutFace), and your state and national legislators.

If you would like to join in the crusade to create mandates for health insurance coverage of conditions of facial difference in your state, you can start by contacting the American Cleft Palate-Craniofacial Association. Ask for a copy of their publication "Guidelines for Legislative Advocacy." This document outlines all the steps that need to be taken when attempting to obtain legislation that will address the health care needs of people with facial difference.

Conclusion

When parents dream about watching their children grow and develop, these dreams usually do not include adversarial scenes filled with legal paperwork, stressful meetings with teams of professionals, or "leisure" time spent poring over laws and interpretations. However, it is extremely important for parents of children with facial difference to know their child's legal rights and entitlements. It is just as important to know how to advocate for those rights: where to go or what to do if you think he is not being treated appropriately or adequately.

Championing your child's rights can be exhausting, frustrating, and not always successful. Along the way, however, you may meet some truly wonderful and dedicated professionals, develop uniquely special relationships with other parents of children with disabling conditions, and become very well educated about your child's condition of facial difference. You may wonder if all of your energy and time will make a difference for your child when he is an adult. Absolutely! Besides obtaining the best care and services for him, you will be teaching him how to navigate systems to obtain what he wants or needs.

When facing legal rights and challenges, try to keep your sense of humor and equilibrium intact. Whenever I think I am moving too fast down a dead-end street, I regain my perspective by remembering what my five-year-old son said when I told him that the doctors did not know why he was born with underdeveloped ears: "Well, what good are doctors for, anyway?" Focus on your child's "big picture," and eventually you will figure out how all of the little pieces fit together.

Parent Statements

We had no problems establishing Tyler's eligibility for early intervention. However, we could have received special services much sooner had a professional told me they were available. Had it not been for one terrific lady involved in our cleft clinic program, I would never have known "free" services existed. State agencies are very slow in following up on children born with clefts.

❈

In our county, a kid has to be delayed 33 percent in one area or 25 percent in more than one area to qualify for early intervention. When Lawrence was 18 months old, he was delayed in speech, but not enough to qualify for the program. By two, he was delayed enough in both speech and fine motor skills to qualify. So we wasted a good six months before he received needed therapies.

❈

Our son's eligibility for educational services was easily determined through a speech evaluation. Currently, his IEP focuses on problems with articulation.

❈

The IEP is a tedious, emotional, but *now* effective tool in providing our son with an education. It requires constant maintenance (including monthly team meetings) to make sure services are provided as they are supposed to be.

❈

Writing IEPs has been a nightmare. All the school sees is the facial differences and not all the numerous anomalies that need to be addressed with services.

❈

Kelly had an IEP from ages four to ten in order to receive speech therapy in the school. When she was ten, we decided to seek private therapy, so her IEP stopped at the end of that school year. We are now in the process of writing a 504 plan for her hearing problems.

Theresa is in special education due to her brain damage. I have requested mainstreaming for years, but the school programs for her are limited. I was told by one school social worker that Theresa would make the other girls in the school's public bathrooms uncomfortable!

My husband's insurance hasn't been very helpful in covering our daughter's needs related to her disabilities, although it does a good job paying for her health needs.

At first the insurance company just paid their part and gave us no problems, but as Michael's bills piled up, they lost claim forms, "accidentally" disconnected me on the phone, and gave us other forms of grief.

We belong to a large HMO, so almost everything has been included. We have been reimbursed for some services that we went outside of the HMO to receive. Our experience has been very positive.

Our insurance would not cover dental services, even though they were related to his congenital condition, would not have occurred if it were not for birth anomalies, and were medically necessary for eating.

Our insurance was fine until we had to get a different policy because of a job change. They will no longer authorize any occupational therapy or speech therapy because the medical advisor claims there is no substantiated medical necessity and it is an educational need. Bull!

It's a hassle finding "preferred providers" who understand our son's rare syndrome.

✖

Our insurance has been *wonderful*, covering all doctors' visits and second opinions, and fully covering all surgeries.

✖

We had some problems with our insurance company. We belong to an HMO and must see the doctor our primary care physician recommends. He would not refer me to the children's hospital where I wanted the operation done. My reason for wanting her to go there was quite simple . . . they have a special craniofacial unit and I felt that if my daughter was to be operated on under aesthesia, it should be done by professionals who dealt only with babies every day. After arguing with the HMO people, they finally let us go to the children's hospital.

✖

Our HMO limited his speech therapy sessions to two months, which was not enough time to correct, maintain, follow up, etc. Any health insurance reform really needs to address this point.

✖

There needs to be a law requiring that dental insurance cover facial differences. We recently saw a prosthodontist, and just a part of his "predetermination of treatment" is approximately $2,300. Our dental insurance will cover $81! This is certainly not a life or death situation, but—do we send him to college or to the prosthodontist?

✖

We need a federal law prohibiting insurance companies from excluding pre-existing conditions. My employers changed health insurance after Clare was born, and the new company wouldn't take Clare. We had to keep her on our old policy. They started out charging us $500 a month just for her and have now raised it to $900 a month.

✖

I only hope that when she tries to get a job, she's not turned down because of her looks.

✖

School is a fairly sheltered environment. What I worry about is acceptance by the work world.

✖

I worry about potential discrimination by future employers due to Emma's appearance and speech.

✖

Laws need to be expanded so that children born with special needs are automatically covered, even though they are *not* considered "handicapped."

✖

Chapter 8

Advocacy

As an infant, my son was evaluated several times by the craniofacial team at an internationally known children's hospital. Their evaluations showed that his physical and intellectual development were on target, but that his speech and language were delayed due to his hearing impairment. The team recommended that he receive speech therapy to enhance his interest in sound and speech, to improve his understanding of language, and to increase his speech skills. Consequently, we tried to enroll our son in a no-cost state program which focused on speech and language stimulation for infants and toddlers with hearing impairments. The staff at this program, however, told us that our son's development was delayed in a number of areas, and that he needed a variety of therapies in addition to speech and language stimulation.

I was faced with the dilemma of whom to believe. Because the staff at the state program had never before seen a child with Treacher Collins syndrome, I decided to follow the recommendations of the craniofacial team. Much to my surprise, the state program then informed me that if I did not give them permission to provide my son all the therapies they recommended, they would deny him speech and language therapy. I withdrew my son from the state program and arranged for private speech and language services. This decision eventually turned out to be the right one, as it became apparent that Sam really *didn't* need therapies other than speech and language therapy.

This story had a relatively happy ending because I was lucky enough to have health insurance that covered private speech therapy. But my family should never have had to resort to private therapy. The state program had no right to refuse my son the speech and language services I had requested. The problem was, I didn't know our rights *or* how to stand up for them. I didn't know how to be an advocate for my child.

What Is Advocacy?

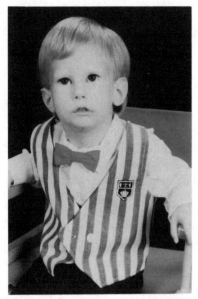

Perhaps you have been told by another parent or a caring professional that you are your child's best advocate. But what exactly *is* an advocate?

The dictionary describes an advocate as one who pleads the cause of another. An advocate can be a lawyer or other professional, or a nonprofessional such as a parent. In either case, an advocate speaks or writes on behalf of someone (such as your child) who cannot do so for herself. An advocate may be interested only in helping one individual obtain what she needs, or can work at obtaining changes for a group with similar needs.

Most parents occasionally advocate for their children—whether or not they know that this is what they are doing. They may need to persuade the soccer coach to let their child play goalie, or convince the teacher to allow their child to turn in an assignment late.

When you have a child with facial difference, you may need to advocate more often and in many different situations. First, you are more likely to encounter people who do not understand what is best for your child, since many people have never before met someone with facial difference. For example, children with facial difference are often assumed to have mental retardation because of their appearance or speech or hearing impairment. Consequently, they may not be treated appropriately by professionals. Second, your child is more likely to need special services or assistance that you may need to advocate for. She may need speech and language stimulation or other early intervention, or medical procedures that your insurance is unwilling to cover (perhaps because they think the procedure is being done for cosmetic reasons only).

As Chapter 7 explains, there *are* some laws that provide standards (usually minimum) for appropriate care and services for children with facial difference. The interpretation of these laws, however, can differ from place to place, from child to child, and from professional to professional. If you want laws to be interpreted to your child's best advantage, you will often need to speak up—to plead your child's case. In addition, many parents believe that existing laws and regulations are woefully inadequate. They feel that county, state, and federal laws should do more to safeguard their child's rights to a normal life or to guarantee needed assistance. These laws will never be passed unless many parents and others join together to advocate for change.

Advocating for Your Child

The idea of advocating may seem very intimidating to you if you have never before had to do so. At first, you may come up with a million reasons why you are unable to advocate for your child. Or you may believe that all the educational and medical professionals in your child's life have her best interests at heart, so there is no need for you to advocate.

Sooner or later, however, something is bound to motivate you to advocate. You may get so angry about unfair treatment of your child that you feel you have to do something. Or you may realize that the official who administers a particular program doesn't share your opinion about what is best for your child. Like it or not, you may find yourself thrust into *case advocacy*—the technical term for working for the rights of one particular individual.

If you are not naturally assertive, you may need to draw upon your guts and determination to develop the new skills, personal attributes, and self-image you need to be effective. It may help to realize that you really are *the* expert on your child. Although others may have more training in specialized aspects of treating facial difference, you have special insights into the unique individual who is your child. Doctors, teachers, and therapists only see your child for limited periods of time in one setting. You see your child at mealtime, play time, and bedtime; in the grocery store, at the park, in McDonald's; with friends and family, with strangers, and with educational and medical professionals. If anyone understands your child's true abilities and disabilities, interests and needs, it is you. You *are* your child's best advocate—at least until she reaches adolescence or young adulthood. After that, she may be willing and able to advocate for herself.

Some parents draw strength from the mere thought that by advocating for their child they may be shattering stereotypes. Some professionals, for instance, think of all parents of children with disabling conditions as helpless victims of fate. Along the way, you might also find out that your child's situation is not an isolated case. You may discover, for example, that all children with your child's condition are routinely denied needed services by your county's early intervention program, or that other parents have similar problems communicating with teachers at your child's school. In these situations, you may feel more confident knowing you are not alone and may want to join with others to advocate for system-wide change.

Getting Started in Case Advocacy

Once you have decided to advocate for your child, how do you begin?

The first step in advocating is to be able to understand and objectively state the problem, as well as who or what is involved in creating or continuing this problem. For example, imagine that your child had a very successful experience in preschool. She made several good friends, and progressed as well, or better, as any other child in most preschool activities. But when she begins kindergarten, she suddenly begins to struggle, both academically and socially. Her spirits are sagging and she is becoming increasingly reluctant to go to school. What is at the root of her problems? Is it that school staff are not helping other children understand and accept your child's differences? Or that your child's hearing impairment is not being accommodated as well as it was in preschool? Or that she is not receiving the special services she needs to succeed in a classroom with so many children?

Questions you may need to have answered in defining a problem like this may include:

- How is the system (educational, medical, etc.) you are dealing with supposed to work? What services are generally available to whom?
- What is the usual process for decision making within the system, and who is involved?
- What are your child's legal rights, if any?

Obtaining the information you need may be a challenge if your child's condition is relatively rare. So, the best way to start gathering information might be to contact organizations knowledgeable about conditions of facial difference. National organizations such as the Alliance of Genetic Support Groups, the Cleft Palate Foundation's CLEFTLINE, or the National Organization for Rare Disorders may be able to refer you to local organizations that can answer your questions. You might also contact organizations described below in the section called "Organizations That Can Help." Addresses and phone numbers for these and other helpful groups are given in the Resource Guide. In addition, you can check the yellow pages of your telephone book under "Social Services," "Human Resources Administration," or "State Department of Health."

Once you have located a support organization, advocacy group, or information service, contact them and explain your problem. Ask if they know of other families who have experienced the same or similar problem, and whether they can put you in contact with these families. See if they have educational materials on legal rights or other subjects you need information about. Ask whether they can help you advocate or give you any advice. Let them know what information you have already gathered, so you can save everyone time and energy which can then be used to solve your child's problem.

If one organization is unable to give you all the information you need, ask them to refer you to another organization that might be able to help. Do not be concerned about offending one organization by asking for referrals to other organizations. Support organizations exist to provide information and support for people; they are glad to provide referrals to other organizations, especially if they are unable to meet all the needs of a consumer.

In your quest for information, it is especially important to gain a clear understanding of your child's legal rights, and what she is eligible for or entitled to. Knowing these legal rights may not only help you decide what your plan for advocacy will be, but how to proceed. You do not need to be a lawyer or hire a lawyer to find out what the laws are or to understand them. A support organization can likely help you with all of this. A Parent Training and Information Center (PTI) can be especially helpful in advising you about laws and their interpretation. The PTI should also be able to help you get a copy of the law or laws that affects your child. (See the Resource Guide for the PTI nearest you.) Copies of laws should also be available from your state senator's or representative's office (if it is a state law), or from your U.S. senator's or representative's office (if it is a federal law).

After you have gathered information about the problem from as many sources as possible, you need to organize this information. How does the information support your feeling that there is a problem? Are there specific sections of specific laws that clearly show that your child's rights are being violated? Are there medical or other professionals who agree that your child's best interests are not being served? For example, is your HMO refusing to pay for needed treatments at a craniofacial center that is outside the HMO system? Are there any publications that back up your position? Gather all of the facts, in writing, if possible. The more documentation you have which clearly explains the situation, the easier it will be to start work on making changes. We live in an age of easy accessibility to photocopy machines—use them!

Once the problem is reasonably clear in your mind, start exploring possible solutions. Think about whether more than one solution would be acceptable to you or how you would be willing to negotiate on solutions. Some solutions may not be perfect and may need modifications over time, but may be helpful in the beginning. Other solutions may just seem totally inappropriate. For example, you may feel as if your child's classroom teacher is not accommodating her hearing impairment as well as she could. To you, the ideal solution might be for the teacher to contact one of the consultants the state provides to assist with the educational problems of students who are deaf or hard of hearing. But if the teacher doesn't do so, despite repeated suggestions from you, you may have to try another solution. Perhaps you will need to go over the teacher's head, and request that the principal or special education supervisor arrange a meeting between the teacher and hearing consultant. You would want to do this as tactfully as possible, so the teacher wouldn't feel as if you were questioning her judgment or competence *and* your child would still benefit from the hearing consultant's advice.

Examine the language in the solution(s) you are thinking of proposing. You may want to write out exactly what you will say, as it is easy to forget things in stressful situations. Is your language wishy-washy or vague? Is it honest? Is it easy to understand and interpret? Is it clear and concise without being accusatory?

In the example above, a less helpful way of wording the problem might be: "The teacher has refused to work with me on Megan's needs because she's rude, cold, and uncaring. She doesn't care about Megan and thinks she isn't worth her time. This school never cares about kids like Megan; they only respond to kids who are attractive, smart, and rich."

More helpful language might be: "I know everyone has Megan's best interests at heart, but I'm not sure they recognize that kids with her condition often have the following needs: . . . . It may take some adjustment within the classroom to accommodate for her needs, but these adjustments can be easily made and the hearing consultant is available to offer information and support. Megan's father and I are always available, too. We all want the best for Megan."

When you have identified both the problem and some desirable solutions, it is time to contact the system (school, program, hospital, agency, insurance company) that is presenting the problem. It is usually best to start with the staff with whom you are most familiar, as long as they have the power to help. Clearly explain what you perceive to be the facts of the situation and the reason why this is a problem for your child. You may want to bring at least one other person along with you to this meeting. This person can give you moral support, offer information to back up your position, remind you of important points to cover, or merely serve as a witness to what is and is not said. Depending on what you are planning to discuss, you may want to ask your spouse, another parent, or a therapist or other professional to accompany you. Just make sure that the person you choose will be supportive and will not work against the situation or make it worse.

Be sure to keep a notebook to document all meetings. Record who said what and when. Also decide on a timetable for the response. When would it be reasonable to expect an answer?

After you have stated the problem and your desired solution, wait for a response! The response you get will indicate what your next step should be.

If you get a response that seems to be positive and in the best interest of your child, ask that the proposed change and how it will take place be put in writing. If you get a response that you believe is not in the best interest of your child, explain that you have a difference of opinion. Mention any laws, research, or other findings that support your position. Ask what the next step is in resolving the conflict.

Moving on to the next step usually means communicating with someone in a higher position in the system. You may feel as if you are starting all over again. At this point, it is important not to feel defeated! As you continue advocating for your child, your skills will become more polished, your strategies will grow more thoughtful, your patience will turn into persistence, and you will make contacts with key people both inside and outside of the system. It is undeniable, however, that the "advocacy road" ahead may be a long one, and you may encounter many roadblocks.

If, at any time, you feel as if you need assistance in continuing your child's advocacy, re-contact the support organizations and ask for help. You might even ask the organizations to refer you to a professional advocate or lawyer familiar with problems like yours. Another possible source of help is through the *Parent Resource Directory* published by the Association for the Care of Children's Health (ACCH). This directory lists parents of children with disabilities throughout the U.S. and Canada who have offered to share information on family-to-family support and networking and on parent/professional collaboration. (See the Reading List for more information.)

Keep in mind that you have not failed—you have only run out of ideas and strategies for handling a problem that other parents have probably faced before. Also keep in mind that if it feels as if the system is failing your child, that could well be happening. If so, now is a good time to think about working to change the system.

Advocating for the Rights of Many Children

As you advocate for your child, you may begin to realize that other children are facing the same problem as your child. Or, as described above, you may discover that the whole system needs to be changed. You may think that if all the parents joined together to advocate in one voice, it would be much stronger than many individual voices. In fact, this is historically what has happened. For instance, coalitions of parents played a critical role in the passage of Public Law 94–142, the original federal law guaranteeing special educational services for children with disabilities. And, more recently, parents and professionals suc-  ceeded in getting eight U.S. states to require health insurance coverage for people with conditions of facial difference. This type of advocacy, which is focused on obtaining long-lasting benefits for a number of people in similar situations, is known as *class advocacy*.

Class advocacy can take place within the government at federal, state, and local levels. Generally, this sort of advocacy is aimed at getting new or improved laws passed related to rights or services. Class advocacy might also occur within an early intervention program, craniofacial center, or other setting where a group of parents would like to see policies or procedures changed.

Usually, parents do not work alone to advocate for legislative change. They may work side by side with health care professionals, educators and therapists, support organizations, and perhaps a professional lobbyist. Parents, however, are a very important part of this team. As constituents, they speak directly to their elected officials about their personal experiences. Most professionals and lobbyists have neither your insight into the needs of your child, nor the passion which comes from experiencing first-hand the chal-

lenges of obtaining the best care and treatment for a child with facial difference.

Getting Started in Class Advocacy

If you have identified an issue that you think should be addressed at a class advocacy level, you can start the ball rolling by
finding out if others share your concerns or thoughts. Contact
those most likely to be interested in the issue, such as your child's
professionals, other parents of children with facial difference, parents of children with special needs who may have similar concerns,
and support organizations. If there seems to be enough support to
move ahead, propose that you join forces and develop a plan of action.

Usually it is helpful to decide on a core group of people or an
organization to take a leadership role. This core group can continue
to gather information and support from a variety of people and organizations in order to further define the problem, develop some
potential solutions, and draw the public's attention to the problem
via the media. (See "Going Public" for information on media exposure.) The core group should include experienced advocates who
understand the legislative process, but less experienced people
who are willing to learn can also be included. Experienced organiz-
ers will tell you, "Never say 'no' to volunteers, just direct their energy!"

If no one in your group has much experience with class advocacy, you may want to obtain the comprehensive "Guidelines for
Legislative Advocacy" prepared by the American Cleft Palate-Craniofacial Association. (See the Reading List for ordering information.) This document focuses on enacting effective state
legislation to improve medical and health insurance coverage for
conditions of facial difference. The principles and strategies of
class advocacy outlined here can also be valuable with other issues,
however.

The League of Women Voters can also help you champion your
cause. They have an office in every state, and offer voter education
at the local, state, and national level. While they don't take a position (politically) on specific issues, they study issues in-depth and
offer forums, discussions, and presentations on specific topics. Your
state Protection & Advocacy (P&A) agency can also offer assistance and information. P&A agencies have been established in

every state to protect the rights of individuals with disabilities and mental illnesses. The National Information Center for Children and Youth with Disabilities (NICHCY), listed in the Resource Guide, can refer you to the P&A office in your state. A PTI, too, should be able to provide assistance with legislative advocacy.

Perhaps you think that your elected representatives could not possibly care what you think about an issue, or that they don't have time to listen to your concerns. This is not true. We elect our government representatives so that they can represent our needs and concerns within our communities, our states, and our country. However, it is impossible for them to know the needs and concerns of all their constituents unless we take it upon ourselves to inform them and educate them. Elected officials rely on their constituents to notify them about important issues, including those related to facial difference.

Your government representatives are available to you and welcome your communication. You can visit their offices, write to them, send them telegrams, or call them. Often, you will not be able to meet with the representative personally, but will instead meet with an aide. Do not feel slighted if this happens. Bear in mind that the aide has direct communication with your elected official, and can be a very effective pipeline of information—especially if you cultivate a cordial relationship with the aide.

If you cannot meet with your elected representatives in person, a letter-writing campaign can also be quite effective. In general, it is best if the members of your group do *not* all send the same form letter. You will get much better results if everyone takes the time to write their own thoughts, and tries to help the representative see them and their families as real people, not just faceless constituents. Sending along a photo of your child and your family can be a big help. To help group members organize their thoughts, your group might want to put together a worksheet or questionnaire, listing specific types of information it would be helpful to include in their letters. For example: What is your child's name and age? What is her condition of facial difference? How will passing/not passing the law under consideration make life easier/harder for your family?

Whether you make initial contact with your elected representative in person, by phone, or through the mail, always follow up! If you don't hear back after a reasonable amount of time has passed, contact the official again. If one strategy doesn't work, try another! It is true that your elected representatives have hundreds of issues to resolve, many of which may affect many more citizens than the issues that concern you. But it is also true that the squeaky wheel gets the grease. Your family's concerns are just as important as any other family's—don't be shy about asking that they be addressed.

If you are not sure who your government representatives are, there are a number of ways to find out. Call the city or town hall where you live; call your local library, newspaper, or League of Women Voters; look in the white pages of your telephone directory under "United States Government - Congress" for representatives and senators; look in the telephone directory under the name of your state under "Governor's Office." These telephone listings usually include a toll-free telephone number for easy access.

Setbacks and Delays

Getting a law passed through class advocacy is a major coup. But that doesn't mean things will improve overnight. Months— even years—may pass between the day a bill is signed into law and the day that you notice any changes for the better.

After legislation is effected and signed into law, it is prepared for printing. *Implementation* must then occur before the new law is actually put into practice. Implementation refers to the process of putting the new law in place through: notifying agencies and organizations that are affected by the new law of the new legal provisions and requirements; training staff who provide services, if necessary; developing a monitoring system to make sure changes are enacted and the public is kept informed. If funding is involved, decisions must be made about who gets funds and for what purpose. And checks and balances need to be developed to make sure the money is spent the way it was intended to be spent. Finally, a method to keep an accurate accounting of how well the new law is doing must be devised.

Even after a new law has been implemented, it may take a while to see any tangible benefits. When changes in laws or policies and procedures are made, there are often a few rough spots in the beginning. For example, staff may resist the changes that come with new policies and procedures. If necessary, be prepared to advocate for your child's rights and benefits under the new law. If the law allows parents to share the responsibility for making the law work well, also be prepared to accept your responsibilities and be watchful that the staff accepts theirs.

Remember: parent victories which change or create new laws, policies, or procedures can be fragile and should never be taken for granted. It is important to thank everyone who helped your dream become a reality, so they will know their efforts were truly appreciated. Unfortunately, as political figures, administrators, and directors change, so too can laws, policies, and procedures. Be prepared to keep an eye on laws, policies, and procedures for changes or proposed changes that will affect your child's well-being. You never know when you will need to jump into the advocacy arena again.

Going Public

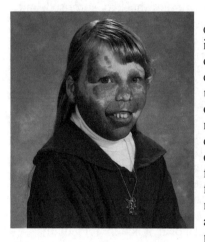

Sometimes an organization or political figure may ask a family to "go public" about their child's facial difference. Or parents might decide to publicize their family's situation on their own. Examples of issues that might be publicized include the effects on the parents, siblings, or family of having a child with facial difference; the genetics of facial difference; health care financing; dealing with professionals or strangers; and psychological and emotional issues.

There are a variety of ways to "go public," including: appearing on a nationally or locally televised talk show or news program; appearing on a telethon or other fundraising broadcast; testifying before Congress, a state legislature, or committee; pleading your child's case before the school board; being interviewed by a newspaper or magazine; being photographed or interviewed for a book or exhibit; writing a letter to the editor of a newspaper or magazine.

"Going public" is a potentially flattering and exciting opportunity for families—sometimes side by side with professionals—to raise public awareness and de-mystify their child's condition. Sometimes, however, "going public" can have an unexpected negative impact on a family. Your words might be taken out of context, for instance, or the thrust of your story may turn out to be different from what you intended.

My own family had an experience that illustrates some of the pros and cons of "going public." When my son was a toddler, the local chapter of a national disability organization invited me to participate in their annual fundraising appeal. Their plan was to interview me for one-half hour on live television. Tapes of this interview would then be distributed throughout the state for rebroadcast in communities by their regional fundraisers. It sounded innocent enough, until I learned that the focus of the interview was to be how awful my family's life had been since my son's birth, how grateful I was to their organization for all the fabulous support they had provided me, and how my life was liveable because of services they had provided. This invitation shocked, surprised, and saddened me. My life had not been awful since my son's birth—it was just different from what I had expected. Besides, I had never received any support from this particular organization—although I had made several calls requesting information and support, my calls had never been returned.

I thought about the invitation for a few days, then called the fundraiser back and declined. She became very angry and expressed outrage that I was unwilling to tell my story so that others could benefit. After I (literally) stopped shaking from this conversation, I called a friend who lived in another state who also had a child with a condition of facial difference. She told me that she too had had a negative experience with her local chapter of this organization, and had heard similar stories from other parents. By the time our conversation ended, I had a plan of action: remedy the situation and regain my feelings of empowerment as a parent.

I wrote a letter detailing my concerns and mailed it to the fundraiser, the director of the state chapter, and a contact I had at the national office. The national office wrote back immediately apologizing for the incident and clarifying the purposes of the organization. A year later, I received an apologetic phone call from the state chapter director. That day she had cleaned out the desk of the fundraiser who had invited me to appear on television. The fundraiser no longer worked there, and the director had found in her desk the letters I had sent both to her and to the fundraiser. The director and I had a lengthy conversation, ending with her inviting me to offer guidance in educating her staff about the needs and sensitivities of parents of children with congenital conditions. As it happened, I was moving out of state the next day, so I was unable to take her up on this offer. The entire incident was, however, a tremendous education for me about how children and families can be exploited, who serves what purpose, and how to handle difficult situations while preserving my dignity and that of my son and family.

Two booklets that should help reduce negative experiences such as the one I narrowly avoided in "going public" are available from the Alliance of Genetic Support Groups (see the Resource Guide). The booklets are entitled "Media Reporting in the Genetic Age: A Guide for Consumers" and "Points to Consider." They provide guidelines to the media for reporting on genetic conditions and people with disabling conditions, and points to consider for individuals who are preparing to "go public." The focus is on providing a sensitive, accurate, and fair portrayal. It includes language to use and not to use and nuts-and-bolts advice on sharing information with the media in writing and in person. The booklets were developed in response to the intense media scrutiny given to Bree Walker, a television news personality. In 1991, Walker was publicly criticized on a major California radio call-in program because she was pregnant a second time after passing her genetic condition, syndactyly, on to her first child. (Syndactyly causes webbing, usually of the fingers, but also sometimes of the toes.) In the months following this broadcast, disability rights organizations rallied to Walker's cause, supporting her freedom of reproductive choice. The media actively followed this course of events. The upshot was that the public was educated about issues rarely publicized, but at considerable cost to Ms. Walker's privacy.

If you are considering "going public," you may want to think about the following questions so that you can decide whether it would be in your family's best interest to do so.*

1. Why are you interested in "going public"? Are your interests personal, political, etc.? What do you hope will result from this experience?

2. What will you communicate about? Do you already know the information, or will you need to do some research?

---

* Some of these questions were originally developed by the Consumer Concerns Committee of the New England Regional Genetics Group.

3. Will you be able to communicate in a style you prefer, or will your responses be provided to you?
4. If you disagree or feel that you are being misunderstood, will you have the opportunity to supply the correct information?
5. Is someone available to provide you with personal support? That is, can someone help you handle any unexpected repercussions of going public? You may, for example, receive letters or phone calls that you find unsettling.
6. Examine your vulnerabilities, doubts, and feelings about personal privacy. Will your privacy be invaded?
7. Can you refrain from responding to certain questions? Or can you choose not to respond? Think about how you would respond to questions which address issues that are sensitive to you, your child, or your family.
8. Is your child's or family's story or situation typical for your child's condition, or is it particular to your family? If it is not typical for your child's condition, how would you paint the broader picture based on your story?
9. What format will be used? Who will interview you and who else will be involved besides you and your child or family? Will the interviewer be knowledgeable about the issues? Will there be an angle?
10. If anything is written about you and your family, will you have an opportunity to edit the written pieces?
11. How and when will the event you participated in be available for public viewing? Will you be paid?

Organizations That Can Help

Whether you are involved in case advocacy or class advocacy, there are a variety of local and national organizations that can help. The section on "Getting Started in Case Advocacy" mentioned some general types of organizations that can support your advocacy and some general ways that they can help. There are also many organizations dedicated specifically to improving the quality of life for people with facial difference. These organizations may be able to help you by providing information on your child's condition or on disability issues; putting you in touch with parents or professionals with similar concerns or experiences; and offering a forum to air your concerns through their newsletter or other publications. The organization as a whole might also decide to take up your cause, thus adding clout to your advocacy efforts.

The American Cleft Palate-Craniofacial Association (ACPA). The American Cleft Palate-Craniofacial Association was founded in 1943 by a group of Pennsylvania dentists. Today it is an international organization of over two thousand professionals from the fields of medicine, dentistry, speech pathology, audiology, nursing, psychology, and other related areas who are committed to improving the quality of life for persons with cleft lip and palate and craniofacial conditions through research and other endeavors. The bimonthly *Cleft Palate-Craniofacial Journal* is an international, professional publication that reports on clinical and research activities in cleft palate and craniofacial conditions, and research in related laboratory sciences.

In 1973, the ACPA founded the **Cleft Palate Foundation (CPF)** to serve as its public link. CPF activities include professional and public education and parent/patient liaison projects (public education activities, awards). CPF also operates the CLEFTLINE, a toll-free number that provides information and referrals to treatment centers and support groups for people with clefts and craniofacial conditions, their families, and professionals; offers informative brochures and fact sheets on conditions of facial difference and related issues; and provides research grants to members of ACPA.

The National Cleft Palate Association. In 1984, the National Cleft Palate Association began through the efforts of Hyman Gardsbane, O.D. Dr. Gardsbane was the grandfather of a child born with cleft lip and palate. Important purposes of this organization were to provide a formal, organized way of bringing together the parent support groups around the United States and to publish a central newsletter. Over the years, advocacy became an important focus for NCPA. In 1992, NCPA formally merged with AboutFace (see below).

AboutFace. AboutFace was founded in 1985 by two women: Betty Bednar, an adult with facial difference, and Laurie Macleod, a nurse and mother of six children, two of whom have facial difference. They believed that all individuals with facial difference, whether congenital or acquired, needed support in coping with looking "different" in a world that puts so much importance on appearances.

In 1991, AboutFace U.S.A. was founded to help address the unique concerns of those living in the U.S. Today, the Canadian and U.S. divisions of AboutFace work closely with the Cleft Palate Foundation to improve the quality of life for people with facial difference and their families. AboutFace provides support to individuals with facial difference by: distributing brochures, pamphlets, and other information about facial differences; offering contact with other individuals with similar concerns through informal group meetings or letter writing; educating the public about the needs and abilities of people with facial difference.

Currently, there are about 50 local chapters of AboutFace across North America. The organization provides assistance to anyone who is interested in starting and maintaining a local chapter.

Let's Face It. In 1984, Christine Piff started an organization in England called Let's Face It. At that time she was recovering from having half of her face removed due to a rare facial cancer. There was nowhere for her to turn for the support she was seeking during and after her surgeries. As a result, she singlehandedly started providing support to other people with facial difference, their families, friends, and professionals—in the process starting Let's Face It. Today, this organization serves people throughout the United Kingdom and the world by providing a support network for anyone with facial difference, along with opportunities for social activities, pen pals, health information, group meetings, newsletters, referral, and, in Ms. Piff's words, "crying, laughing, and dying." Professionals are also encouraged to become involved in Let's Face It activities and to help organize group meetings.

In 1987, Ms. Piff's idea was brought to the United States by Betsy Wilson. Ms. Wilson directs the American activities of Let's Face It with the aim of linking people with facial difference, their families, friends, and professionals so they can share experiences, strengths, and hopes. Group members actively participate in educating the public and professionals to "value the person behind the face" by working with medical schools and appearing on television programs. The group also publishes the annual *Resources for People with Facial Difference*, which has evolved into the "yellow pages" of information for people with facial difference, their families, and professionals. Included in this directory are organizations, publications, educational materials including videos and games, and educational opportunities. Ordering information for the directory is included in the Reading List.

Condition Specific Organizations. Over the years, a variety of organizations such as the Treacher Collins Foundation have been founded to provide information, support, and education about specific conditions of facial difference. These are listed in the Resource Guide. In addition, some hospitals and physicians have started support organizations for their patients. Your craniofacial center can tell you if there are any of these organizations in your area. Also, CLEFTLINE can refer you to groups they are aware of. If there is not a local support group in your area, consider starting one. You can look to the established groups such as About-Face for guidance in getting started.

Keys to Successful Advocacy

Unfortunately, there are no foolproof methods of advocating for your child's needs; no guarantees that those in a position to help you actually *will* help you. I have, however, found that there are certain strategies that increase your chances of success when advocating for your child. These include compromise and negotiation; listening and communicating; choosing your battles; and reframing negative situations into positive situations.

Compromise and Negotiation

It would certainly be a wonderful world if everything we needed and requested for our children with facial difference was cheerfully offered and given. Unfortunately, this doesn't always happen. It is certainly important to set your sights high for your child, but you must also keep in mind that all of your expectations may not be met, or may not be met in the way you would prefer. If you show a willingness to compromise and negotiate, however, your flexibility will generally be appreciated and your child will often receive at least some of what you are asking for. Something is better than nothing, and you can always continue working toward getting more of what your child needs.

Listening and Communicating

In advocating for your child, it is important to listen to what is actually being said and then respond to it. Situations may not always be as they first appear. There may be political or financial reasons why you are not getting what you request, or there may be

personality conflicts involved. If at first you meet with resistance to what you're seeking for your child, you must continue to communicate with those in a position to effect change. If you are perceived as closed or unwilling to communicate, the process can come to a standstill.

In the situation that I described at the beginning of the chapter, communication played a major role in my eventual decision not to pursue speech and language services through the state program. As I was making my decision about what to do and whom to believe, I talked to several workers I trusted. At first they were reluctant to answer my questions. When they finally did, they indicated that they didn't necessarily agree with the recommendation that my son receive multiple therapies, but they felt as if their hands were tied because the recommendation came from their supervisor. These comments let me know what type of "battle" I might be in for. The information helped me decide not to continue to argue with the people in the program. If I hadn't pursued this information and listened carefully to the answers, I might not have found out what I needed to know to make a decision.

Choosing Your Battles, or "Don't Sweat the Small Stuff"

At the birth of a child with facial difference, everything can seem so overwhelming and equally important. In time, life settles down and in, and some things seem less important and others more. How does this happen? As parents, we start selecting what needs attention and how fast, and what can slide (we prioritize, in other words). As we continue doing this, year after year, we get very good at it. The day is only twenty-four hours long, and if we put an equal amount of time and energy into everything that came our way, there would be no time or energy left to enjoy our children and live our lives.

The importance of choosing my battles really hit home just days before my son and I were scheduled to leave for his fourth outer ear surgery in ten months. Out of the blue, I was informed that Sam was behind his peers in academics because he had missed so much school due to his three previous operations. Therefore, he would probably need to have an aide assigned to him the next year to help him catch up. This news really caught me off guard, as I believed that he was academically in the middle of his class and fit right in.

Instead of arguing about whether Sam really needed an aide, I chose to focus my energy instead on preparations for travel and surgery. I decided to look at the importance of kindergarten within the educational system and the scheme of life, and to put this experience into perspective. Within this perspective, I decided that no one single experience was a prophesy for Sam's success in life. Plenty of people who are happy and successful become this way despite the words and actions of doomsayers. If Sam ended up with a classroom aide the next year, it really would not be the end of the world.

As it turned out, Sam was not assigned an aide, as he didn't meet the criteria for needing one-on-one support. And the new teacher agreed to be trained by me and a hearing consultant in techniques that would enhance Sam's ability to hear in the classroom.

Reframing Negative Situations

Every time you go to bat for your child, you can view the situation as a learning experience. Whether you're successful or unsuccessful, what you learn can help you the next time you need to advocate for your child. Even if you fail utterly to achieve what you were after, you may gain tremendous insights into how the educational or medical system works, into the laws that guarantee your child specific rights or benefits, or just into human nature. No matter how successful or unsuccessful you are, you need to recognize the positive aspects of the advocacy process. If you don't, you will have trouble continuing to advocate for your child. If positive support doesn't come from others, you need to learn how to create some for yourself. Finding something positive in a negative experience is one way of doing that. You are also providing a good model for your child, who will one day need the tools to advocate for herself.

To return to the example above, I was determined that something positive would come out of Sam's experiences in kindergarten. I was determined to establish better lines of communication about Sam's special needs in the classroom. A week before the next school year started, I therefore encouraged the special education director at his school to schedule a meeting with Sam's new teacher, all the other adults who would work with him, the hearing consultant, and my husband and me. At this meeting, we offered everyone information on Sam's hearing and facial difference, dispelled myths, and answered questions. This meeting should have occurred before Sam began kindergarten, but it didn't. I truly believe, however, that it is never too late to reframe a negative situation into a positive one.

Conclusion

I like to think that advocates are made, not born. I never thought of myself as an advocate for any cause, or that I had the skills or abilities to be an advocate. Then my son was born. From the day of his birth onward, I learned that a child with a condition of facial difference can be a curiosity to professionals and the public. I also learned that my son's self-esteem and our family's life could be hurt by this curiosity. Soon I realized that I wanted my son and our family to live a normal life, as unencumbered as possible by this curiosity. The seeds of my advocacy were sown in the nursery!

I can't say that all of my advocacy efforts have produced the precise results I would have wished for. People and bureaucracies are not always as welcoming or flexible as we would like them to be, although things are generally better today than they were years ago. I can say, however, that I have never regretted my advocacy and have always tried to learn a little something from each experience. I can also say that my son's life up to the present and his future prospects are better than they would have been if I hadn't decided to stick up for his rights. What "they" say is really true: You *are* your child's best advocate.

Parent Statements

I have contacted dozens of support organizations. It was very helpful to speak to other parents, and I am now returning the favor and speaking to new parents of children with my daughter's condition.

�֎

I have probably contacted almost every support organization possible. I rely a lot on friends, family, and professionals for emotional support. Now I want to be a resource parent and help others who are going through similar experiences.

✖

The only support groups in our area are for kids with Down syndrome or severe handicaps. My daughter's in the middle, and there's nothing for her.

✖

We haven't had any trouble getting the school to do as we wish. This may be because I can be loud and abrasive and I know how to write letters if things don't go according to plan. I'm usually on top of everything, so they don't slack off on care to my son.

✖

Having Michael has forced me to be more assertive and persistent.

✖

The school generally wants to provide less speech therapy than our craniofacial team has recommended. But after I demand it, they provide what I want. Still, the school seems to stretch out the time limits from testing to providing the service. School starts August 17. Speech therapy starts October 1 and ends in April!

✖

When Robert was ill for so long with severe ear problems, we had to beg for a tutor. At first we were told there was a "waiting list." Wrong! After several phone calls, they gave him a tutor.

✖

All children born with facial differences should have a better life.

❈

I hate fundraiser TV programs. I would, however, participate in radio or TV interview shows whose goal was to increase awareness of facial differences.

❈

I took part when our PBS channel filmed a short program on craniofacial disorders. It aired over a hundred times in one year. I'd definitely do something like this again.

❈

Our family, including Scott, participated in a Health Awareness for Charities Day. So did Scott's surgeon. I think it made a big difference in how much money was raised for our local cleft society.

❈

Because Jamie's condition is so rare, health care providers do not know much about it. I find myself educating them. At first, this was very frustrating.

❈

We need to let our elected officials know that a facial difference is not just a matter of surgery: there are dental problems, speech therapy needs, auditory problems, increased risk of infection.

❈

You don't realize how assertive you can be until you are looking out for your child. More than once, I had to be assertive with the nurses who took care of Clare after surgery. They never had her pain medication ready and were in no hurry to get it.

❈

The speech therapists my insurance company sent me to had no experience with cleft lip and palate. I had to really fight the insurance company to be able to take her to a therapist with experience.

❈

A parent of a "special needs" child must *always* be assertive by asking questions, calling for meetings to discuss your child, obtaining several opinions to determine the best approach for treatment. The parent is the one who coordinates meetings between professionals and follows up to get the necessary information disseminated in the right directions. The parent has to stay on top of medical claims to make sure they are processed properly, and, when they are refused, the parent must argue as to why they should be paid.

He makes us realize how many barriers are out there, and how many people we need to educate.

GLOSSARY

accommodations - any changes made to the regular school program that will help a child succeed. Includes changes in teaching methods, services provided by a professional other than a classroom teacher, special technology or equipment, or changes to the physical classroom.

ADA - Americans with Disabilities Act. A sweeping civil rights law designed to prohibit discrimination against people with disabilities by employers, by public and private services, by "public accommodations," and in the area of telecommunications. Failure to make "reasonable accommodations" is defined as discrimination.

adenoids - lymphatic tissue in the back of the throat.

advocacy - supporting or promoting a cause; speaking out.

amblyopia - diminished vision in one or both eyes due to lack of use.

American Sign Language - form of sign language in which people use their hands to make signs which represent ideas.

anesthesiologist - physician who specializes in administering drugs and gases to produce a state of sleep and a loss of feeling in the body so that a surgical procedure can take place.

anomaly - a change or deviation from what is considered typical.

anotia - congenital absence of external ear(s).

anthropologist - scientist who specializes in monitoring and charting the size, weight, and proportion of the parts of your child's body, especially the bones; may also be known as a *medical anthropometrist.*

antimongoloid - downward slanting eyes.

aortic arch anomalies - malformation (such as narrowing) of one of the arteries originating from the aortic arch of the heart.

apnea - stoppage of air flow for longer than ten seconds before the child starts breathing again.

apnea monitor - device that is attached to electrodes on your child's body and makes a loud noise whenever your child's respirations do not occur in a normal pattern.

Apert syndrome - a condition of facial difference (craniosynostosis) characterized by a large skull, widely spaced eye sockets, bulging eyeballs, tilted eyelids, underdevelopment of the upper jaw, misalignment and crowding of the teeth, webbed fingers, toes or both; can also include cleft palate and mental retardation.

articulation - the ability to move and control the lips, tongue, jaw and palate to produce the sounds of a language.

assessment - process to determine a child's strengths and weaknesses. Includes testing and observations performed by a team of professionals and parents. Term is often used interchangeably with *evaluation.*

asymmetry - both sides are not equally affected, such as one side of the face is different from the other side.

atresia - closing or absence of a normal body opening, such as the ear canal.

audiogram - electrical study of hearing plotted on a graph.

audiologic assessment - hearing test.

audiologist - health professional who determines how well your child hears by administering tests and evaluating the presence of fluid in the ears.

Auditory Brainstem Response (ABR) - objective test to assess hearing in an infant; also known as *Evoked Response Audiometry (ERA).*

auditory canal - tube that connects the outer ear to the middle ear.

auditory word discrimination - ability to hear sounds within words.

aural - hearing.

auricle - external or outer ear; also known as *pinna.*

autosomal dominant inheritance - a pattern of genetic inheritance; anyone who carries an autosomal dominant gene has a 50:50 chance with each and every pregnancy of passing it on to offspring; for example, Treacher Collins syndrome, Crouzon syndrome, Apert syndrome.

autosomal recessive inheritance - pattern of genetic inheritance; affected child receives an altered gene from *both* his mother and his father; e.g., Carpenter syndrome.

autosomes - 22 of the 23 pairs of chromosomes present in each human cell; they contain the genes that determine all characteristics except gender.

bilateral - related to both sides.

binaural - using two hearing aids.

bonding - process by which an infant and parent, most often the mother, psychologically attach to one another.

bone distraction - surgical bone lengthening technique also known as distraction osteogenesis.

brachydactyly - short fingers.

canalplasty - surgical opening of the ear canal.

cardiopulmonary - lung and heart.

Carpenter syndrome - condition of facial difference characterized by an asymmetric tower-shaped skull, short neck, webbing of fingers and toes, and extra fingers.

case advocacy - working for the rights of one particular individual.

CAT scan - *See* CT scan.

Child Find - program designed to identify children with special needs prior to the beginning of age-appropriate schooling (usually kindergarten). Through Child Find, school districts are required to notify the public that they offer developmental assessments to children who reside within their geographic boundaries.

choana - passage leading from the back of the nasal cavity into the nasopharynx.

choanal atresia - narrowing or closure above the soft palate between the nose and throat which can obstruct breathing; atresia can be due to soft tissue only or a bony obstruction.

chromosome - a threadlike string of genes; each cell ordinarily has 46 chromosomes located in the nucleus.

class advocacy - advocating for long-lasting benefits for a number of people in similar situations.

cleft - split in an anatomic structure, such as a cleft lip or cleft palate.

cleft lip (or palate) feeder - special feeding bottle and nipple designed for babies who have a cleft lip and/or palate. Often useful for babies with other conditions of facial difference.

cleft palate team - interdisciplinary team made up of the family of a child with a cleft lip and/or palate, the child, and health care professionals who specialize in treating children with cleft lip and palate.

cochlea - spiral tube forming part of the inner ear which is the essential organ of hearing.

collaboration - families and professionals working together toward the same goal(s).

coloboma - notching of the eyelid, iris, or retina.

conditioned orientation reflex (COR) - response made by a child to a sound.

conductive hearing loss - hearing impairment that originates in the outer or middle ear due to a blockage in the sound passageway.

congenital - present at birth.

content of language - what the words mean.

cosmetic surgery - surgery that is performed to reshape normal structures of the body in order to improve the patient's appearance and self-esteem.

craniofacial - pertaining to the head and face.

craniofacial abnormalities (anomalies) - conditions of facial difference characterized by underdevelopment, overdevelopment, absence of, or past trauma to, the bones and soft tissues of the head and face.

craniofacial surgeon - plastic surgeon who specializes in correction of conditions of facial difference. *See* plastic surgeon.

craniofacial team - interdisciplinary team made up of health care professionals who specialize in treating patients with facial difference, the family of a child with facial difference, and the child.

craniosynostosis - premature closing of the seams between the bones of the skull.

Crouzon syndrome - condition of facial difference (craniosynostosis) characterized by an underdevelopment of the bones in the middle third of the face and skull; a high, flat, prominent forehead and increased head width, bulging of the eyes, strabismus, receded upper jaw, high and narrow palate.

CT or CAT scan - diagnostic procedure in which a computerized machine takes cross-sectional x-ray pictures of the body.

decibel (dB) - unit of measurement for intensity (loudness) of sounds.

dentist - a professional who diagnoses and treats problems with your child's teeth and the inside of his mouth. See also *pedodontist*.

depression - a condition characterized by symptoms such as poor appetite or overeating; sleeping too little or too much; low energy or fatigue; low self-esteem; poor concentration or difficulty making decisions; feelings of hopelessness.

dermoid cyst - congenital sacs containing a liquid or semi-solid substance, sometimes bone, hair, and teeth (in ovaries).

due process hearing - part of the procedures established to protect the rights of parents and children with special needs during disputes under IDEA (Public Law 101–476). These are hearings before an impartial hearing officer to review the identification, evaluation, placement, and services by a child's educational agency.

dyspraxia - partial loss of ability to perform coordinated movements; for example, difficulty planning the movements needed to pronounce sounds.

early intervention - the specialized way of interacting with infants and toddlers to minimize the effects of conditions that can delay early development. *See* Part H.

"educationally handicapped" - label given to a child if he has one or more of the handicapping conditions listed in the law, and if that condition has a significant impact on the child's functioning at school.

encephalocele - a condition in which the brain, meninges (membranes surrounding the brain and spinal cord), or both protrude through an opening in the skull.

epidemiologist - scientist who specializes in studying the frequency, distribution, and causes of health problems, including facial differences.

epiphoral - excessive tearing of the eyes.

evaluation - *See* assessment.

Evoked Response Audiometry (ERA) - *See* Auditory Brainstem Response (ABR).

exorbitism - bulging of the eye because the bony cavity (orbit) around the eye is too small and shallow. Also known as *exophthalmos.*

exposure keratitis - inflammation of the cornea.

expressive language - the ability to use language to express oneself to others.

expressivity - the degree to which a genetic disorder affects the body structures.

extubation - removal of the breathing tube from the nose or mouth that was used during general anesthesia.

facial difference - generic term for a variety of conditions that can affect a child's head and face.

Family and Medical Leave Act of 1993 - federal law which stipulates that if you work for a business which employs at least 50 people, your employer must allow you to take up to twelve weeks of unpaid leave to care for a child with a serious health condition (Public Law 103–3).

feeding specialist - professional who is trained to help infants and young children who have problems with the physical process of eating or behavioral problems associated with eating.

feeding tube - tube made of soft plastic used for feeding children who are not able to get enough nutrition through regular feeding and eating. *See* naso-gastric (NG) tube, gastrostomy (G-tube) tube, and gavage tube.

fine motor - related to the use of the small muscles of the body.

finger spelling - using the hands to spell out words.

fluency - the way speech flows.

Freeman-Sheldon syndrome - a genetic condition of facial difference characterized by microstomia (small mouth), flat mid-face, webbing of the neck, contractures of the hands and fingers, and club feet. Also called "whistling face syndrome." The condition can run in families or occur spontaneously.

frequency - hearing: number of times per second the sound causes the fluid in the middle ear to vibrate; genetics: number of members of a population (1 in 10,000).

fronto-orbital advancement - operation on the front of the skull and upper eyes to expand (bring forward) these structures.

gastrostomy (G-tube) tube - feeding tube that is inserted through an incision in the abdomen directly into the stomach.

gavage tube - feeding tube that is inserted through the mouth and into the stomach.

genes - bits of chemical information (DNA) in every body cell that serve as a blueprint for our development, determining such characteristics as hair color and stature.

genetic - related to a person's genes. *Genetic conditions* are caused by the presence of one or more altered genes or by the absence of one or more genes.

genetic counselor - professional who specializes in informing families about the risks and nature of inherited conditions and syndromes; this person typically holds a master's degree.

geneticist - physician who specializes in identifying inherited conditions and syndromes and advising families about their risks and nature.

genioplasty - a surgical procedure to alter the position or appearance of the chin.

germline mosaicism - a condition in which someone who appears to be unaffected by a genetic condition has a group of cells (eggs or sperm) that carry the gene for the condition.

glossoptosis - backward-positioned tongue.

Goldenhar syndrome - one of many names for hemifacial microsomia, also known as oculo-auriculo-vertebral syndrome.

graft - procedure of transferring bone and tissue from one site in the body to another.

gross motor - relating to the use of the large muscles of the body.

Haberman Feeder - special feeding bottle and nipple designed for babies who have a cleft palate; sometimes also used for babies with other conditions of facial difference.

harvesting - removal of bone and tissue from one site in the body to be used at another site.

hearing aid - device which amplifies sound; types include: body level, behind-the-ear, in-the-ear.

hearing threshold - decibel level at which a person's brain starts to respond to sound.

hemangioma - a usually harmless tumor made up of blood vessels that can occur as a birthmark or develop later in life. Can be flat or raised; found anywhere in the body, but usually in the skin. Types include: "strawberry" or "raspberry" marks, port wine stains, cavernous.

hemifacial microsomia - condition of facial difference characterized by an underdevelopment of facial bones and soft tissue on one side of the face. Common features include: underdevelopment of the cheekbone and lower jaw, chewing muscles, temple, outer and middle ear, facial nerve and facial muscles, hearing loss, dental problems, notch at the corner of the mouth (macrostomia). Also known as oculo-auricular-vertebral syndrome.

Hertz (Hz) - cycles per second; unit used to measure frequency. 1 Hz = 1 cycle per second.

HMO - Health Maintenance Organization. A system of health care delivery in which all the health care services its members need are offered within the HMO system. HMOs therefore may not agree to refer or financially cover health care professionals or services outside of their HMO system.

holoprosencephaly - a congenital condition in which the brain fails to divide into two cerebral hemispheres. Characteristics include cleft lip and palate, ear anomalies and deafness, eye anomalies, microcephaly, mental retardation, and infant mortality.

hypernasal - voice that sounds too nasal.

hypertelorism - *See* orbital hypertelorism.

hyponasal - voice that sounds "plugged up," as if the child has a cold.

hypopharyngeal obstruction - obstruction of the opening into the larynx and esophagus.

hypoplasia - underdevelopment of a structure.

IDEA - **I**ndividuals with **D**isabilities **E**ducation **A**ct, the federal law that guarantees all children with "handicapping conditions" (as specified in the law) the right to a free appropriate public education; it is Public Law 101–476.

identification - the determination that a child should be evaluated as a possible candidate for special education services.

IEP - Individualized Education Plan. The written plan that describes the services and goals that the local education agency has agreed to provide a child with special needs.

IFSP - Individualized Family Service Plan. The written plan that details who will provide what services to a child aged birth through two who has a developmental delay or is at risk of a developmental delay. It is developed by professionals and families working together as a team.

inner ear - contains the cochlea, auditory nerve, and vestibular canals.

interdisciplinary team - team of parents and professionals from a variety of professions with the intent of working together towards a common goal. *See* multidisciplinary; craniofacial team.

intervention - steps taken to accomplish an end or a goal intended to benefit another; used when discussing surgery, therapy, etc.

intubation - placement of a breathing tube into the nose or throat used with general anesthesia.

language - the expression and understanding of human communication.

Least Restrictive Environment - the requirement under IDEA (Public Law 101–476) that children with "handicapping conditions" who receive special education must be made a part of the regular school to the fullest extent possible. Included in the law as a way of ending the traditional practice of isolating children with disabling conditions.

Local Education Agency (LEA) - the agency responsible for providing educational services on the local (city, county, and school district) level.

localize (sound) - ability to recognize what direction sounds come from.

lower face - area of the face below the nose.

macrostomia - excessive width of the mouth, usually one-sided, as in hemifacial microsomia.

major life activity - includes caring for oneself, performing manual tasks, walking, seeing, hearing, speaking, breathing, learning, and working. *See* Section 504 of the Rehabilitation Act of 1973.

malocclusion - malposition of the two jaws resulting in the faulty meeting of the teeth.

mandible - lower jaw.

mastoid bone - cranial bone directly behind the outer ear.

maxilla - upper jaw.

maxillofacial abnormalities - differences that occur in jaw areas of the middle to lower face.

maxillofacial surgeon - surgeon who specializes in operations to treat skeletal problems of the lower half of the head and face.

Medicaid - health insurance program for people with low income and limited assets. Application procedure and qualifications for eligibility differ from state to state, but in most states, children who receive SSI benefits also qualify for Medicaid.

medical anthropometrist - *See* anthropologist.

medically necessary care for facial disfigurement - includes appropriate and reasonable assessment, treatment, and follow-up care. Medically necessary care may include medical-surgical treatment; hearing and speech evaluation and management; psychological and psychiatric evaluation and care; dental evaluation and treatment; medical supplies and devices; dental and prosthetic appliances; and other services as prescribed by qualified health care providers. Care is medically necessary for the purposes of treating infection, pain, ulceration, bleeding, and disease; for the improvement of speech, sight, breathing, swallowing, chewing, hearing, emotional functioning, etc.; for restoration of facial function and form needed for a more normal appearance, and social acceptance.

mental health professional - generic term for a professional who is trained in understanding human behavior, emotions, and how the mind works; this professional can be a psychologist, counselor, social worker, psychiatrist, etc.

mental retardation - a condition that begins before the age of 18 years and is characterized by intellectual functioning of approximately 70 or below on an individually administered IQ (Intelligence Quotient) test, as well as impairments in at least two areas of adaptive behavior (skills that enable an individual to function independently). Examples of adaptive behavior include communication, self-care, home living, and social/interpersonal skills, use of community resources, self-direction, functional academic skills, work, leisure, health, and safety skills.

microcephaly - small head size in relation to the rest of the body; below the third percentile on growth charts.

micrognathia - underdevelopment of the lower jaw.

microphthalmia - small eye.

microstomia - a mouth that is smaller than usual.

microtia - underdeveloped outer ear.

middle ear - the air-filled cavity between the outer and inner ears that contains the three tiny bones (malleus, incus, stapes) which make up the ossicles.

middle face - area of the face which extends from the eyebrows to the bottom of the nose.

mixed hearing loss - conductive hearing loss in combination with a sensorineural hearing loss.

Moebius syndrome - a condition of facial difference characterized by paralysis of the seventh (sometimes sixth) cranial nerve(s), microtia, and sometimes chest and limb anomalies (extra or webbed fingers or toes), cleft palate, hearing impairment, and a small mouth and jaw.

monaural - using one hearing aid.

motility - the ability to move; children with motility problems with their eyes have difficulty moving their eyes in a coordinated fashion.

multidisciplinary team - team made up of professionals representing a variety of disciplines, parents, and child. *See* interdisciplinary; craniofacial team.

multifactorial inheritance - pattern of inheritance which cannot be traced to any one cause. It is probably caused by the interaction of both genetic and environmental factors; for example, cleft lip and palate.

mutation - a permanent change in a gene that occurs by chance.

Nager syndrome - a condition of facial difference commonly characterized by flat cheeks and downslanting eyes, almost total absence of the eyelashes, lowset cupped ears, very small lower jaw, asymmetric underdevelopment of the thumbs and forearms.

naso-gastric (NG) tube - feeding tube that is inserted through the nose, down the esophagus, and into the stomach.

nasopharynx - part of the pharynx (throat) above the soft palate.

neurosurgeon - surgeon who specializes in operations on the brain and correction of the upper skull (cranium).

nevus - a pigmented or nonpigmented spot on the skin; may be flat or raised, hairy, smooth, or warty. Some types include: nevus flammeus (port wine stain—a flat, purple-red mark, usually on face or neck); nevus vasculosus (strawberry mark—a bright red, raised mark that increases in size); systematized nevus (a widespread congenital nevus that follows a pattern).

nutritionist - professional with expertise in how the human body takes in and uses nutrients for growth, energy, and maintenance.

obstructive apnea - stoppage of air flow for several seconds because of an obstruction in the upper airway.

obturator - a device worn in the mouth to decrease nasal air flow during speech.

occupational therapist - professional who helps a child work on small muscle strength and coordination so that he can improve his self-care skills, as well as leisure and work skills such as handwriting.

O.M.E.N.S. - classification system used to help medical professionals document and study treatment of hemifacial microsomia. O = orbital symmetry; M = mandibular hypoplasia; E = ear deformity; N = nerve involvement; and S = soft tissue deformity.

open bite - when teeth on the upper and lower jaws do not make complete contact when clenched; can be either anterior (front teeth) or posterior (back teeth).

operation - surgical procedure.

ophthalmologist - physician who specializes in diagnosing and treating eye problems, prescribes medication, and is skilled at delicate eye surgery.

optician - specialist trained to make prescription lenses used for correcting vision.

optometrist - specialist trained to examine the eye and prescribe corrective lenses, such as eyeglasses or contact lenses, to improve vision.

orbital hypertelorism - widely spaced eyes, also known as "hypertelorbitism."

orbits - eyes.

orphan - *See* rare.

orthodontia - devices such as braces and retainers that gradually exert pressure to move the teeth into a better position.

orthodontist - dentist who aligns and straightens teeth by using braces, retainers, etc. and who monitors and treats malocclusions.

oscillator - vibrator on a bone conduction hearing aid; it sends vibrations or sound waves through the bone of the skull.

osseointegration - implants screwed into bone for attaching teeth, prosthetic body parts such as ears, or appliances such as a hearing aid.

ossicles - the three small bones in the middle ear: incus, malleus, stapes.

osteotomy - cut made in bone.

otitis media - inflammation of the middle ear which is often accompanied by a build-up of fluid in the space normally filled with air.

Otoacoustic Emissions Test - a hearing screening test used in early infancy to determine whether the cochlea is vibrating normally to sound stimulation and whether the middle ear responds normally to sound.

outer ear - the part of the ear that is visible outside of the head. *See* pinna; auricle.

palate - roof of the mouth, separated into the hard and soft palate.

Part B - section of IDEA (PL 101–476) which provides for educational services for children ages 3–21. *See* IDEA.

Part H - section of IDEA (PL 101–476) which provides for educational services for children birth-3. *See* IDEA.

Passey-Muir valve - valve used to plug a tracheostomy so that air passes around the tube and into the mouth and nose.

PCA (patient controlled analgesia) - self-administration of a prescribed dose of pain medication into the intravenous line; controlled by a computer to prevent over-dosage.

pediatrician - physician who specializes in the general medical care of children.

pedodontist - dentist who specializes in treating children.

Pfeiffer syndrome - a condition of facial difference (craniosynostosis) characterized by a tall head that is flat in the front, bulging of the eyes, a receded midface, high arched palate, crowded teeth, broad thumbs and big toes, and usually normal intelligence.

pharynx - throat.

physical therapist - professional who uses activities and exercises to help a child overcome problems with movement and posture, usually involving large muscles of the body.

Pierre Robin sequence - a condition of facial difference characterized by severe underdevelopment of the lower jaw, a backward-positioned tongue, and usually a cleft palate. If other problems are noted, the child has a syndrome.

The two conditions that most commonly cause Pierre Robin sequence are *Stickler* and *velocardiofacial (Shprintzen)* syndromes.

pinna - outer ear; also known as auricle.

pitch of a sound - highness or lowness of a sound.

P.L. 94–142 - The Education of all Handicapped Children Act; the predecessor of IDEA.

P.L. 101–476 - *See* IDEA.

plagiocephaly - asymmetric (twisted) skull, usually caused by compression while within the mother's uterus ("deformation plagiocephaly"). Rarely caused by premature fusion of sutures ("synostotic plagiocephaly"). Most commonly, the forehead suture closes prematurely (unilateral coronal synostosis).

plastic surgeon - surgeon who builds, constructs, reconstructs, corrects, or improves the shape and appearance of body structures.

play audiometry - method of testing hearing using play activities.

polygenetic disorders - conditions that are caused by a combination of altered genes, rather than a single altered gene; for example, familial cleft palate.

polyhydramnios - excess amniotic fluid.

port wine stain - a flat, purple-red birthmark. *See* hemangioma; nevus

post-op - after the operation.

pre-existing condition - term used by insurance companies to indicate that a child's medical condition existed before he was put onto the policy; can be a reason to deny or reduce insurance coverage.

pre-op - before the operation.

pressure equalization tubes (PE) - tiny ventilating tubes inserted in the eardrums to equalize the pressure of the middle ear.

prosthodontist - dentist who specializes in making oral appliances such as dentures and bite plates.

psychiatrist - physician who specializes in the study, treatment, and prevention of mental disorders.

psychologist - professional trained in understanding human behavior, emotions, and how the mind works.

ptosis - "droopy" eyelids, due to an abnormality of the muscle that elevates the eyelids.

Public Law 101–476 - *See* IDEA.

rare - as classified by the National Organization for Rare Disorders (NORD), a condition diagnosed in 200,000 or fewer Americans.

reasonable accommodation - efforts made to remove the obstacles that stand in the way of accessibility but do not result in an unreasonable financial burden.

receptive language - the ability to understand other's language.

reconstructive surgery - surgery performed on atypical structures of the body, caused by congenital problems, developmental differences, trauma or injury, infection, tumors or disease. It is generally performed to improve function, but may also be done to approximate a "normal" appearance (per the American Society of Plastic and Reconstructive Surgeons).

residual hearing - degree of hearing a child with hearing impairments is born with or has without the use of hearing aids.

respiration - breathing in and out.

respite care - skilled or unskilled child care and supervision that can be provided in a family's home or the home or site of a caregiver; may be available for several hours on a regular basis or overnight stays.

retruded - sloping backward.

Saethre-Chotzen syndrome - a condition of facial difference (craniosynostosis) characterized by asymmetric head and face, low-set hairline with turned-up hair follicles, droopy eyelids (ptosis), low-set ears, beaklike nose, deviated septum, short fingers with some possible fusing.

scaphocephaly - "boat"-shaped skull.

Section 504 of the Rehabilitation Act of 1973 - civil rights law which prohibits any program or activity that receives federal funds from discriminating against people with disabling conditions.

self-esteem - an individual's feelings and opinion about himself.

sensorineural hearing loss - hearing impairment which originates in the inner ear or auditory nerve.

sex chromosome - chromosome which determines gender. Females have two x chromosomes; males have one x and one y.

sign language - language that is not spoken, but is performed by making signs with one's hands. *See* American Sign Language; Signed English

Signed English - form of sign language in which spoken language is translated word for word into gestures; people use their hands to make signs that represent words or to spell words.

sleep apnea - at least thirty episodes during a seven-hour period of sleep during which the air flow stops for longer than ten seconds before the child starts breathing again.

social worker - professional who monitors and assists the social, emotional, and psychological growth and development of a child and family.

soft palate - fleshy area at the back of the roof of the mouth; contains the muscles that elevate the palate during eating and speaking.

sound booth - small room where the audiologist can close the door and regulate sound without interference from outside noises; used as a testing environment for hearing.

special education - a package of specially designed instruction and services (such as occupational or speech-language therapy) tailored to meet the individual needs of a child with a disabling condition.

special needs - needs generated by a person's disabling condition.

speech and language pathologist - professional who specializes in analyzing difficulties with speech and communication and ways to improve these skills.

S.S.I. - Supplemental Security Income. A program administered by the Social Security Administration to provide financial assistance for people with lower incomes who are blind, aged, or have disabling conditions; eligibility is based on income and need, not on past earnings.

stages of coping - stages generally involved include: shock; denial; sadness, anger and anxiety; adaptation; and reorganization.

stenosis - narrowing.

Stickler syndrome - a condition of facial difference which is characterized by skeletal abnormalities, arthritis, and eye problems, in addition to features of *Pierre Robin sequence.*

strabismus - misaligned ("crossed") eyes due to imbalance of the muscles or other causes.

Sturge-Weber syndrome - a congenital condition characterized by a port wine stain, usually on one side of the face, and a hemangioma on the brain. May also include seizures, glaucoma, developmental delays, and enlarging of the eye on the side of the port wine stain.

submucous palatal cleft - cleft in the palate that is not visible; there is separation of the muscles of the soft palate, but not in the skin covering the muscles.

Supplemental Security Income - See *S.S.I.*

sutures - seams between the bones of the skull which permit the skull to expand as the brain grows in size.

symmetry - when both sides are affected equally or to a similar degree, such as in Treacher Collins syndrome.

syndrome - a recognized pattern of differences, occurring in different areas of the body, considered to have a single and specific cause.

synostosis - abnormal and premature joining of the skull bones.

synostotic plagiocephaly - oblique or twisted skull due to premature closure of a suture—usually the coronal suture; rarely the lambdoid suture.

telecanthus - increased distance between the inner angles of the eyes.

temporomandibular joint (TMJ) - joint between the side of the skull and lower jaw.

tetralogy of Fallot - a complex malformation of the heart in which there is ventricular septal defect (VSD, a hole between ventricles), pulmonary stenosis (narrowing of the artery to the lungs), dextroposition of the aorta (aorta exiting from the right, rather than left, side of the heart), and hypertrophy (enlargement) of the right ventricle. The condition causes cyanosis ("blue baby")—lack of enough oxygen in the blood.

total communication - using a variety of methods to communicate, including speech, sign language, finger spelling, lipreading, and anything else that might be helpful.

trachea - windpipe.

tracheostomy - tube placed in the throat to make sure there is adequate oxygen flow.

transdisciplinary - across disciplines.

transposition of the great vessels - a condition in which the aorta comes off the right side of the heart (carrying unoxygenated blood) and the pulmonary artery comes off the left side of the heart (carrying oxygenated blood); this is the opposite of usual. Results in insufficient oxygenation of blood. Also called aortic dextroposition and is a component of tetralogy of Fallot.

Treacher Collins syndrome - a condition of facial difference characterized by bilateral and symmetric underdevelopment of the bones and soft tissue of the head and face. Common features include: downward slanting eyes, notching of the lower eyelids, sparse or absent eyelashes in the inner one-third of the lower eyelids, underdevelopment of the cheekbones, lower jaw and upper jaw, bite problems, small face, underdeveloped and/or unusually formed outer ears, and hearing loss.

trigonocephaly - triangular-shaped skull, due to premature fusion of the interfrontal (metopic) suture.

trismus - spasms of the jaw muscles.

unilateral - on one side, vs. bilateral, on both sides.

upper face - area of the face which extends from the eyebrows to the hairline.

velocardiofacial (Shprintzen) syndrome - a condition of facial difference, characterized by flattening of the cheeks, a receded lower jaw, prominent nose with a square-shaped root, narrow eyelid openings, narrow nasal passages, long and thin upper lip with down-slanting mouth, cleft palate or submucous cleft palate, abnormalities of the heart, and learning disabilities. Some infants exhibit Pierre Robin sequence.

voice - speech sounds coming from the larynx.

zygoma - cheekbone, malar bone.

READING LIST

This Reading List is a compilation of materials that may be of interest to families of children with facial difference and the professionals who serve them. It is organized to coincide with each chapter in this book. We are lucky, however, that this list is not inclusive of every publication available—more pamphlets, books and booklets, guides, and packages are being written all the time. Your interests may also change over time. To keep current with materials, refer to the annual publication, Resources for People with Facial Difference, published by Let's Face It, P.O. Box 29972, Bellingham, WA 98228–1972.

Chapter 1

AboutFace (P.O. Box 93, Limekiln, PA 19535). Booklets: *Apert, Crouzon and Other Craniosynostosis; Making the Difference: Caring for the Newborn and Family Affected by Facial Disfigurement - An Orientation Package for Health Care Providers;* Pamphlets: *My Newborn Has a Facial Difference; You, Your Child and the Craniofacial Team.*

Batshaw, Mark and Yvonne Perret. *Children with Disabilities: A Medical Primer.* Baltimore, MD: Brookes Publishing Co. (P.O. Box 10624, 21285–0624), 1992. This sourcebook includes general and specific information on a variety of disabling conditions, including such facial differences as cleft lip and palate and Treacher Collins syndrome. Entire chapters address genetics and heredity, prenatal diagnosis and fetal growth, premature birth, technology assistance, feeding, dental care, hearing, language and communication, ethical dilemmas, and coping.

Berkowitz, Samuel. *The Cleft Palate Story.* Carol Stream, IL: Quintessence Publishing Co. (551 N. Kimberly Dr., 60188–1881), 1994. This is a practical guide designed to allay parent anxieties by describing how cleft palates can be managed and a successful outcome facilitated. Includes information on the definition of a cleft palate, feeding, heredity of clefts, speech and hearing, dental problems, social and emotional issues, closing of the cleft, and health care providers, insurance, and support organizations.

Buyse, Mary Louise (editor-in-chief). *Birth Defects Encyclopedia.* Dover, MA: Center for Birth Defects Information Services (Dover Medical Bldg., 30 Springdale Ave., Box 1776, 02030. 508–785–2525.), 1990. This encyclopedia is a comprehensive reference source for the diagnosis, cause, occurrence, prevention, and treatment of human anomalies known as birth defects. For the most current information on a condition, contact the center, which continually updates their database.

Children's Hospital of Wisconsin, Craniofacial Team. *A Team Approach to Children with Cleft Lip and Palate: A Resource Guide for Families.* Order from: Maxishare, P.O. Box 2041, Milwaukee, WI 53201. This booklet is designed to answer parents' questions about caring for a child with cleft lip and/or cleft palate. Covers types of cleft lips and palates, repair, feeding, speech and hearing.

Cleft Palate Foundation (1218 Grandview Avenue, Pittsburgh, PA 15211). The following is a listing of their current publications; contact the Foundation for pricing information: Booklets - *For Parents of Newborn Babies with Cleft Lip/Palate (available in Spanish); Cleft Lip and Cleft Palate: The First Four Years (available in Spanish); Cleft Lip and Cleft Palate - The Child from Three to Twelve Years; Information for the Teenager Born with a Cleft Lip and/or Palate; Feeding an Infant with a Cleft (available in Spanish); The Genetics of Cleft Lip and Palate.* Fact Sheets - *Information about Choosing a Cleft Palate or Craniofacial Team, Information about Crouzon's Disease, Information About Dental Care, Information about Financial Assistance, Information about Pierre Robin Malformation Sequence, Information about Submucous Cleft, Information about Treacher Collins Syndrome, Information about Treatment for Adults with Cleft Lip and Palate.*

Connecticut Cleft Lip and Palate Parent's Group. *There's a Little Problem, BUT...* Newington, CT: Newington Children's Hospital and the Connecticut Lip and Palate Parent's Group (Cleft Palate Center/Dept. of Speech Pathology, Newington Children's Hospital, 181 E. Cedar St., Newington, CT 06111), 1984. This booklet offers information on the Connecticut Parent's Group, emotions, feeding equipment and procedures, health professionals, and first surgery.

Craniofacial Institute. *Building on Today: A Guide to the Diagnosis and Treatment of Craniofacial Deformities.* Dallas, TX: Craniofacial Institute (Medical City Dallas Hospital, 7777 Forest Lane, 12th Floor, Suite C700, 75230–9988). This booklet describes conditions of facial difference and the treatment approach at the Craniofacial Institute.

Craniofacial Team - British Columbia's Children's Hospital. Vancouver, British Columbia, Canada: Craniofacial Team (British Columbia's Children's Hospital, 4480 Oak St., V6H 3V4), 1989. This parent-oriented booklet is written in very simple language. It offers information on: characteristics, genetics, multidisiplinary craniofacial team management, and information for teachers and schools for dealing with teasing.

Fearon, Jeffrey. *A Guide to Understanding Apert Syndrome, A Guide to Understanding Craniosynostosis, A Guide to Understanding Hemifacial Microsomia, A Guide to Understanding Microtia, A Guide to Understanding Treacher Collins Syndrome.* Children's Craniofacial Association: Dallas, TX (9441 LBJ Freeway, Suite 115, 75243), 1993. These parents' guides are designed to answer questions that are frequently asked by the parents of a child with that condition.

The Genetic Resource. Blatt, Robin J.R., Wayne A. Miller, Paula K. Haddow (editors). Boston, MA: MA Genetics Program (MA Dept.of Public Health, 150 Tremont, 7th Floor, 02111). A publication of the New England Regional Genetics Group (NERGG), this journal focuses on key developments in genetics that affect medical practice by sharing current information on new research, developments, trends and ideas in the field of genetics.

Human Genome News. Contact: Human Genome Management Information System, Betty Mansfield, Oak Ridge National Laboratory, P.O. Box 2008, Oak Ridge, TN 37831–6050. This is the newsletter for the Human Genome Project. It reviews meetings which take place around the world along with a calendar of upcoming events and conferences. Upon request, the staff can assist readers in locating genetic researchers and materials on genetics and genetic conditions.

Informed Consent: Participation in Genetic Research Studies. Chevy Chase, MD: Alliance of Genetic Support Groups (35 Wisconsin Circle, Suite 440, 20815). This pamphlet covers common pros and cons of participation in genetic research studies, and discusses important considerations to bear in mind when deciding whether to take part.

Loyola University of Chicago. *Craniofacial Surgery.* Maywood, IL: Loyola University Mulcahy Outpatient Center (Craniofacial Center, 2160 S. 1st Ave., Bldg. 106, Rm. 2532, 60153). This illustrated booklet was written for parents of children with craniosynostosis (scaphocephaly, plagiocephaly, brachycephaly, trigonencephaly, and Crouzon and Apert syndromes).

March of Dimes. White Plains, NY: March of Dimes Birth Defects Foundation (Supply Division, 1275 Mamaroneck Ave., 10605). Publications available include: *Cleft Lip and Palate Public Health Information Sheet* (1988), *Birth Defects* (1992), *Genetic Counseling* (1992).

McDonald, Eugene and Asa Berlin. *Bright Promise: For Your Child with Cleft Lip and Cleft Palate.* Chicago, IL: National Easter Seal Society (Publications Department, 70 East Lake St., 60601), 1987 (English); 1980 (Spanish). Written in question and answer format, this booklet covers multidisciplinary management along with prenatal development, possible causes, anatomy, surgical management, and feeding, speech, intelligence, hearing, dental, emotional issues. Illustrations and photographs included.

Miller, Nancy. *Nobody's Perfect: Living and Growing with Children Who Have Special Needs.* Baltimore, MD: Brookes Publishing Co. (Box 10624, 21285–0624), 1994. This book was written by a social worker and a group of "moms." Parents' thoughts and strategies are outlined. A parent's story of the birth of her child with Pierre Robin malformation sequence is recounted.

Moffitt, Karen, John Reiss, and John Nackashi. *Special Children, Special Care.* Tampa, FL: Florida Diagnostic and Learning Resources System of the University of South Florida (University of South Florida Bookstore, 4204 E. Fowler Ave., 33620–6550, Attn.: General Books). This guide is for parents of children who are medically complex and technology dependent. Includes daily charts that can make life at home more manageable, along with information on emotional aspects, insurance and health financing, legal and medical issues, and education and social services.

Moller, Karlind, Clark Starr, and Sylvia Johnson (editors). *A Parent's Guide to Cleft Lip and Palate.* Minneapolis, MN: University of Minnesota Press (2037 University Ave. SE, 55414), 1990. This book offers chapters on the types of clefts and embryology, team approach, surgical care, feeding, ear problems, dental care, speech concerns, social and psychological development, genetic counseling. Illustrations, photographs, case histories, and resources are included.

Mulliken, John and Dorothy MacDonald. *Cleft Lip and Palate: Questions and Answers for Parents.* Boston, MA: The Children's Hospital (300 Longwood Ave., 02115).

National Organization for Rare Disorders in collaboration with Dowden Publishing Co. *Physicians' Guide to Rare Disorders.* Montvale, NJ: Dowden Publishing Co. (110 Summit Ave., 07645–9895), 1995. This reference book offers easy-to-read medical information on "rare" conditions and resources for support or to find out more about the condition. A variety of conditions of facial difference are included.

Neiman, Gary and James Lehman Jr. *A Parent's Guide: Cleft Lip and Palate and other Craniofacial Problems.* Akron, OH: Plastic and Reconstructive Surgeons, Inc. (Akron Craniofacial Center, Children's Hospital Medical Center of Akron, 300 Locust St., Suite 380, 44302), reprinted 1990. This booklet provides text, medical illustrations, and photographs about anatomy, causes, and the multidisciplinary management of children with clefts.

Parameters for Evaluation and Treatment of Patients with Cleft Lip/Palate or Other Craniofacial Anomalies. Pittsburgh: American Cleft-Craniofacial Association (1218 Grandview Ave., 15211.), 1993. This booklet outlines what the American Cleft Palate-Craniofacial Association considers to be optimal care for children with facial difference. A good resource to refer to when selecting a craniofacial team for your child.

Reich, Elsa. *Treacher Collins Syndrome: An Overview.* Norwich, VT: Treacher Collins Foundation (P.O. Box 683, 05055), 1992. This booklet provides an overview of information about Treacher Collins syndrome, including information about genetics, health problems related to the condition, research, treatment, selecting a craniofacial team, and psychological aspects.

Snyder, Gilbert, Samuel Berkowitz, Kenneth Bzoch, and Sylvan Stool. *Your Cleft Lip and Palate Child: A Basic Guide for Parents.* Evansville, IN: Mead Johnson Nutritionals (order through your local representative), 1986. This booklet offers general information about the different types of clefting, genetics, feeding, surgeries, dental care, ear and speech concerns, secondary surgeries, and emotional aspects. Spanish available.

Wynn, Sidney, MD. *Team Approach to the Cleft Lip and Palate Child.* Milwaukee, WI: Milwaukee Children's Hospital (Cleft Lip and Palate Center, 1700 W. Wisconsin Ave., 53222), 1981.

Chapter 2

The Exceptional Parent. P.O. Box 3000, Dept. EP, Denville, NJ 07834. This is a magazine for parents of children with disabling conditions. Articles are written by parents and professionals. A regular column, Search & Respond, provides an opportunity for readers to share information on treatment, supplies, services, family experiences, and conditions.

Leff, Patricia Tanner and Elaine H. Walizer. *Building the Healing Partnership.* Cambridge, MA: Brookline Books (P.O. Box 1046, 02238), 1992. Brief vignettes based on parents' responses to a questionnaire which help the reader experience caring for a child who is chronically ill.

Marsh, Jayne, and Carol Boggis (editors). *From the Heart: On Being the Mother of a Child with a Disability.* Bethesda, MD: Woodbine House, 1995. This book gathers together the insights, worries, hopes and dreams, and anecdotes of nine women who participated together in a support group for parents of children with disabilities or serious medical problems.

Meyer, Donald (editor). *Uncommon Fathers: Reflections on Raising a Child with a Disability.* Bethesda, MD: Woodbine House, 1995. Fathers of children with a variety of disabling conditions reflect on the emotions that go along with parenting a child with special needs, as well as on the many ways such parenthood has changed their lives.

Simons, Robin. *After the Tears: Parents Talk about Raising a Child with a Disability.* San Diego, CA: Harcourt Brace Jovanovich, 1987.

Pinkava, Mary J. *A Handful of Hope: Helpful Suggestions for Grandparents of Children with Disabilities.* Phoenix, AZ: Pilot Parent Partnerships (2150 E. Highland Ave., Suite 2105, 85016). Written for grandparents of a child who has recently been diagnosed with a disabling condition.

Schleifer, M.J. (1988). "I Wish Our Parents Would Help Us More. Understanding Grandparents of Children with Disabilities." *Exceptional Parent*, 18, 62–68.

Seligman, Milton and Rosalyn Benjamin Darling. *Ordinary Families, Special Children: A Systems Approach to Childhood Disability.* New York: The Guilford Press, 1989.

Chapter 3

American Dental Association. *Caring for the Disabled Child's Dental Health.* Chicago, IL: American Dental Association, Bureau of Health Education and Audiovisual Services (211 E. Chicago Ave., 60611), 1982.

American Society of Plastic and Reconstructive Surgeons. *Cleft Lip and Palate Surgery (cheiloplasty and palatoplasty).* Arlington Heights, IL: ASPRS (Order Department, 444 E. Algonquin Rd., 60005), 1984. This booklet discusses selected surgical techniques of cleft lip and palate repairs accompanied by non-medical type illustrations.

American Society of Plastic and Reconstructive Surgeons. *Surgery of the Nose (rhinoplasty).* Arlington Heights, IL: ASPRS (Order Department, 444 E. Algonquin Rd., 60005, 708–228–9900), 1984. This booklet offers information about the surgical procedure and recovery period, along with non-medical color illustrations.

Bennett, Virginia, and Sheila Farnan. *Feeding Young Children with Cleft Lip and Palate.* St. Paul, MN: Minnesota Dietetic Association (1910 W. County Rd. B, Room 212, 55113), 1991. Non-medical illustrations accompany a comprehensive text on general nutrition information and special considerations for infants with clefts.

Berkowitz, Samuel. *The Road to Normalcy: For the Cleft Lip and Palate Child.* Evansville, IL: Mead Johnson Nutritionals (order through local representative), 1985. This booklet outlines surgical management, timing, expectations regarding appearance, and the goal of "normal" function and appearance through text and photographs.

Berkowitz, Samuel. *Steps in Habilitation: For the Cleft Lip and Palate Child.* Evansville, IL: Mead Johnson Nutritionals (2404 Pennsylvania Ave., 47721; order through local representative), 1972. This booklet includes photo studies of 6 children followed through surgical and dental/orthodontic management.

Brizee, Lori and Barbara Anderson. *Feeding Your Baby: Tips for the Baby with Cleft Lip and Palate (Birth to 3 Months).* Olympia, WA: Department of Health (PCHS Warehouse, 7741–A Arab Road SE, Mailstop MK-14, 98504), 1988. In a simple question-and-answer format, this pamphlet offers suggestions regarding bottle and nipple choice, how to feed the baby, frequency and amount of feeding, and breastfeeding.

Brizee, Lori and Barbara Anderson. *Ready for Solid Foods? Tips for the Baby with Cleft Palate.* Olympia, WA: Department of Health (PCHS Warehouse, 7741–A Arab Road SE, Mailstop MK-14, 98504), 1988.

This pamphlet offers suggestions regarding food readiness, foods to start at each age, "problem" foods, and dental hygiene.

Clapper, Diane, and Ginny Dixon-Wood. *Feeding an Infant with Cleft Palate: An Aid for Parents and Professionals.* Gainesville, FL: University of Florida Craniofacial Center (Box J-166 JHMHC, 32610), 1985. This pamphlet addresses positioning, modifying common equipment (nipples), and supportive information.

Clark, Gloria Frolek. "Special Needs in the Lunchroom." *Exceptional Parent*, March 1995, 45–46. This article discusses the laws that require schools to provide specially prepared meals for children with feeding problems, as well as accommodations that may be requested.

Connecticut Developmental Disabilities Council. *A Parent Guide for Doctors' Visits.* E. Hartford, CT: Connecticut Developmental Disabilities Council (90 Pitkin St., 06108), 1987.

Danner, Sarah Coulter, and Edward Cerutti. *Nursing Your Baby with a Cleft Palate or Cleft Lip.* Waco, TX: Childbirth Graphics, Ltd. (WRS Group, P.O. Box 21207, 76702–1207), 1990. This illustrated booklet suggests alternatives and modifications for breastfeeding.

Friends of the Family (audiotape). This tape holds 26 songs, some of which address hospitalization (Celebration Shop, Box 355, Bedford, TX 76095).

Grady, Edith. *Nursing My Baby with a Cleft of the Soft Palate.* Franklin Park, IL: La Leche League International (P.O. Box 1209, 60131–8209), August 1983. Based on a case study, practical information is presented about adjustments made in breastfeeding techniques needed to adapt to the needs of an infant with a soft cleft palate. Additional information is included on the needs of an infant with a cleft lip only and a cleft of the hard palate. Illustrations of technique are not provided.

Klein, Marsha Dunn. *O.T.R. Feeding Techniques for Children Who have Cleft Lip and Palate.* Tucson, AZ: Therapy Skill Builders/Communication Skill Builders (3830 E. Bellevue, P.O. Box 42050, 85733), 1988. This pamphlet provides information and illustrations of different types of clefts and infant feeding along with numerous suggestions for improved feeding techniques and nipple choices.

Minnesota Department of Health. *Guidelines of Care for Children with Special Health Care Needs: Cleft Lip and Palate.* Minneapolis, MN: Minnesota Dept. of Health (Services for Children with Handicaps, 717 SE Delaware St., P.O. Box 9441, 55440), 1991.

Novy, Marge, and Marcia Aduss. *Feeding Your Special Baby.* Chicago, IL: Center for Craniofacial Anomalies (University of Illinois College of Medicine, P.O. Box 6998, Rm. 476, CME M/C 588, 60680). This booklet provides information and photographs on breastfeeding, use of a breast pump, guidelines for bottle feeding, oral hygiene, and resources for support and equipment. Also available in Spanish.

Poulton, Donald R., and John Dann III. *Orthognathic Surgery: Reshaping Your Face with Orthodontics and Corrective Jaw Surgery.* Daly City, CA: Krames Communications (312 90th St., 94015–1898), 1990. Designed for patients who are contemplating orthognathic surgery, this booklet outlines and illustrates the sequence of orthodontic and surgical management.

Sargent, Larry A. *Craniofacial Surgery: Treatment of Deformities of the Face and Skull.* (Tennessee Craniofacial Center, Erlanger Medical Center, T.C. Thompson Children's Hospital, 975 E. 3rd St., Chattanooga, TN 37403). The primary purpose of this booklet is to inform health care professionals, as well as parents, of the treatment that is available at the Tennessee Craniofacial Center for various types of craniofacial deformities, including cleft lip and palate, outer ear reconstruction, craniosynostosis, craniofacial dysostosis, orbital hypertelorism, and Treacher Collins syndrome.

Sargent, Larry A. *Craniosynostosis: Diagnosis and Current Surgical Treatment.* (Same address as above.) This booklet informs health care professionals and parents of the diagnosis, evaluation, and current surgical treatment of craniosynostosis at the Tennessee Craniofacial Center.

Ware, William, Jeffrey Fujimoto, and Calvin Lee. *Patient Information for Orthognathic Surgery.* Roseville, CA: River City Publications (P.O. Box 899), 1988. This booklet reviews pre- and post-operative procedure routines, answers common questions, and addresses possible risks.

Chapter 4

Abbott, Marcia. *My Face.* Piedmont, CA: Marcia Abbott (59 Sylvan Way, 94610). Marcia wrote this book about her daughter, Natalie, and for her. Natalie has Moebius syndrome.

Bergen, Bernice. *Face Value: Corrective Cosmetic Camouflage.* Gainesville, FL.: University of Florida Craniofacial Center (Box J-166 JHMHC, 32610), 1988. This handout offers makeup tips for young women and adults who have cleft lip scars.

Beuf, Ann Hill. *Beauty is the Beast: Appearance Impaired Children in America.* Philadelphia, PA: University of Pennsylvania Press, 1990. This book examines the stigmatization of children who deviate from acceptable American standards of physical appearance. Using theory and methodology from sociology, anthropology, and psychology the author analyzes the effects of this stigmatization on children and the strategies they use to cope with it.

FACE, P.O. Box 1424, Sarasota, FL 34230. *Why Am I Different?* In question and answer format, this booklet describes many types of "differentness," such as skin color, clefting, hearing impairment, etc., and positive coping strategies.

Fishbaough, Michael. *Someone Like Me - A Booklet for Children Born with Cleft Lip and Palate.* Noblesville, IN: Becky Meeks (306 Redbay Drive, 46060).

Grealy, Lucy. *Autobiography of a Face.* New York: Houghton Mifflin, 1994. This book documents the author's life, from her diagnosis of facial cancer at age nine through subsequent treatment and reconstructive surgeries.

Jammine, Georgia Haitas. *Michael Has a Cleft Lip and Palate.* South Africa: Genetic Services (Dept. of National Health and Population Development, Private Bag X 63, Pretoria 0001 South Africa). This paperback book offers children (and adults) engaging, realistic color illustrations along with accurate information.

Kaleidoscope. *Kaleidoscope: A Spectrum of Articles Focusing on Families.* East Hartford, CT: Kaleidoscope (Connecticut's University Affiliated Program on Developmental Disabilities, The University of Connecticut, 991 Main St.), 1988.

Krahl, Rhonda. *Rebuilding Your Dream Family: Life with a Disabled Child.* Iowa City, IA: The University of Iowa (Campus Stores, MI050H, 52242.)

Krementz, Jill. *How It Feels to Live with a Physical Disability.* New York: Simon & Schuster, 1992. This book is composed of mini-autobiographies (text and photos) of twelve children who have physical differences. Of special interest is Francis Smith, age 16, who has Treacher Collins syndrome. Francis tells his story and speaks about his life, accomplishments, disappointments, hopes and fears, goals and dreams.

MacGregor, Frances Cooke. *After Plastic Surgery: Adaptations and Adjustment.* Westport, CT: Greenwood Press Publishing Group (Box 5007, 88 Post Road West, 06881).

Meyer, Donald J. and Patricia F. Vadasy. *Sibshops: Workshops for Siblings of Children with Special Needs.* Baltimore, MD: Brookes Publishing Co. (Box 10624, 21285–0624), 1994. This details the work of the Sibling Support Program at Children's Hospital and Medical Center of Seattle, WA. It also describes the process of the SibShop—social opportunities for siblings of children with special needs to spend time together and explore their similarities and differences.

Peckinpah, Sandra Lee. *Rosey—The Imperfect Angel.* Westlake Village, CA.: Scholars Press (Dasan Productions, Inc., 4201 Hunt Club Lane, 91361), 1990. An illustrated fairy tale book in which an "imperfect" angel with a cleft is chosen to journey to "The Land Called Below." The message is that there is beauty in imperfection. Suitable for children and adults.

Pediatric Projects. *A Buyer's Guide to Medical Toys & Books for Toddlers through Teens.* Tarzana, CA: Pediatric Projects (Box 571555, 91357–1555). This publication describes products (including toys and books) which help children understand health care, illness, disability, and hospitalization.

Pruzinsky, Thomas (1990). "Collaboration of Plastic Surgeon and Medical Psychotherapist," *Medical Psychotherapy,* Vol. 3, p. 103–116. (Single copy available from Let's Face It, P.O. Box 29972, Bellingham, WA 98228–1972. Send SASE.) This article discusses the role of the medical psychotherapist in the treatment of people with congenital conditions of facial difference. It describes the psychological assessment and interventions conducted by medical psychotherapists with patients undergoing reconstructive plastic surgery for congenital deformities of the face and skull. It advocates for the specialized role of the medical psychotherapist on the craniofacial treatment team.

Pruzinsky, Thomas (1992). "Social and Psychological Effects of Major Craniofacial Deformity," *Cleft Palate-Craniofacial Journal,* Nov. 1992, Vol. 29, No. 6, p. 578–84. This article discusses the social and psychological experiences of patients with the most severe forms of craniofacial differences. A conclusion is drawn that individuals with the most severe forms of craniofacial differences are at risk for experiencing social and psychological stress and may have their quality of life negatively affected by the experience of having a facial difference.

United Cerebral Palsy. *The Discovery Book.* Petaluma, CA (1180 Holm Road, Suite C, 94954). This book is an exploration of the social and psychological aspects of childhood disability, written by children with physical disabilities.

Chapter 5

Breitenfeldt, Dorvan, and Ted Harper. *Questions Relating to the Use of a Speech Appliance to Treat Nasal Speech.* Spokane, WA: Spokane County Health District (Cleft Lip and Palate Program, West 1101 College Ave., 99201), September 1988. This illustrated pamphlet describes the use, placement, and follow-up management with a speech appliance.

Center for Craniofacial Anomalies. *Pharyngeal Flap.* Chicago, IL: Center for Craniofacial Anomalies (University of Illinois College of Medicine at Chicago, P.O. Box 6998, Room 476, CME M/C 588, 60680), 1987. This handout outlines general information on the speech mechanism, surgical anatomical changes, and postoperative care for this procedure. A videotape is also available.

Hammond, Linda Brewer. *FM Auditory Trainers: A Winning Choice for Students, Teachers and Parents.* Minneapolis, MN: Gopher State Litho Corp. (Order from: Hearing Resources, P.O. Box 4506, Hopkins, MN 55343), 1991. This booklet is meant to serve as a practical guide to the selection and use of an FM system to be used in the classroom or at home. Written in generic terms for parents, educators, therapists, audiologists, and hearing aid dispensers, it describes FM systems and the different types available, and managing the system after purchase.

Lansky, Vicki. *Koko Bear's Big Earache: Preparing Your Child for Ear Tube Surgery.* New York: Bantam Books, 1988. This book has two written passages on each page: one for children and one for adults; along with an accompanying drawing. Written at a simple reading level.

MacDonald, Susan Kelley. *Hearing and Behavior: In Children Born with a Cleft Palate.* West Roxbury, MA: Prescription Parents, Inc. (P.O. Box 161, 02132.) This booklet explains the relationship of hearing loss and cleft palate and its treatment.

Patrick Gets Hearing Aids. Available from Phonak, Inc., 850 E. Diehl Rd., P.O. Box 3017, Naperville, IL 60566. 1–800–777–7333; 708–505–7007. This beautifully illustrated children's book tells the story of Patrick, a bunny who can't hear well. He visits the audiologist, is tested, and fitted for hearing aids.

Ross Laboratories. *Your Child and Otitis Media.* Columbus, OH: Ross Laboratories (Division of Abbott Laboratories, order through local representative), March 1989. Through photographs and diagrams, this booklet describes ear anatomy, a normal and inflamed eardrum, and position of the eustachian tube. A sample chart for medication administration is included.

Chapter 6

AboutFace. *A School Program to Introduce Facial Differences: We All Have Different Faces.* (P.O. Box 93, Limekiln, PA 19535).

Anderson, Winifred, Stephen Chitwood, and Deidre Hayden. *Negotiating the Special Education Maze: A Guide for Parents and Teachers.* Bethesda, MD: Woodbine House, 1990. This is a step-by-step guide to making the system work for children who require special accommodations at school or are in early intervention programs. Many worksheets and exercises are included to help with all stages of the process from evaluation to development and monitoring of the IFSP/IEP.

Coleman, Jeanine. *The Early Intervention Dictionary.* Bethesda, MD: Woodbine House, 1993. This dictionary defines and clarifies terms and abbreviations used by the many different medical, therapeutic, and educational professionals who provide early intervention and special education services.

Garrity, C., et al. *Bully-Proofing Your Classroom: A Comprehensive Approach for Elementary Schools.* Longmont, CO: Sopris West (P.O. Box 1809, 1140 Boston Ave., 80502–1809), 1994. This 368–page book is a step-by-step program to be used in the school classroom.

Handbook for the Care of Infants and Toddlers with Disabilities and Chronic Conditions. Lawrence, KS: Learner Managed Designs, Inc. (2201 K West 25th St., 66047). This handbook contains information about care that is helpful at home, in day care centers, early intervention programs, and schools.

National Information Center for Children and Youth with Disabilities (NICHCY). NICHCY publishes a number of free publications on special education issues. Titles include: *Parent's Guide to Accessing Programs for Infants, Toddlers, Preschoolers with Disabilities; Planning for Inclusion; Education of Children & Youth with Special Needs: What Do the Laws Say?* Contact NICHCY at 800–695–0285 to request any of these publications or a current publications list.

Nuegelbauer, Bonnie (editor). *Alike and Different: Exploring Our Humanity with Young Children.* Redmond, WA: Exchange Press (Box 2890, 98073–2890). This book explores how teachers can guide young children to appreciate differences.

Plumridge, Diane, Robin Bennett, Nuhad Dinno, and Cynthia Branson. *The Student with a Genetic Disorder: Educational Implications for Special Education Teachers and for Physical Therapists, Occupational Therapists, and Speech Pathologists.* Springfield, IL: Charles C. Thomas, 1993. This book covers the basic principles of genetics and inheritance, special education laws, resources, and a host of other subjects pertinent to education professionals.

Project School Care. *Working Towards a Balance in Our Lives: A Booklet for Families of Children with Disabilities and Special Health Care Needs.* Boston, MA: Children's Hospital, Boston (Gardner 610, 300 Longwood Ave., 02115), 1992. This booklet, written by and for parents, lists questions parents should ask, state and national resources, and offers ideas on how parents can work towards a balance.

Project School Care. *Children Assisted by Medical Technology in Educational Settings: Resources for Training.* Boston, MA: Project School Care (Children's Hospital, Gardner 610, 300 Longwood Ave., 02115), 1991.

What Is Inclusion in Child Care? This brief pamphlet answers common questions parents and child care providers have about including children with special needs in typical child care programs. Available from Child Care Plus, Rural Institute on Disabilities, The University of Montana, 51 N. Corbin, Missoula, MT 59812.

Chapter 7

The Americans with Disabilities Act: Questions and Answers. Available free from the U.S. Equal Employment Opportunity Commission, 1801 L St., N.W., Washington, DC 20507. 800–669–3362. This booklet explains the major provisions and limitations of the ADA, discussing such concepts as "reasonable accommodation" and "auxiliary aids and services" in detail.

Best's Insurance Reports: Life-Health. Oldwick, NJ: A.M. Best Co. (Ambest Rd., 08858). Look for this expensive annual report in the library. Features statistics and ratings for U.S. and Canadian life and health insurance companies.

Federal Social Security Office. *Disability* (Publication No. 05–10029); *Social Security and SSI Benefits for Children with Disabilities* (Publication No. 05–10026); *Understanding Social Security* (Publication No. 05–10024). Call 1–800–772–1213 for the most current editions of these publications.

Health Insurance Association of America. *The Consumer's Guide to Health Insurance.* Washington, DC: Health Insurance Association of America (1025 Connecticut Ave., NW, 20036–3998), 1992. This booklet answers frequently asked questions about health insurance.

Health Insurance Association of America. *Report of the ACLI-HIAA Task Force on Genetic Testing 1991.* Washington, DC: Health Insurance Association of America (1025 Connecticut Ave., NW, 20036–3998, 202–223–7780), 1991.

Health Insurance Resource Guide. Chevy Chase, MD: Alliance of Genetic Support Groups (35 Wisconsin Circle, Suite 440, 20815). Topics covered in this booklet include: The Pre-Existing Condition Dilemma, Obtaining and Keeping Health Insurance, Important Provisions to Note when Assessing Your Health Care Coverage, The Price You Pay for Your Policy, Strategies for Reimbursement, Income Taxes and Medical Expenses, Government Assistance Programs, When All Else Fails.

Larson, Georgianna and Judith A. Kahn. *How to Get Quality Care for a Child with Special Health Needs. A Guide to Health Services and How to Pay for Them.* St. Paul, MN: Lifeline Press (2500 University Ave. West, 55114), 1990.

McManus, Margaret A. *Understanding Your Health Insurance Options. A Guide for Families Who Have Children with Special Health Care Needs.* Washington, DC: McManus Health Policy Inc. (3615 Wisconsin Ave. NW, 20016), 1988.

New England SERVE. *Paying the Bills: Tips for Families on Financing Health Care for Children with Special Needs.* Boston, MA: New England SERVE (MA Health Research Institute, 101 Tremont St., Suite 812, 02108), 1992. This booklet was written by parents who have children with special needs. It shares information and strategies for getting payment for children's health care and includes tips on how to make the system work.

United Cerebral Palsy of Minnesota. *Health Care Coverage and Your Disabled Child: A Guide for Parents.* St. Paul, MN: United Cerebral Palsy of Minnesota (1821 University Avenue, 55014), 1983.

Chapter 8

Bishop, Kathleen Kirk with Josie Woll and Polly Arango in collaboration with Families and Professionals. *Family/Professional Collaboration for Children with Special Health Needs and Their Families.* Burlington, VT (Dept. of Social Work, University of Vermont, 499B Waterman Building, 05405–0160), 1993. This monograph describes more than 10 years of dialog on what is necessary and important in the collaborative relationships between families of children with special health needs and their professionals.

Des Jardins, Charlotte. *How to Get Services by Being Assertive: For Parents of Children with Disabilities and Their Helpers.* Family Resource Center on Disabilities (20 E. Jackson Blvd., Room 900, 60604. 312–939–3513), 1993. Written to empower parents, this book offers step-by-step instructions on obtaining services for children through assertive communication techniques.

Des Jardins, Charlotte. *How to Organize an Effective Parent/Advocacy Group and Move Bureaucracies.* Chicago: Family Resource Center on Disabilities (20 E. Jackson Blvd., Room 900, 60604. 312–939–3513), 1993. This book offers information on how parents can organize effective advocacy groups that work with bureaucracies to choose services for each child. Topics covered include: recruitment of members and volunteers, choice of leaders, communication within the group, getting results through school districts, learning to lobby, getting out messages through the media, organizing conferences and coalitions, and training other parents to be advocates.

The Exceptional Parent Annual Directory of National Organizations. Lakewood, NJ: Richardson Specialty Books (1905 Swarthmore Avenue, 08701). This yearly publication is a comprehensive resource for support, information, and educational organizations which serve children with special needs and their families.

Exceptional Parent Reprints. Psy-Ed Corporation, 1170 Commonwealth Ave., Boston, MA 02134. Reprints of interest include: *Parent Written Care Plans: Instruction for the Respite Setting* (1988); *Respite Services: A*

National Survey of Parents' Experiences (1989); *Funding Technology: Ways Through the Maze* (1987).

Guidelines for Legislative Advocacy. Pittsburgh, PA: American Cleft Palate-Craniofacial Association (1218 Grandview Ave., 15211). Topics covered include: Preparation for the Introduction of Legislation, A Model Bill, Preparation for Testimony before the Legislative Committee(s), If Legislative Attempts Fail, Tips on Testifying, and Establishing Contact with Legislators.

Human Services Group. *Becoming Informed Consumers: A National Survey of Parents' Experience with Respite Services.* Cambridge, MA: Human Services Group (2336 Massachusetts Ave.), 1989.

Let's Face It, P.O. Box 29972, Bellingham, WA 98228–1972. A sample of publications available is listed below. Contact Let's Face It for cost.

- *Resources for People with Facial Difference* (annual publication)

Reprints:

- April 1993 search of medical literature pertaining to the psychosocial aspects of facial difference.

- A Bibliography of Favorite Articles Recommended for Parents of Young Children with Special Needs.

- Harvard Law Review (1990). "Facial Discrimination: Extending Handicap Law to Employment Discrimination on the Basis of Physical Appearance."

- Macgregor, Francis Cooke (1990). "Facial Disfigurement: Problems and Management of Social Interaction and Implications for Mental Health."

- Pruzinsky, Thomas (1990). "Collaboration of Plastic Surgeon and Medical Psychotherapist."

Madara, Edward J. and Abigail Meese (editors). *The Self-Help Sourcebook: Finding and Forming Mutual Aid Self-Help Groups.* Denville, NJ: St. Clares-Riverside Medical Center, 07834.

National Council on the Handicapped. *Toward Independence: An Assessment of Federal Laws and Programs Affecting Persons with Disabilities - with Legislative Recommendations.* Order from Superintendent of Documents, Washington, DC 20402. Ask for publication #052–03–01022–4.

Owen, M.J. (1991). "What Has the Social Security Administration Done for You Lately?" *Exceptional Parent,* 21(4), 40–42.

Pacesetter Newsletter, Parent Advocacy Coalition for Educational Rights (PACER), 4826 Chicago Ave., Minneapolis, MN 55417. This quarterly newsletter focuses on helping parents use advocacy to obtain quality educations for children with disabling conditions. It includes updates on new legislation or threats to existing legislation affecting people with disabilities.

The Parent Resource Directory. Bethesda, MD: National Center for Family Centered Care (7910 Woodmont Ave., Suite 300, 20814. 301–654–6549). A listing of parents of children with special needs from throughout the U.S. and Canada who have offered to be available to others. Parent Training and Information Centers are also listed.

Shapiro, Joseph. *No Pity: People with Disabilities Forging a New Civil Rights Movement.* New York: Times Books, 1993. Joe Shapiro, reporter for *U.S. News & World Report,* has written a chronicle of the struggle of people with disabling conditions from the 17th century to the passage of the Americans with Disabilities Act of 1990. Poignant personal stories are told.

Wide Smiles, P.O. Box 5153, Stockton, CA 95205–0153. Contact: Joanne Greene, Editor. This newsletter focuses on cleft lip and cleft palate. Articles are written by professionals along with families and individuals with these conditions.

VIDEOS

Over the past several years, a variety of television programs have featured children and adults with facial difference along with their health care providers. Some of these programs have taken cameras into homes, operating rooms, schools, and health care facilities. The list of these programs is too lengthy to print in this book, and, unfortunately, there is no central source for obtaining videos of these programs or written transcripts. Some of the larger generic support organizations for facial difference (see *Resource Guide*) or condition-specific support organizations for facial difference may have lending copies of videos and transcripts of these programs.

The Center for Craniofacial Anomalies at the University of Illinois at Chicago has produced a variety of videos on subjects related to the needs of children with cleft lip and palate and their parents: *What is Going to Happen to My Baby?*, *Feeding Your Special Baby*, *Your Baby's Surgery*, *Being Misunderstood*, *Pharyngeal Flap*, *SOM: A Silent Disease*, and *Put on a Happy Face*. All videos are available in English and some are also available in Spanish. For rental or pricing information contact: Marcia K. Aduss, Center for Craniofacial Anomalies, University of Illinois at Chicago, P.O. Box 6998, Room 476 CME M/C 588, Chicago, IL 60680.

Cleft Lip and Palate - Feeding the Newborn presents a variety of methods for feeding an infant with a cleft lip and/or palate. For pricing information contact: Sylvia Schippke, Coordinator, Cleft Lip and Palate Program, The Hospital for Sick Children, 555 University Avenue, Toronto, Ontario Canada M5G 1X8.

Forward Face has produced the *"Face Facts"* videos on five conditions of facial difference: cleft lip and palate, craniosynostosis, hemifacial microsomia, orbital hypertelorism, and Treacher Collins syndrome. Each tape includes an overview of the condition and interviews with health care professionals, family members, patients, and educators. For pricing information contact: Pat Chibbaro, RN, Forward Face, Institute of Reconstructive Plastic Surgery, NYU Medical Center, 560 1st Ave., New York, NY 10016.

Home Tracheostomy Care for Infants and Young Children was produced by the University of Colorado Health Sciences Center School of Nursing. In it, a parent describes her feelings as she learns to manage her baby's tracheostomy. Manual also available. For pricing information contact: Learner Managed Designs, Inc., 2201 K West 25th St., Lawrence, KS 66047.

Human Genome Project (#24754) produced by the National Center for the Human Genome. This video describes the goals of the project and how it might be important to you and your family. Loaned free-of-charge from: Modern Talking Picture Service, 5000 Park St., St. Petersburg, FL 33709.

Meeting the Medical Bills is available from: National Center for Clinical Infant Programs, 2000 14th St. N., Suite 380, Arlington, VA 22201–2500. This video describes methods a family can use for payment of their child's medical care.

"Rare" Should Not Mean "Alone" describes Treacher Collins syndrome from the perspective of children and adults with the condition along with their families and the variety of health care professionals who serve them and offers an overview of the services available from the Treacher Collins Foundation. For ordering information contact: Treacher Collins Foundation, P.O. Box 683, Norwich, VT 05055.

Slim Goodbody's The Before Tour is for children aged 3 to 11 who are preparing for surgery. In an entertaining manner, children will learn about the admission process, diagnostic procedures, surgical environment and medical staff. For pricing information contact: Slim Goodbody Corporation, 27 E. 20th St., Suite 1207, New York, NY 10011.

Teasing and How to Stop It videotape and manual. For pricing information contact: Edna Durbach, British Columbia Children's Hospital, 4480 Oak St., Vancouver, B.C., Canada V6M 1K8. By watching the video and their own behavior, children who are teased learn how to analyze their own situation with the guidance of an adult "coach." The video and manual can be purchased by a school or other community center for access to children with facial difference and other children who might encounter teasing.

Understanding People with Disabilities is a collection of award-winning videos which includes *Mirror Mirror,* a documentary about living with a facial difference. For Let's Face It "special pricing" contact: Filmmakers Library, 124 East 40th St., New York, NY 10016.

RESOURCE GUIDE

This Resource Guide includes a variety of national resources that may be helpful to families of children with facial difference and the professionals who serve them. Due to space limitations, not every resource is listed. And, for resources listed, names, addresses, and phone numbers can change. If you are not able to find a resource you are seeking, it might be helpful to refer to the most up-to-date issue of the annual publication, *Resources for People with Facial Difference,* published by Let's Face It, P.O. Box 29972, Bellingham, WA 98228–1972. Other helpful places to go for information include your local library (inquire about interlibrary loan), medical or university library, parent-to-parent organization, and reference books.

For information on state resources, a good starting point is to contact NICHCY, the National Information Center for Children and Youth with Disabilities, at 1–800–695–0285. NICHCY offers "State Sheets," which list addresses and phone numbers of state special education and early intervention agencies, protection and advocacy agencies, Parent Training and Information Centers, condition-specific support groups, and other state resources.

National and International Organizations

Facial Difference Support Organizations

The organizations listed below provide a variety of services that can be of help to you and your child with facial difference. Some organizations are affiliated with a hospital or physicians's office. Some groups have a national office and state or local chapters. For further information about any of these organizations, call or write and request a copy of their newsletter or other publications.

AboutFace - Canada
99 Crowns Lane, 4th Floor
Toronto, Ontario
CANADA M5R 3P4
1–800–665–3223
    International support and information organization for people with facial difference and their families. Resources include newsletter, parent support

training, booklets, videos, lending library, chapter development, and an annual meeting.

AboutFace - USA
P.O. Box 93
Limekiln, PA 19535
1–800–225–3223
American office for AboutFace.

Apert Support and Information Network
1626 Redwood Ave.
Redwood, CA 94061
   This organization was designed to provide support and information about Apert syndrome. Newsletter and networking meetings available.

Carpenter Syndrome Network
Box 4215–48,
26661 Bear Valley Rd.
Tehachapi, CA 93561
   This support and information organization links parents of children with Carpenter syndrome.

Children's Craniofacial Association
9441 LBJ Freeway, Suite 115–LB46
Dallas, TX 75243
1–800–535–3643
   This organization offers physician referrals and patient financial assistance, produces educational booklets, and hosts an annual support meeting.

Cleft Palate Foundation
1218 Grandview Ave.
Pittsburgh, PA 15211
1–800–24–CLEFT
   This organization is the public service and education component of the American Cleft Palate Craniofacial Association (listed under "Professional Organizations"). Resources include: 24–hour CLEFTLINE service, fact sheets on cleft lip and palate and some craniofacial conditions, bibliography, brochures, referrals, and an annual meeting.

Craniofacial Foundation of America
Tennessee Craniofacial Center
T.C. Thompson Children's Hospital
975 E. Third St.
Chattanooga, TN 37403
1–800–418–3223
   This foundation offers financial support for non-medical expenses to patients traveling for evaluation and treatment to the Tennessee Craniofacial Center. Resources also include a variety of educational materials and opportunities to network with other patients and families.

Crouzon's/Meniere's Parent Support Network
P.O. Box 12791
Prescott, AZ 86304–2791

FACE (The Friends for the Aid, Correction and Education of Craniofacial Disorders)
P.O. Box 1424
Sarasota, FL 34230
Local support organization offering resources which include puppets, videos, and publications for outreach and education. Publications include handouts about craniosynostosis, jaw surgery, port wine stains, clefts, and preparing for surgical procedures.

Face to Face
473 Live Oak Dr.
El Cajon, CA 92020
This organization offers phone consultation to parents and a parent's article about having a child with Crouzon syndrome.

FACES
The National Association for the Craniofacially Handicapped
P.O. Box 11082
Chattanooga, TN 37401
1–800–332–2373
This organization provides financial support for non-medical expenses to patients traveling to a craniofacial center for treatment. Eligibility is based on financial and medical need. Resources include: newsletters, information about craniofacial conditions, and networking opportunities.

Forward Face: The Charity for Children with Craniofacial Conditions
317 E. 34th St., Suite 901
New York, NY 10016
1–800–393–3223
This organization is affiliated with the Institute of Reconstructive Plastic Surgery at New York University Medical Center. They offer practical and financial support to people with craniofacial conditions. Activities and resources include an active group for teenagers and young adults, a newsletter, videos, and information, support meetings, and workshops in New York City.

Foundation for Faces of Children
P.O. Box 1361
Brookline, MA 02146
This organization is affiliated with the Craniofacial Centre at Children's Hospital, Boston. Resources include a newsletter, fundraising to support projects at the Centre, parent support, library, and meetings.

Foundation for Miller and
  Nager Syndromes
333 Country Lane
Glenview, IL 60025
1–800–507–3667

This organization provides information about Miller and Nager syndromes, has a lending library, and newsletter.

Freeman-Sheldon Parent Support Group
509 E. Northmont Way
Salt Lake City, UT 84103
801–364–7060
This organization offers information on Freeman-Sheldon syndrome, peer support, registry, and links between researchers and families. Resources include newsletter membership directory, telephone "helpline," and pamphlets.

Happy Faces Support Group
1331 N. 7th Ave, Suite 250
Phoenix, AZ 85006
This organization offers meetings and family visits along with education and support for people with facial difference.

Holoprosencephaly - Fighters of Defects Support Group
3032 Brereton St.
Pittsburgh, PA 15219

Information and Support for DiGeorge & Shprintzen Syndrome Families
27859 Lassen St.
Castaic, CA 91384

Let's Face It
P.O. Box 29972
Bellingham, WA 98228–1972
This organization offers information and network support for people with facial difference, their families, friends, and professionals. Offers the annual publication, *Resources for People with Facial Difference*, along with a variety of reprints of articles and excerpts from journals and books. See *Reading List* for more information on publications.

Meniere's Network
2000 Church St.
Box 111
Nashville, TN 37236

Mobius Syndrome Foundation
Box 993
Larchmont, NY 10538
This organization is dedicated to supporting research for Mobius (Moebius) syndrome and providing educational opportunities such as a newsletter, meetings and networking opportunities.

Mobius Syndrome Network
6449 Gerald Ave.
Van Nuys, CA 91406
This networking organization offers a newsletter and networking opportunities for people with Mobius syndrome.

National Foundation for Facial Reconstruction
317 E. 34th St., Room 901
New York, NY 10016
This foundation sponsors programs at the Institute for Reconstructive Plastic Surgery at New York University Medical Center. Resources include: lending library, videos, and a newsletter.

Nevus Network
1400 S. Joyce St., #1225
Arlington, VA 22202

New Moms, New Babies
Box 262481
Houston, TX 77027–2481

Orafacial Outreach
13962 Wake Ave.
Irvine, CA 92718

Prescription Parents
P.O. Box 161
West Roxbury, MA 02132
This organization offers an active support network in New England for people with cleft lip and/or cleft palate. Offers outreach to parents of newborns, newsletter, social activities, and legislative advocacy.

Sturge-Weber Foundation
Box 418
Mt. Freedom, NJ 07920
1–800–627–5482
This organization is a clearinghouse of information on Sturge-Weber syndrome. Resources include a newsletter, resource guide, and annual meetings.

Treacher Collins Foundation
P.O. Box 683
Norwich, VT 05055–0683
This foundation is an organization of families, individuals, and professionals who are interested in developing and sharing knowledge and experience about Treacher Collins syndrome and related conditions. Resources include networking opportunities, newsletter, educational publications, lending library, resource list, and video.

Velo-Cardio-Facial Syndrome Educational Foundation
3331 Bainbridge Avenue
Bronx, NY 10467

Velo-Cardio-Facial Syndrome (Shprintzen Syndrome) Parent Support Group
110–45 Queens Blvd.
Forest Hills, NY 11375–5501

Books

These are sources of books on various subjects related to special needs, including facial difference. Most offer a free catalog.

Association for the Care of Children's Health (ACCH)
7910 Woodmont Ave., Suite 300
Bethesda, MD 20814
1–800–808–2224
Request their annual Resource Catalogue of books and videos.

Books for Special Needs
Albert Whitman Company
6340 Oakton St.
Morton Grove, IL 60053–2723

Children with Special Needs Collection
In many B. Dalton Bookseller and Barnes & Noble stores nationwide several shelves of the "Family" and "Child Care" sections are devoted to children with special needs

Disability Bookshop
Box 129
Vancouver, WA 98666

Special Needs Project (book store)
3463 State St.
Santa Barbara, CA 93105

Trace Research and Development Center
1500 Highland Ave., S-151
Madison, WI 53705–2280

Uncle Bear's Book Service
53 Glenwood Dr.
Westerville, OH 43081

Woodbine House
6510 Bells Mill Rd.
Bethesda, MD 20817

Child Care

Child Care Plus
Rural Institute on Disabilities
The University of Montana
51 North Corbin
Missoula, MT 59812
1–800–235–4122

This national program is focused on inclusive child care for children with disabling conditions. For families and professionals, they offer written materials, training, consultation, and support.

Ears, Hearing, Speech, and Language

Financing for hearing aids: Financial assistance can be found through a variety of sources. Check your health insurance policy for coverage, Medicaid, and your local state health department. Service groups may also be particularly interested in supporting the needs of children who have a hearing loss. Some of these groups include: Lions club (Sight and Hearing Committee), Fraternal Order of the Eagles (Jimmy Durante Children's Fund provides assistance for children with disabilities under the age of fifteen for the purchase of assistive listening devices, hearing aids, and other types of equipment), American Legion, and Veterans of Foreign Wars Association. Check your phone book for local or state chapters of these groups.

Alexander Graham Bell Association for the Deaf
3417 Volta Place, NW
Washington, DC 20007
An organization designed to empower persons who are hearing impaired to function independently by promoting universal rights and optimal opportunities for such persons to learn to use, maintain, and improve all aspects of their verbal communications. Offers newsletter, magazine, journal; scholarship programs; meetings; purchasing of books.

American Society for Deaf Children
814 Thayer Ave.
Silver Spring, MD 20910
1–800–942–2732
This organization offers information and support for parents of children who are deaf or hard of hearing. Newsletter included with membership.

Better Hearing Institute
P.O. Box 1840
Washington, DC 20013
1–800–327–9355
Information about hearing loss and aid for people with hearing impairments. Publishes a newsletter, has a speaker's bureau, and receives consumer complaints.

Captioned Films and Videos for the Deaf
Modern Talking Picture Services
5000 Park St. North
St. Petersburg, FL 33709
1–800–237–6213
Service which offers "loaner" videos free of charge on a variety of subjects.

EAR (Ear Anomalies Reconstructed - The Atresia/Microtia Support Group)
72 Durand Rd.
Maplewood, NJ 07040
This organization offers networking and medical information about atresia
and microtia of the ear. Resources include meetings and phone support.

The Geoffrey Foundation
P.O. Box 1112
Kennebunkport, ME 04046
207–967–5798
This foundation provides financial assistance to families and children with
hearing loss who would like to pursue the Auditory-Verbal approach to communication—using amplified residual hearing to listen and speak, rather than sign
language.

Hear Now
9745 E. Hampden Ave., Suite 300
Denver, CO 80231–4923
1–800–648–HEAR
To individuals with financial need, this organization offers hearing aids, financial assistance for cochlear implants, and fundraising opportunities to help
cover the costs of assistive hearing device.

Hearing Aid Helpline (National Hearing Aid Society Helpline)
20361 Middlebelt Rd.
Livonia, MI 48152
1–800–521–5247
Provides information on hearing loss and hearing aids and national referrals
to qualified hearing aid specialists. Has a newsletter and library.

Hereditary Hearing Impairment Resource Registry
Boys Town National Research Hospital
555 N. 30th
Omaha, NE 68131
1–800–320–1171

Huggie Aids
837 N.W. 10th St.
Oklahoma City, OK 73106
This company produces and sells a variety of headbands and accessories
used to keep hearing aids on children. These bands are popular for children
with microtic outer ears.

John Tracy Clinic
Correspondence Program
806 West Adams Blvd.
Los Angeles, CA 90007
1–800–522–4582
The Clinic offers a free international correspondence program to parents
of hearing impaired children ages birth - 6. Provides lessons and activities for

home use; information about hearing aids, IFSP's, IEP's, legal rights of people who are hearing impaired; and resources referrals.

National Association for Hearing and Speech Action
10801 Rockville Pike
Rockville, MD 20852
1–800–638–8255
    Information and resource center for the American Speech/Language/Hearing Association.

National Information Center on Deafness
Gallaudet University
800 Florida Ave., NE
Washington, DC 20002
    Information office at Gallaudet University, the only university in the U.S. for students who are deaf or have hearing impairments.

National Institute on Deafness & Other Communication Disorders
NIH Building 31, Room 3C35
Bethesda, MD 20892
1–800–241–1044

Nobelpharma USA, Inc.
5101 South Keeler Ave.
Chicago, IL 60632
1–800–347–3500
    This company is in the process of producing an implantable hearing aid. Contact for the status of their research.

Self Help for Hard of Hearing People, Inc. (SHHH)
7910 Woodmont Ave., Suite 1200
Bethesda, MD 20814
    International organization devoted to the welfare and interests of those who cannot hear well but are committed to participating in the hearing world. Resources include: advocacy services, workshops, newsletter, library, speaker's bureau.

Tripod
2901 N. Keystone St.
Burbank, CA 91504
    The GRAPEVINE (1–800–352–8888 USA;1–800–346–8888 CA) is a hotline staffed to provide answers to questions about raising and educating a child with a hearing impairment. The purpose of the hotline is to help parents make confident, well-informed decisions that are appropriate for their child and their family.

Xomed Treace
6743 Southpoint Dr. North
Jacksonville, FL 32216
1–800–874–5797
This company produces and sells the Xomed Audiant, an implantable hearing aid.

Education

Alliance for Parental Involvement in Education
P.O. Box 59
East Chatham, NY 12060–0059

The American Council on Rural Special Education
Miller Hall 359
Western Washington University
Bellingham, WA 98225

Early Education Intervention Network
376 Bridge St.
Dedham, MA 02026

National Association for the Education of Young Children
1509 16th St. NW
Washington, DC 20036–1426

National Association of Private Schools for Exceptional Children
1522 K St. NW, Suite 1032
Washington, DC 20005

National Assn. of State Directors of Special Education
1800 Diagonal Rd., Suite 320
Alexandria, VA 22314

National Information Center for Educational Media (NICEM)
P.O. Box 40130
Albuquerque, NM 87196

PACER Center (Parent Advocacy Coalition for Educational Rights)
4826 Chicago Ave. South
Minneapolis, MN 55417–1098
612–827–2966
The PACER Center is dedicated to helping parents understand special education laws and obtain appropriate educations for their children. Offers many publications (some free of charge), including several newsletters, and provides workshops for parents of children with disabilities.

Zero to Three/National Center for Clinical Infant Programs
2000 14th Street N, #380
Arlington, VA 22201–2500

Feeding

Gerber Consumer Information Service (cleft palate NUK nipples)
1–800–4–GERBER

La Leche League International
9616 Minneapolis Ave.
Franklin Park, IL 60131
1–800–LA-LECHE
Support and information for breastfeeding mothers.

Mead Johnson (cleft palate bottles)
Consumer Affairs
812–429–6321

Medela, Inc.
P.O. Box 660
McHenry, IL 60051–0660
1–800–435–8316 or 1–800–835–5968 (Breastfeeding National Network - 24
    hours/day)
Manufactures breastpumps and the Haberman Feeder, which was designed by a mom whose baby had Pierre Robin sequence and was developed
for babies with severe feeding problems or poor sucking abilities.

Genetics

In the United States, there are ten regional genetics networks. Networks
receive federal funding for research; training; hemophilia diagnosis and treatment; genetic diseases screening, counseling and referral; and maternal and
child health improvement project grants. Each region identifies needs, shares
resources, and enhances communication and coordination among states within
the region. Participants include health professionals such as genetic service
providers, public health planners, federal and state Maternal and Child Health
personnel, consumers of genetic services, and consumer organizations. Council
of Regional Networks for Genetics Services (CORN) is a national coalition of
the regional networks, public health officials, consumers, and professionals.
Consumers' representation with CORN is through the Alliance of Genetic
Support Groups.

Alliance of Genetic Support Groups
35 Wisconsin Circle, Suite 440
Chevy Chase, MD 20815
1–800–336–GENE
Network of people with genetic conditions, parents, and professionals who
have an interest in the "consumer" approach towards genetics. Holds confer-

ences, publishes newsletters and publications (*Directory of National Genetic Voluntary Organizations, Media Guide, Health Insurance Resource Guide*), and gives awards.

Council of Regional Networks for Genetic Services (CORN)
Emory University School of Medicine
Pediatrics/Genetics
2040 Ridgewood Dr.
Atlanta, GA 30322

Genetics Network of New York State, Puerto Rico and the Virgin Islands
    (GENES) - New York, Puerto Rico, Virgin Islands
New York State Dept. of Health, WCL&R
Laboratory of Human Genetics
Empire State Plaza
P.O. Box 509
Albany, NY 12201–0509

Genetics Services Branch
Maternal and Child Health Bureau
U.S. Dept. of Health and Human Services
5600 Fishers Lane
Rockville, MD 20857

Great Lakes Regional Genetics Group (GLaRGG) - Indiana, Illinois, Minnesota, Ohio, Wisconsin
328 Waisman Center
1500 Highland Ave.
Madison, WI 53705–2280

Great Plains Genetics Service Network (GPGSN) - Arkansas, Iowa, Kansas, Missouri, Nebraska, North Dakota, Oklahoma, South Dakota
University of Iowa, Dept. of Pediatrics
Division of Medical Genetics
Iowa City, IA 52241

Mid-Atlantic Regional Human Genetics Network (MARHGN) - Delaware, Washington, DC, Maryland, New Jersey, Pennsylvania, Virginia, West Virginia
260 Broad St., Suite 1900
Philadelphia, PA 19102–3865

Mountain States Regional Genetics Services Network (MSRGSN) - Arizona, Colorado, Montana, New Mexico, Utah, Wyoming
Colorado Dept. of Health
Medical Affairs and Special Programs
4300 Cherry Creek Dr.
Denver, CO 80222

New England Regional Genetics Group (NERGG) - Connecticut, Maine, Massachusetts, New Hampshire, Rhode Island, Vermont
P.O. Box 670
Mt. Desert, ME 04660

Pacific Northwest Regional Genetics Group (PacNoRGG) - Alaska, Idaho, Oregon, Washington
901 E. 18th Ave.
Eugene, OR 97403

Pacific Southwest Regional Genetics Network (PSRGN) - California, Hawaii, Nevada
State of California Dept. of Health Services
2151 Berkeley Way, Annex 4
Berkeley, CA 94704–1011

Southeastern Regional Genetics Group (SERGG) - Alabama, Florida, Georgia, Kentucky, Louisiana, Mississippi, North Carolina, South Carolina, Tennessee
Emory University School of Medicine
2040 Ridgewood Dr.
Atlanta, GA 30322

Texas Genetics Network (TEXGENE) - Texas
Texas Dept. of Health
Bureau of Women and Children
1100 West 49th St.
Austin, TX 78756–3199

Other National Genetics Organizations

Council for Responsible Genetics
5 Upland Rd., Suite 3
Cambridge, MA 02140

National Center for Human Genome Research
Ethical, Legal and Social Implications Program
National Institutes of Health
Building 31, Room 4B09
Bethesda, MD 20892

U.S. Dept. of Energy
Ethical, Legal and Social Implications (ELSI) Program
Los Alamos National Laboratory
MS-A 187
Los Alamos, NM 78545

U.S. Dept. of Energy
Human Genome Project
Office of Health and Environmental Research
Washington, DC 20545

Headbands

Goody Products, Inc.
969 Newark Turnpike
Kearney, NJ 07032
Goody Products manufactures the #28100 Terry Sports Bands, which can be used to keep a bone conduction hearing aid on the head of a child with microtic outer ears.

Huggie Aids
837 N.W. 10th St.
Oklahoma City, OK 73106
This company produces and sells a variety of headbands and accessories used to keep hearing aids on children. These bands are popular for children with microtic outer ears.

Insurance

Family Voices - A National Coalition Speaking for Children with Special
    Health Care Needs
Box 769
Algodones, NM 87001
This family-founded organization attempts to ensure that the principles of family-centered, community-based, and coordinated care are woven into health, education, and social service initiatives.

Health Insurance Assn. of America
1001 Pennsylvania Ave., N.W.
Washington, DC 20004

Institute for Child Health Policy
University of Florida
5700 SW. 34th St., #323
Gainesville, FL 32608

National Association of Insurance Commissioners
120 W. 12th St., Suite 1100
Kansas City, MO 64105

World Institute on Disability
Bob Griss, c/o United Cerebral Palsy Assn.
1522 K Street, N.W., Suite 1112
Washington, DC 20005

Medical Information

National Health Information Center
P.O. Box 1133
Washington, DC 20013–1133
    This system can link you to the specific federal agency or organization that can answer questions about health care, insurance, and medical conditions. Operated by the Department of Health and Human Services.

Computer Information Sources

Major commercial sources for on-line medical information:

America Online
1–800–827–6364

CompuServe
1–800–848–8199

Prodigy
1–800–776–3449

Other on-line sources:

Black Bag BBS
on-line 610–454–7396
    Computerized list of medical bulletin boards.

Index Medicus
    A monthly bibliography that lists medical journal articles by subject. Available at medical libraries. To locate a medical library open to the public in your area, contact the National Network of Libraries of Medicine at 1–800–338–7657.

MEDLARS: MEDLINE
1–800–638–8480
    Computerized database of medical information available through the National Library/Dept. of Health and Human Services. May be available through public libraries. Fees vary.

Medical research firms

    The following medical research firms will, for a fee, provide you with medical information tailored to your needs. Ask for a price estimate.

The Health Resource
1–800–949–0090
501–329–5272

For a fee, provides up to 250 pages of medical information tailored to the user's needs.

Medical Data Exchange
503–471–1627

Medical Data Source
1–800–776–4673

Medical Information Service
1–800–999–1999

MedScan
1–800–633–8145

Planetree Health Information Service
415–923–3681
For a fee, provides up to 50 pages of medical information tailored to the user's needs.

Schine On-Line
1–800–346–3287

The World Research Foundation
818–907–5483
For a fee, offers a library search of books and periodicals that contain alternative medical therapies, and a computer search of more than 5000 medical journals, including pharmaceutical and surgical information.

Parent Advocacy, Legal, & General Disability Information

Accent on Information
P.O. Box 700
Bloomington, IL 61702

Association of Birth Defect Children
827 Irma Ave.
Orlando, FL 32803
This organization offers information and resources for parents of children with environmentally caused congenital conditions. Offers a newsletter, for a fee, and will produce a personalized report on your child's condition.

Center for Birth Defects Information Services, Inc.
Dover Medical Building
Box 1776
Dover, MA 02030–1776

Center on Human Policy
Syracuse University
200 Huntington Hall
Syracuse, NY 13244–2340

Children in Hospitals
21 Wilshire Park
Needham, MA 02192

Children's Defense Fund
25 E Street NW
Washington, DC 20001

Clearinghouse on Disability Information
Office of Special Education and Rehabilitative Services
U.S. Dept. of Education
400 Maryland Avenue, S.W.
Room 3132, Switzer Building
Washington, DC 20202–2524

Council for Exceptional Children
1920 Association Dr.
Reston, VA 22091–1589

Direct Link for the Disabled
P.O. Box 1036
Solvang, CA 93464

Family Empowerment Institute
2545 Koshkonong Road
Stoughton, WI 53589

Family Support Network
University of North Carolina
CB #7340
Chapel Hill, North Carolina 27599–7340

Federation for Children with Special Needs
95 Berkeley St., Suite 104
Boston, MA 02116–3104
    Staffed by parents of children with special needs, this organization focuses on child advocacy and information for families of children with special needs. It is also the main office of several national projects. Offers a newsletter, information sheets, conferences, and workshops.

Indian Health Service
Parklawn Building, Room 2014
5600 Fishers Lane
Rockville, MD 20857

March of Dimes Birth Defects Foundation
1275 Mamaroneck Ave.
White Plains, NY 10526
914–428–7100
    The goal of this organization is the prevention of birth defects. Has state and local chapters, health education and community service programs, fact sheets, and newsletter.

National Association of Protection and Advocacy Systems
900 2nd St. NE, Suite 211
Washington, DC 20002

National Center for Education in Maternal and Child Health
2000 N. 15th Street, Suite 700
Arlington, VA 22201
This organization provides education, information, and publications on maternal and child health.

National Center for the Law and the Deaf
Gallaudet University
800 Florida Ave., NE
Washington, DC 20002

National Center for Youth with Disabilities
University of Minnesota
420 Delaware Street, SE
Box 721
Minneapolis, MN 55455–0392
1–800–333–6293

National Center on Parent Directed Family Resource Centers
Parents Helping Parents
3041 Olcott St.
Santa Clara, CA 95054
This organization provides consultation and technical assistance to people interested in implementing parent-to-parent programs.

National Easter Seals Society
230 W. Monroe
Chicago, IL 60606
The Society works to help people with disabilities increase their independence through advocacy, publishing and distributing information on rehabilitation, and other services. There are many local affiliates throughout the country.

National Health Information Center
P.O. Box 1133
Washington, DC 20013–1133
1–800–336–4797

National Information Center for Children and Youth with Disabilities
(NICHCY)
P.O. Box 1492
Washington, DC 20013–1492
1–800–695–0285
This clearinghouse provides information on disabling conditions and disability-related topics focused on children aged birth to 22. NICHCY offers fact sheets on a variety of disabilities, information packets, a newsletter, and "State

Sheets," which list each state's resources for people with disabilities. Parents can call or send in requests for free information or a publication list.

National Information Center for Orphan Drugs and Rare Disorders (NICODARD)
P.O. Box 1133
Washington, DC 20013–1133
1–800–456–3505

National Information Clearinghouse for Infants with Disabilities and Life-Threatening Conditions
University of South Carolina
Benson Building, First Floor
Columbia, SC 29208
1–800–922–9234 x201 (US outside of SC); 1–800–922–1102 x201 (SC)
This organization provides information and referral to community and national services for infants with disabilities.

National Institute of Dental Research
NIH Bldg. 31, Room #2C-35
Bethesda, MD 20892

National Oral Health Information Clearinghouse
1 NOHIC Way
Bethesda, MD 20892–3500
This clearinghouse offers information on special care in oral health. Resources include: database, materials published by the clearinghouse, and mailing list updates.

National Organization for Rare Disorders (NORD)
P.O. Box 8923
New Fairfield, CT 06812
1–800–999–6673
This organization provides information on rare disorders, educates the public and professionals, and focuses national attention on the needs of people with rare disorders. Offers newsletters, referrals, networking, information on specific conditions, and meetings.

National Parent Network on Disabilities
1600 Prince St., Suite 115
Alexandria, VA 22314
This organization is a coalition of parents and parent organizations. They provide a national voice for parents of people with disabilities.

National Parent to Parent Support and Information System
Box 907
Blue Ridge, GA 30513
1–800–651–1151

Parent Care
9041 Colgate St.
Indianapolis, IN 46268–1210

This organization works to improve the newborn intensive care experience and future for babies, families, and caregivers. Offers newsletter and referrals.

Parentele National
8331 Kimball Ave.
Skokie, IL 60076

Parents for Parents, Inc.
125 Northmore Dr.
Yorktown Heights, NY 10598

Pathfinder Resources, Inc.
2324 University Ave. W.
Suite 105
St. Paul, MN 55114

Pike Institute on Law and Disability
Boston University School of Law
765 Commonwealth Ave.
Boston, MA 02215

Rural Institute on Disabilities
52 Corbin Hall
University of Montana
Missoula, MT 59812

Senate Document Room
Hart Building
Washington, DC 20515
202–224–7860
To obtain a copy of a federal bill or law (such as IDEA or ADA), contact this office.

Sexual Abuse and Young People with Disabilities Project (SAYPD)
The McCreary Centre Society
c/o Sunny Hill Hospital
3644 Slocan St.
Vancouver, B.C.
CANADA V5M 3E8

STOMP: Specialized Training of Military Parents
c/o WA PAVE
12208 Pacific Highway 10
Tacoma, WA 98499

World Institute on Disability
510 16th Street, Suite 100
Oakland, CA 94612–1502

Professional Organizations

The following organizations cover the various disciplines of professionals who serve children with facial difference. Some possible reasons to contact these organizations include: to get a referral to professionals, to inquire about publications, to learn about the relationship between the discipline and your child's condition, to find out about workshops or committees, to receive research updates, and to file a complaint.

American Academy of Facial Plastic and Reconstructive Surgery
1110 Vermont Ave., NW, #220
Washington, DC 20005

American Academy of Pediatrics
P.O. Box 927
Elk Grove Village, Il 60009–0927

American Assn. for the Advancement of Science
Project on Science, Technology, and Disability
1333 H Street, NW
Washington, D.C. 20005

American Association of Hospital Dentists
211 E. Chicago Ave.
Chicago, IL 60611

American Association of University Affiliated Programs for Persons with Developmental Disabilities
8630 Fenton Street, Suite 410
Silver Spring, MD 20910

American Cleft Palate-Craniofacial Association
1218 Grandview Ave.
Pittsburgh, PA 15211

American Occupational Therapy Association
4720 Montgomery Lane
P.O. Box 31220
Rockville, MD 20824

American Physical Therapy Association
1111 N. Fairfax Street
Alexandria, VA 22314

American Psychological Association
750 1st Street NE
Washington, DC 20002

American Society of Human Genetics
9650 Rockville Pike
Bethesda, MD 20814

American Society of Plastic and Reconstructive Surgeons
444 E. Algonquin Rd.
Arlington Heights, IL 60005

American Speech-Language-Hearing Association
10801 Rockville Pike
Rockville, MD 20852

The Deafness Research Foundation
9 E. 38th St., 7th Floor
New York, NY 10016

Family/Professional Collaboration Project
499B Waterman Building
Dept. of Social Work
University of Vermont
Burlington, VT 05405–0160
    Research project which explores the collaborative inter-relationships be-
tween professionals and families of children with special health needs.

International Society of Nurses in Genetics
c/o Shirley L. Jones, M.S.
Genetics & IVF Institute
3020 Javier Rd.
Fairfax, VA 22031

National Association of School Nurses, Inc.
P.O. Box 1300
Scarborough, ME 04070–1300

National Association of Social Workers
750 1st Street, NE, Suite 700
Washington, DC 20002

National Foundation of Dentistry for the Handicapped
1800 Glenarm Place, Suite 500
Denver, CO 80202

National Society of Genetic Counselors
233 Canterbury Dr.
Wallingford, PA 19086

Society for Developmental Pediatrics
P.O. Box 23836
Baltimore, MD 21203

Society for Ear, Nose and Throat Advances in Children (SENTAC)
Children's Hospital of Philadelphia
ORL Department
34th St. Civic Center Blvd.
Philadelphia, PA 19104

Sibling Support

Sibling Support Project
Children's Hospital and Medical Center
P.O. Box 5371, CL-09
Seattle, WA 98105

Siblings for Significant Change
105 E. 22nd St.
New York, NY 10010
Siblings of Disabled Children
535 Race Street, Ste. 220
San Jose, CA 95126

Support Organizations

ARCH National Resource Center (Access to Respite Care and Help)
800 Eastowne Dr., Suite 105
Chapel Hill, NC 27514

Association for the Care of Children's Health (ACCH)
7910 Woodmont Ave., Suite 300
Bethesda, MD 20814
1–800–808–2224
This international organization of health care professionals and parents focuses on the many aspects of appropriate health care for children with special health needs. Offers booklets, resource catalog of videos and books, bibliographies, a journal, *AACH Parents' Resource Directory*, and meetings.

Beach Center on Families and Disability
c/o Institute for Life Span Studies
The University of Kansas
3111 Haworth Hall
Lawrence, KS 66045
This center focuses on families: how they cope, what they need, and how other people can help. Holds meetings; offers publications and a catalog of resources.

Love Letters, Inc.
P.O. Box 416875
Chicago, IL 60641
Contact: Linda Bremner, Executive Director
Provides emotional support through the mail to children ages 3 to 21 who are dealing with long-term or catastrophic illness.

Mothers United for Moral Support (MUMS)
150 Custer Court
Green Bay, WI 54301
This is a national Parent-to-Parent organization for parents or care providers of a child with any disability, disorder, chromosomal abnormality, or health

condition. The main purpose is to provide support to parents by matching parents with other parents whose children have the same or similar condition, including rare conditions. Over 1,500 disorders are listed.

National Self-Help Clearinghouse
CUNY Graduate School, University Center
25 W. 43rd St., Room 620
New York, NY 10036

Project COPE
9160 Monte Vista Ave.
Montclair, CA 91763

Self-Help Clearinghouse
St. Clares Riverside Medical Center
6 Hinchman Ave.
Denville, NJ 07834

Toys

Kids on the Block
9385–C Gerwig Lane
Columbia, MD 21046
1–800–368–KIDS
   Company which manufactures and sells specially designed puppets and puppet shows which are focused on issues of difference.

Next Store Neighbors
2642 Baumgardner Rd.
Westminster, MD 21158
   Company which manufactures and sells specially designed puppets and puppet shows which are focused on issues of difference.

Teddy Bears
18617 Jirete Rd.
Odessa, FL 33556
   Custom made teddy bears with your child's facial difference are available.

Index